SLOVAK SHORT STORIES

TWENTY-FIVE CONTEMPORARY

IN SEARCH OF HOMO SAPIENS

Pavol Hudík

Editor

2002

Bolchazy-Carducci
Publishers

The Publishing House
of the Slovak Writers Society

In Search of Homo Sapiens
(Twenty–Five Contemporary Slovak Short Stories)

Published by The Publishing House of the Slovak Writers Society
(Vydavateľstvo Spolku slovenských spisovateľov) Bratislava, SR
and
Bolchazy-Carducci Publishers, Inc. Wauconda, Illinois, USA

Editor: Pavol Hudík

Translated by Heather Trebatická
American english editor: Lucy Bednár

The publication of this book has been made possible by grants from:
The Slovak-American International Cultural Foundation, Inc.
The Center for Information on Literature (Slolia), Bratislava
Tipos, Ltd., Bratislava
Stephen J. Schostok, Esq.

Bolchazy-Carducci Publishers, Inc.
1000 Brown Street, Unit 101
Wauconda, IL 60084 USA

www.bolchazy.com

First Edition 2002

ISBN 80-8061-118-1 (SR)
ISBN 0-86516-532-7 (USA)

Library of Congress Cataloguing-in-Publication Data

In search of homo sapiens : twenty-five contemporary Slovak short stories / editor
Pavol Hudík ; [translated by heather Trebatická; American english editor: Lucy Bednár].
-- 1st ed.
     p. cm.
  ISBN 0-86516-532-7 (alk. paper)
     1. Short stories, Slovak--Translations into English. 2. Slovak fiction--20th
century--Translations into English. I. Hudík, Pavol. II. Trebatická, Heather. III. Bednár,
Lucy.

PG5545.E8 I5 2002
891.8'730108--dc21   2002022872

CONTENTS

THE WIND OF FUTURE WORDS *(PAVOL JANÍK)*

JÚLIUS LENKO: AN EVENING SEARCH FOR MAN

JÚLIUS BALCO
— Holes in the Ground

MÁRIA BÁTOROVÁ
— Tells

MARÍNA ČERETKOVÁ-GÁLLOVÁ
— The Actress

ETELA FARKAŠOVÁ
— A Sky Full of Migrating Birds

ANDREJ FERKO
— Intra muros populis

ALEXANDER HALVONÍK
— Fear

PETER HOLKA
—Love as a Crime

IVAN HUDEC
— The Undeniable Likeness of Twins

ANTON HYKISCH
— A Free Royal Town

ANDREJ CHUDOBA
— Snow and Rooks

PETER JAROŠ
— Making Faces

ĽUBOŠ JURÍK
— The Road Sweeper

JÁN LENČO
— On the Way to P.

DUŠAN MIKOLAJ
— The Man with the Weak Heart

RÓBERT MÜLLER
— The Question

GABRIELA ROTHMAYEROVÁ
— In a Danger Zone

PETER ŠEVČOVIČ
— Near to Eternity

VINCENT ŠIKULA
— Grannie

VIERA ŠVENKOVÁ
— Pharaoh's Smile

LADISLAV ŤAŽKÝ
— A Parting Gift

JÁN TUŽINSKÝ
— A Murmur

MILAN ZELINKA
— The Blue Carp

HANA ZELINOVÁ
— The Order of Wolves

A DIVERSE CONTRIBUTION TO SHORT-STORY LITERATURE

(PAVOL HUDÍK)

THE WIND OF FUTURE WORDS

It sometimes seems there is nothing new to be discovered on this planet Earth, but, thanks to this book, for many readers a new island has appeared on the map of world literature – Slovakia.

Our beautiful and hospitable land lies in the heart of Europe. Our neighbors are Austria, the Czech Republic, Hungary, Poland and Ukraine. We have now had almost ten years of Slovak independence, yet our cultural traditions have contributed to central Europe for over a thousand years. We know the world well, as the world knows us, even though for the most part under the name of one or another of our neighbors.

Reliable sources estimate that in the United States alone there are as many Slovaks and their descendants as there are in Slovakia itself. In the course of history our capital city Bratislava has been known to the world by a number of names: in Latin it was Istropolis or Posonium, in German Pressburg, in Hungarian Pozsony and in Slovak Prešporok, for several months in 1918 even Wilson.

The Slovak Writers Society, whose traditions reach back to 1923, and which brings together outstanding figures in the world of Slovak literature, has made the maximum effort to enable our country to speak to the world through works representative of its contemporary literature. They say it is better to see something once than to hear about it a hundred times. In the case of literature it is certainly better to have the opportunity to read a literary work for oneself than to rely on the evaluations and opinions of others.

Concerning the development of our writers' organization, a variety of subjective views have always been expressed, as well as differing interpretations influenced by their times. In spite of the vagaries of historical developments, it has always been a voluntary, selective, professional institution, whose aim is to support the development and publication of Slovak literature at home and abroad, as well as to search untiringly for new talents and gradually incorporate them in literary life.

The Slovak Writers Society also made an exceptional contribution to democratic changes in the former Czecho-Slovakia, and it is one of the spiritual platforms of modern Slovak statehood. It systematically makes contacts in the sphere of literature in the interests of future international exchanges of cultural values based on the universal ideas of humanism, peace, mutual understanding and a growing familiarity with the distinctive features of contemporary writing.

PAVOL JANÍK
Secretary
Slovak Writers Society

... Wisdom lies in understanding people,
their breath, gaze, walk, silence,
their anger, song, love and lack of it.
But in a world wrapped up in words,
people have been lost. Somewhere at the bottom.
And then you meet a non-human.
What did you get from this meeting?
With a butterfly, yes, a stream, a tree, yes.
But people like to be non-humans. They take on
sharp edges like rocks, they are cold within as caves,
proud as eagles, only on occasion
does a splinter of their lives bring you together
and you see yourself in them. You join them
in the search for truth. That, however, lies in a pile of words.
You push them aside, you carry them off,
as many remain as ever there were,
and dressed as a clown you walk beside the cart
in the hope that when the slag is removed
you'll discover the ore...

Július Lenko: An Evening Search for Man (an extract)

JÚLIUS BALCO

- prose writer;
born in Cífer (1948)

Július Balco has worked as an editor for the literary journals *Romboid* and *Literika*.

He writes both for adults and for children. He made his debut as a writer with a short novel **Voskovožlté jablko** (*The Shiny Yellow Apple*, 1976) – an intimate story about the fate of man in his search for ways to achieve justice in life. He made use of exotic gypsy motifs in the ballad-like prose work **Husle s labutím krkom** (*The Swan-necked Fiddle*, 1979). In his collection of short stories about love **Ležoviská** (*Lairs*, 1986) he reflects on situations in which young people are confronted with what is often the harsh reality of life. The novella **Cestujúci tam i späť** (*Traveling There and Back*, 1988) is the story of an editor in which he discovers the significance of times gone by and comes to terms with a crisis, while the beauty of a love relationship is compared with hard reality.

Július Balco combines the real with the imaginary in an unconventional way, especially in his works for children – the trilogy **Strigôňove Vianoce** (*The Wizard's Christmas*, 1991), **Strigôňove prázdniny** (*The Wizard's Holiday*, 1994) and **Strigôňov rok** (*The Wizard's Year*, 1999).

He is the author of television scenarios for animated fairytales.

The story "Jamky" ("Holes in the Ground") is from **Ležoviská**.

In his own words:
(About the collection of short stories Ležoviská):
I should like to emphasise that the book *Ležoviská* is a **collection** of already published short stories, prose works which differ in length, time, theme and perhaps even genre. One of them took me nineteen years to develop, another more or less a single night, and I'm fondest of this one, perhaps because I never again experienced such a pleasant surprise in the form of a short story. I worked very hard on yet another, and I suspect that it is the "most peculiar" of

1

them all. If there is anything that unites them, it is what I have always aimed at in my writing: purity of expression.
(1986)

(About his trilogy and children's literature):
Wizards as supernatural fairytale beings are often villains and must come to a bad end, so that the tale can have a happy ending. They are not usually the main character, but in my books they are. This means that they cannot be as bad as they are generally thought to be. The Carpathian wizard casts spells to amuse his grandchildren, just as I conjured up the first book in the series for my daughter Kamilka. Before that I had written only for adults and I had had no experience whatsoever with writing for children. It was clear to me, however, that she preferred to listen to classical fairytales, rather than modern ones full of incomprehensible sophistry and void of plot. I kept to this and I tried to write in such a way that she could understand them and – what is most important – enjoy reading them....

If a parent wishes to give his or her child the pleasure of childhood, they cannot, they must not, steal their books.
(1999)
JÚLIUS BALCO

HOLES IN THE GROUND

When the old vineyards were being dug up, Viktor Móder was just seventeen years old. The sun was more lively then, it rubbed against you affectionately like a cat and it didn't burn at all.

The school holidays had begun.

Everything, even the bare plains, seemed very near.

Rudo's father worked for the co-operative and had arranged a holiday job for them. They wanted to buy racing bikes in the autumn. The teacher's son had been exercising his muscles with dumbbells all winter and now he walked around in a T-shirt with his arms hanging unnaturally away from his sides, as if his biceps were getting in his way. It was obvious he would dig the most holes. A year later the holes for concrete posts were dug out by machines and lots of new vineyards were planted to grow along wire trellises.

They climbed uphill until they almost reached the forest. The tools were stored in a workman's trailer and they could see a group of holiday workers already spread out over the slope. The work was shared out by a self-important university student, who occasionally dug with the others and counted and measured the holes at the end of the shift. They had to be a prescribed depth but no wider than allowed, because they would be filled with expensive cement. That's why the bottoms were broken up the hard way, with crowbars with sharp wedge-like ends, and people were paid according to the number of holes they dug.

A tubby blond with a broad, phony face wrote down their names, handed out the tools and led them to the edge of the slope, which rolled over into the bushes, beyond which lay the forest.

Viktor was to dig at the very edge only a few meters from a deep ditch hollowed out by the rush of water long before. It was overgrown with prickly acacias, briars and brambles, wild cherry trees and hops. It smellled of virgin forest, and Viktor, already covered in sweat, breathed in deeply. They slipped off their rucksacks and all three took gulps of the raspberry juice they had brought. The marked-out slope dropped away from them sharply. At the foot of it, in the meadows, shone the surface of an irrigation pond, and looking into the sun, they could see the whole town with its chimneys and towers.

They pulled out the first wooden stakes and set to work. The teacher's son was already digging his second hole while Viktor's first still seemed too shallow. He was making slow progress because his mind was elsewhere, on something reflected in the surface of the pond, which his eyes wandered to every few minutes. The same image was mirrored in it all the time: slipping out of her dress like a butterfly out of its chrysalis, she had looked as if she were growing. Lost in her dress, small and thin, she suddenly seemed to him quite different. He told her he hadn't wanted to take a blanket with him, but now he'd like to stretch out in comfort. She had nodded gravely, saying he could if he would carry it on the way back. He had been a bit taken aback by that and said he would think about it and went off to have a swim.

When he emerged from the water, she was lying quietly with her arm under her head, the soft down showing in her armpits and curly hairs peeping thickly from the edge of her suit. He quietly let himself down next to her, but she immediately opened her eyes and smiled. "I've got some cream in my bag," she said. "Would you rub it on my back?"

The ground was hard, as if a path had once run along the edge of the bushes. Solid lumps of clay, full of stones, broke away from the crowbar. A morning haze rose over the little town, the reservoir shimmered coldly like a scale from a large fish. Sweat trickled down all three of them. Those to the left were already a bit ahead of them; Viktor had the feeling he was behind in every way.

3

If only he had wings, he would stretch them wide and fly down like a wild duck: splash onto the water!

He went over to the bushes, sat down beside his rucksack and pulled out his bottle of raspberry juice. It was still cool and he drank and drank, relishing every gulp. Then he looked at the other two. They were diligently digging like moles, with visions of bicycles driving them on. For a while he watched them thoughtfully. Rudo and he were good friends, they shared a desk at school. He ought to tell him, but on the other hand, she was no beauty, at least no one had ever said so. After yesterday, though, she seemed to him more than just pretty.

Bicycle visions were replaced by visions of Jana. Inconspicuous, modest Jana, who the boys had overlooked, because none of them had rubbed cream on her back and then on her legs, too; no one had stroked her where Viktor had and she had certainly never kissed anyone the way she had kissed him.

He had to leave it at that. He knew where the nursery was and he wanted to see her. They had talked about it the day before. He had promised her he would come to see her. He slung his rucksack over his shoulders and strode off up the hill, with not so much as a backward glance.

"Where's he off to?" asked the schoolteacher's son.

"Probably looking for mushrooms," said Rudo.

"Or for girls. He'll earn zilch, instead of a bike," he spat and rammed the crowbar into the ground.

Victor strode up the steep slope, skirting the bushes and soon he was in the forest. It was cool under the trees and his shirt was in his rucksack. He halted for a minute, savoring the pleasant feeling. Cool and refreshing, penetrating through his skin. In a moment he would catch sight of her. It was very near. He sensed that she wanted it. Just imagine – she wanted it. She really wanted it with him and he knew it. She must have fallen for him. No doubt about it – she was in love with him!

A woodpecker began tapping a tree.

He took a short cut, straight across a meadow, past a hollow tree where not so long ago young woodpeckers had clamored for food. They had already flown the nest. He remembered how they had tweeted so urgently, so joyfully, even though they had always been hungry, had always wanted to eat.

There were bell flowers growing in the meadow. He smiled as he picked them. They rang in his hands. Jan-ka, Jan-ka....

When he looked over the fence of woven branches and caught sight of her among the other girls loosening the soil around the saplings, she was again wearing nothing but her bathing suit. She was the most beautiful of them all and he resolved to tell Rudo where he had been. He didn't mind if he knew. He didn't mind if they all knew.

She was the first to see him and she came over to him. No one was watching, no one even noticed.

And what if they had.

She came, and when he gave her the bell flowers, she snuggled up to him like a cat that must have company.

"Where did you pick them?" she asked eagerly.

"Here in the meadow. Come on! I'll pick them all for you."

"Is it allowed?"

"No, it isn't."

"Really?"

"Cross my heart." He could feel her heart beating, she was breathless with excitement.

"Are you sure?"

"Sure."

"That's...wonderful!"

"Then come on!" he took her by the hand and led her to the opposite side of the meadow. She clasped his hand tightly with her soft, childlike fingers.

"We'll sit down here," he said, once they were among the trees. The tall, fluffy grass in seed rippled in the gentle breeze like the surface of a pond, grey-green like mist, delicate as a cobweb.

"No one will find us here," he whispered, "no one will see us." And when he put his arms around her, they couldn't see anything either, drowned in the meadow. It was very simple, the way she let him pull off her suit, and after their first love-making the whole forest burst into song. When he made his way back, the sun was already shining from the opposite side. His legs were giving way beneath him, because he had suddenly grown wings. He flapped them and soared into the air. He flew over the deep ditch hollowed out long ago by the rush of water, through the thorny bushes; with the wings he had grown everything was possible. Fly through the sky! Who could do that?

Suddenly he was back on the hillside with Rudo. If he had wanted to, he could dive down to the pond or float over the tower in the town – with these wings of his that too was within his reach.

Rudo stared at him in astonishment.

See? I've got wings, thought Viktor. That's something, huh?

"You're scratched all over and your trousers are torn," Rudo commented.

"I took a short cut through the ditch."

"You could have taken a serious fall."

He smiled proudly: "I've got wings. Aha – feathers."

A feather was stuck to his ragged elbow. He picked it off and blew on it gently. "See? Feathers!!"

Rudo laughed, Viktor laughed, too. "Where's the body builder?"

"He did twenty holes and went for a swim," he nodded in the direction of the pond. His face was red, flushed from exertion. He was glad Viktor had come at last and they could go home. "I've done fifteen," he boasted. "What about you?"

"I've done one."

"Will you ask them to write it down?" he grinned. "I'm going to get that blond guy."

"Maybe tomorrow," he shrugged and went to have a look at the holes they had dug. There really were twenty in that row, deep and narrow, perfect work. He didn't notice the blond student who passed him carrying a measuring rod and notebook, looking into every hole, but not bothering to measure them. It was obvious at a glance that they were just as they should be. Viktor's mind was elsewhere, entangled in the cobwebs of the forest clearing, his thumb stroked the feather in his palm.

"Name! What's your name?" the curly blond fellow was suddenly beside him. His fist closed around the feather.

"Me? Viktor Móder."

"Módr, Módr...," muttered the curly-haired student, "where've I got you?"

He pretended to be looking through his notebook, but he was observing him out of the corner of his eye.

Viktor stood staring at the ground, his mind elsewhere. The blond fellow could see that he was pretty exhausted. Broad-shouldered guy, he thought to himself and wrote down the number seventeen.

Just at that moment Viktor happened to glance at the page.

He snapped the notebook shut and looked at Viktor. Had he noticed? Or hadn't he? Anyway, he could have made a mistake. He smiled sweetly and nodded his fleecy head in a friendly manner.

"Keep it up, young man!"

Viktor nodded indifferently.

Curlyhead gave him a broad smile and winked conspiratorially, as if he wished to confirm his first judgement that here was the kind of hard worker he liked.

Viktor just flapped his wings at him.

Rudo, on the other hand, walked along beside him, counting out loud. Curlyhead didn't like that type at all. He commented on the depth and width, haggled over every hole, but in the end he accepted them all. On the other hand, he waved cordially to Viktor, who flapped his wings in return.

"He's a thief. There are twenty of them and he only put seventeen down by my name. – "Thief of holes!" he shouted when the fellow's head and shoulders were all that could be seen over the crest of the hill. "Do you see that thief of holes?!" he pointed to him, laughing. "Do you see him?"

"Incredible...," said Rudo. "You really are in luck!"

"Luck? I don't need it! What for?" and he flapped his wings hard, breathing in the hot summer air, heavy with the smell of soil and sun.

MÁRIA BÁTOROVÁ

- prose writer, literary scholar;
born in Trenčín (1950)

Mária Bátorová worked at the Literary Institute of the Slovak Academy of Sciences, and at present she is at the Academy's Institute of World Literature. She lectured for some time on the history of Slovak literature at the university in Cologne on the Rhine.

Her first book was a literary-history monograph **Roky úzkosti a vzopätia** (*Years of Anguish and Resistance*, 1992), about the trends in Slovak literature between 1938 and 1945. Her latest work is a monograph entitled **Jozef Cíger Hronský and Modernism – Myth and Mythology in Literature** (2000).

In the sphere of fiction, her first book was a collection of novellas and short stories set in the present, **Zvony v kameni** (*Bells in Stone*, 1993). The intimate short stories in **Tíš** (*Tranquility*,1996) are psychological sketches, in particular of the relationships between men and women. There is in her work a clear tendency to combine without sentimentality a woman's sensitivity and the rational view of the scholar. There is an increasing inclination towards more complicated compositions with a number of different interpretations and situations overlapping each other, supplemented by verses which correspond in their associations. Her other, philosophically even more demanding book of prose, **Tell** (*Tells*, 1999), from which the story of the same name is taken, is composed in a similar manner.

In her own words:

If the artist is to "open our eyes to our own world" (Nietzsche), if therefore he or she is to clarify and explain, they can do it if they have the right "key," if they know how to communicate the "universal primordial images," the "original ideas," which, according to Jung, all of us carry within us. But the task of explaining is only one of the roles of the literary work. The word as both a challenge and an action is our accepted basis in the Štúr tradition. It is said that the nation that hasn't had to fight for its own freedom, cannot value it; it is only a gift it has received. Štúr and his followers remained single to carry on their struggle, their revolution. Many intellectuals of this century, even though they had families, took up arms and fought against the violence of fascism. As a woman and as a mother, I am against arms, against violence in any form whatsoever. I believe that politicians and diplomats can solve problems without armed conflict, if they want to. If they don't want to, they call for assistance from any source, writers included. Writers are not usually good strategists. They do not have the right sense of perspective. Their hearts are full, their heads are full, but their eyes are not in focus; they see too far ahead or too close, and they see a great deal. Writers write for life. It is the twilight of culture when they are called to death....

Reaching out to people, the desire to communicate through creative work, the reproduction of oneself in a creative act, the reflection of which can be immediately seen in the eyes of another person – that is freedom....

Life is too short to drink bad wine, one wise man said. And too short for us to live without dreams and ideals.

(1999)

MÁRIA BÁTOROVÁ

TELLS

"Won't you give me some loose change?" A tall, thin girl with short hair and a cigarette behind her ear stuck out her hand. Her narrow black jeans made her young body look long and arched, as if she had rickets. She darted here and there among the oncoming crowd, taking tiny steps, while a sandy-brown Pekingese leaped behind her in the same rhythm. People turned their heads away from the blue rings under her eyes. The crowd swept on, swallowed in the dark narrow exits to the street, or pouring down the stairways leading in all directions towards the metro.

The palm used to the occasional small hard coin automatically puckered to grasp the banknote. She wasn't certain, because the donor had come up from behind and the crowd had flowed on. The next day in the same place she again received a whole day's earnings, so she could sit beside the fountain, while Benny licked himself after half a hamburger. It was the same all week. She was now certain, she had seen the same man from behind: long grey hair, cut and combed on the crown, spread out in wisps over his shoulders, a leather jacket on his thin, bony back, blue jeans which always looked as if they had just been ironed.

"Your feet fascinate me," a deep voice with a foreign, Russian accent came from above her. He was blocking out the sun, so when she looked up, she at last saw him for the first time from the front. A pointed, obstinate chin, deep-set blue eyes below a high forehead, pronounced furrows around the eyes and running down the cheeks. She saw that his eyes really were resting on her tennis shoes and it seemed so ridiculous that she suddenly burst into loud laughter. Benny quickly lifted his nose, one eye open wide, the other lid drooping slightly, and he wagged his tail. He thought they were going to have some fun and games.

"My feet? It's my soles you're looking at," the girl said, still laughing.

"Exactly," he replied, and his sharp, troubled gaze passed slowly from her tennis shoes to her smiling face. "I can't understand how you can dance through the world on such small soles."

"Well, it could hardly be said I dance through the world," the girl said with a sudden frown. Hearing that tone of voice, Benny once more crouched low on the pavement, pressing his side against her left shoe. There would be no fun and games.

"Do you like modern music? Would you like to go to a concert with me today?" he asked quickly. "It's out of town, in an old tower. I'll pick you up here at half past five. My name's Leonard," he added and, not waiting for a reply, he left. Once more she saw his flowing hair and confident step.

She sat for a while and pondered what it meant. She looked at her tennis shoes and couldn't help laughing. Men usually admired her eyes, her face, her large breasts. Boys would say to her: you say such cool things.... No one had yet looked as far as the soles of her feet. She considered for a while whether she should go to the concert or to Magnus, her usual haunt, for a beer, a drop of something, the same old chatter, usually ending with having to see some befuddled guy home....

There were still two whole hours to go before half past five. She stretched out on the warm, stone edge of the fountain and placed Benny on her tummy. The moment he heard the beating of her heart, he began snoring rhythmically.

The most pleasant thing about this town is that no one notices anyone. All anomalies are allowed and taken as a person's right to be himself. It is not aloofness, it is an agreeable, cultivated tolerance. This town is freer than Paris.

"Well, I'm here," she was woken by a deep voice over her head. "I see you're waiting for me."

"Not really," she half opened her eyes, "I've just not budged from here."

"Well, let's go. My motorbike is around the corner."

"On a motorbike? I...I haven't got a helmet, a jacket.... I've got a dog and I'm scared of motorbikes...."

He gazed at her for a while and the penetrating blue eyes seemed to soften.

"Wait here, or come with me...," he grasped her hand and led her into one of the streets. "Choose which one you like," he pointed to a row of helmets of various colors.

She tried on a red one and immediately took it off. "Looks as if I'm asking for blood. What color's your motorbike?" she asked abruptly.

"Black."

"Well, what about this silver one with pink stripes?"

"And this light jacket to go with it. Try it on!"

"No. And I'll leave you the helmet afterwards. Maybe it'll come in useful for someone else," she bowed to him coquettishly.

He tilted the machine as they took the corners and then sped down the highway, weaving in and out between the cars. He was showing off and she thought they must have an accident any moment. She closed her eyes and pressed up against his back, till Benny whined in the rucksack on her chest.

"That was the last time...," she said, when she climbed off.

"And how do you want to get back?" he grinned.

They walked from a parking lot landscaped like the Schönbrunn gardens in the direction of the tower. The sun was just setting behind it, so against the blackness of the ruins the windows seemed to be burning, with figures flitting among purple flames. She stopped in amazement at the sight. Leonard turned around and for a moment couldn't tear his gaze away from the girl and the dog.

"Come on, it'll be beautiful in the evening, too."

They strolled slowly through the little courtyard, full of small clusters of people. Many of them greeted Leonard. Hi, Leo! was heard here and there and no one took any notice of her. Her unusual appearance looked ordinary in this eccentric company and that was agreeable. Suddenly, in almost a whisper, a little loud speaker over the entrance began calling the people inside.

"Come on, first we'll take a look at the other side, with a view of the valley."

They ducked under a little stone gateway in the wall and stood on a ledge overhanging a deep drop. The girl quickly scooped Benny up in her arms, because he was standing on the edge, stretching out his neck and sniffing, while trembling all over. There was a river meandering along the bottom of the valley.

"He's scared of heights. He's terribly scared of heights. Anyway, there should be a railing here," she turned around and crept back.

They entered the tower. There were torches burning in brackets on the inside wall. Through a black upholstered door they passed into the first room on the right. A young man was standing in the middle of a half circle. He was dressed all in black and even his long hair was black, combed smooth and tied up at the back of his neck. He had an instrument something like a violin, but he held it against his side instead of under his chin. It had only two strings and he was drawing from it a wonderfully gentle, almost monotonous sound. The others were sitting along the walls almost on the floor, on low benches covered with furs. Leonard remained standing near the door, although someone beckoned to him. The girl sat down on the ground and, hearing these sounds, Benny crouched on the floor, pushing his nose under her shoe. A rustling sound made her turn around and all she saw was Leonard's back, so she quickly got up and closed the door behind her. They moved in this way from door to door. There was always a different instrument and no more than two musicians, each of whom played their own thing. As they went up the narrow stairways, they passed people in little groups or by themselves, who in the course of the three hours moved around as they liked in the three-story tower. Applause broke out in one room when Leonard entered. He bowed, found a seat for the girl and slowly sat down himself. A red-haired girl with a flute began the last passage once more. The flute wailed, yowled as only a flute can yowl. Benny growled quietly. Dogs are said to hear things six times louder than humans. And these were dissonant sounds. She therefore picked him up and carried him out, then up the stairs to the balcony at the very top of the tower. Dusk was falling, the sky had a greenish tinge, turning to red on the horizon, where the sun was setting. Across it floated bears, frogs, hedgehogs, a dynasty of kings with long beards and empty eyes like in Goya's paintings, changing in a moment to the profile of a grandmother or her silhouette from behind, carrying a bowl of cakes, which a while later became a lone camel. Who was it who said that everything can be seen in the clouds?

The balcony was secured all around with a wooden parapet. She suddenly heard a quiet murmur and when she looked down inside the tower, she smelled the faint smoke from the torches, she could see heads along the balustrade on each floor and music came from half-opened doors, the sounds mingling to create a quiet, agreeably irregular symphony. Benny clung tightly to her arms, not wanting to be put down for anything in the world, because he could sense the depths below him.

"Well, how do you like it?" Leo came up to her.

"It's...certainly, unusual.... I was expecting a concert, either something at a stadium, sports hall or a classical one...this is... but I like it, it's...natural somehow.... The people playing seem to be part of the setting, as if they rounded it off, a pleasant accord.... I don't know how to describe it in any other way. What do you think?"

Leonard was silent. Leaning against the parapet, with his back to her, he was gazing into the twilight valley.

"Did I say something wrong?"

"No. In fact you expressed it very well. Not one of the critics has said that about this music. Maybe that it was in accord not with the setting, but with nature, with something people are born with.... That's what music is for. Music is art at its most free, it has no bounds, just like the wind, the sea, the sky...."

"Does that mean you object to classical music?"

"What do you mean by classical? I was thinking that it's a real sin to pin tones down to form a composition, well, it may be camouflage, a drilled circus act...."

"I can't agree with that. That's to deny creative work, combinations, structures...."

"Hm, it looks as if you've studied it...."

"I might have, a bit. My father is a well-known Moscow violinist. But that's neither here nor there...."

"You can speak Russian? You can't tell from your accent."

"You can from yours. And what about those who interpret, if you don't acknowledge composers. And if you don't want notes, why do you let people interpret your things?"

Leonard was clearly amused to see her getting so excited. "The more I know about you, the better it is. Other times the opposite has been true. All my expectations have turned to disappointment."

"It just seems like that because you don't expect anything any more."

"Listen. It's lovely when you're gazing at the clouds in an evening sky."

They listened. The tones rose from the cone of the tower and they were closer to the clouds than to the ground; suddenly the evening sky really stretched to infinity....

"Why did you leave my music? Didn't you like it?" Leo asked as they were about to get onto his motorbike.

"Maybe I did, but Benny was unhappy. It's very dissonant. I think perhaps I prefer more melody, too."

* * *

"You went slowly on the way back," the girl said, when he dropped her off in front of an Art Nouveau building from 1902.

"If you think about your dog, why shouldn't I think about you and then...perhaps I wanted to spend more time with you."

The girl stared at him with her green eyes, but quickly looked down. "Thank you for an unusual evening."

"I don't even know your name."

"Ester."

"Ester, where can I find you next time?"

At that moment Ester realized that Leo didn't want to see her at the underground station where he had seen her so far.

"But I've no choice," she said, as if he had actually said it.

"Won't you invite me for a cup of tea in return for that lovely evening?"

"Not now. But come tomorrow around four. That balcony up there with the recess is ours."

"O.K. See you then."

When he was approaching the house the next day, he saw Ester slowly walking along with Benny in her arms, dragging her little tennis shoes one after the other. When he spoke to her outside the house, she turned around and even before he saw her face, he caught sight of Benny's large, deformed, bloodshot eye.

"Some mongrel bit his good eye," she announced instead of greeting him. "I want to take him to see the vet immediately, but I'm just going to get something from upstairs. Come tomorrow."

Leonard waited in the doorway opposite and he saw Ester come out again, go into the pawn shop at the end of the street and then disappear around the corner. When she returned an hour later, he was still standing there.

"I wanted to tell you that I can't come tomorrow or the rest of the week; I'll be away.... What did they say?"

"That he's old...," she repeated lethargically. "But come in, we'll make that cup of tea."

They climbed up to the third floor. The apartment had a hall, toilet and a large L-shaped room. There was a shower cubicle behind the door, a sink and a hotplate, a folding table with an overhead frame from which the kitchen utensils hung, two chairs, one old armchair, an old television and bookshelves all along the walls. The other part of the L was divided horizontally in the middle to form an upper "floor" with a short ladder.

"That's where I used to sleep when Grandma was alive," Ester commented as she filled a large old Russian teapot with water. "She slept on the bottom bed. I've got my writing desk there now."

"Not a centimeter wasted. When did she die?"

"Last year. Everything around me is dying...," Ester said in a weary voice. Then she sat down facing him. They heard the water bubbling quietly. "She spent her last month in the hospital. She couldn't move at all. Have you ever seen bed sores?" Ester didn't wait for an answer. Now, for the first time, a year later, she had to pour out to this stranger at least some of what still haunted her, waking her up in the middle of the night: "Greyish, dying flesh, open wounds covered with excrement.... When I turned her over, washed her, called for the nurse and she sprayed and disinfected it all, I saw how it kept seeping into the wounds, again and again.... She knew how to suffer, or she couldn't feel anything any more, because she used to give me a wonderful smile and whisper: "Esty, Esty...my little girl.... And for a year before that she was in this little room.... Sometimes she was irritable and bad tempered and sometimes very good. In spite of the fact that she could hardly move, she wanted to go out. It was hot last summer. Every day I took her down these three floors, scared that I wouldn't be able to hold her on the way down...and on the way up I almost carried her in my arms. Then with Benny, and so it went on, day after day. That's when I stopped going to lectures. In the last month, I just kept praying that she would die...."

There was a long silence.

"Didn't you start studying again?"

"No. What for? Everything around me is dying...."

"What connection do you have with Russia?" Leonard was looking at the teapot and cups. He had forgotten her reference to her father.

"Grandma was a Russian German or a German Russian. As you like. She was born here during the First World War to a German mother and a Russian officer. She lived there and after the Second World War she moved here. I came to join her when my parents divorced." Ester got up, so she wouldn't have to go on and she put Benny, who was staggering here and there with his nose to the ground, in front of his bowl of water. "He can't even find that. He's completely blind," she said almost in a whisper. But Benny only took two licks and staggered on, bumping his little forehead into everything that got in his way. She put him back on a soft cushion in a basket under the bookcase.

* * *

When Leonard came by a week later, he saw on a chair in the middle of the room a box, in which Benny was lying on his right side on a cushion, his paws folded in front of him like a child. A candle was burning nearby.

"He fell from the balcony," Ester whispered. "Actually...he jumped after my voice.... I told him: Benny, I'm going to buy you your favorite liver, because he was getting better, it looked as if he could see, he was more lively outside...he asked to go out onto the balcony, I told him, look out for me, I'll be back soon...and when I left he really was sitting at a safe distance from the railing, as he always did. He used to wait for me like that...I was only away for a while, who would have thought...a friend of mine from next door called out to me, we chatted a bit, I was just laughing at something she said, when I suddenly heard a dull thud behind me...he was lying on the ground, jerking and making a rattling sound...it didn't last long...how could he jump like that, when he was so terrified of heights? You know what I still feel. How he pressed his little head so hard up to my neck, like a young child...."

"Come on, Ester, let's bury him. I know a place."

Ester covered Benny with a cloth from the basket, Leonard shut the box and they blew out the candle.

"It's nice here, especially in winter. It reminds me...," Leonard didn't finish.

Ester didn't ask what it reminded him of. Showing no sign of interest, she climbed back on the motorbike and took a last look at the place where they had buried Benny. They got off at Neuer Markt.

"Will you have something? It's on me."

Ester nodded absent-mindedly. So they moved along with the crowd. All of a sudden Leonard reached down to grasp her hand and stop her. Next to one of the entrances to Kaufhof four men were preparing to play, in black tails, white shirts with bow ties. The first violinist was over fifty, with a wavy mane of grey hair. He tossed a white cloth over his shoulder and the tense posture of a violinist indicated what was to follow. On the notice next to a violin case they read: Moscow Chamber Orchestra. Performances for private celebrations. At the first notes a circle formed around them, but there were also many people with rucksacks on their backs who passed by indifferently. The dark-skinned Neuer Markt madman, who walks around barefoot in winter and summer, letting out dreadful sounds and spitting on the ground under people's feet, was also a disturbance.

"And these people won the war," Ester said. "I'm ashamed to be one of them.... A beggars' empire!" she cursed quietly.

"It's not that simple. And that you of all people should say so...."

Ester fell silent. The enthusiastic street audience clapped and showered coins into the violin case. Leonard wrote something on a cigarette packet, went over to the first violinist and stuffed it in his pocket.

"Do you belong to the Russian Mafia?" she asked him.

"No. I've just been in touch with the music scene here for quite a while. I've sent them to the rich mansions on the Rhine. Every evening they'll earn as much there as they would in the street the whole winter. I don't usually do this, but they were really good. Listen, Ester, do you know how to avoid getting bruised? I mean the corner we might bump into," Leo asked silent Ester in a little coffee bar.

Ester sipped her kölsch and didn't answer. Perhaps she ought to get up and go to the Magnus. What nonsense was this?!

"Don't look at me like that. I'm thinking of how I can protect you.... The important thing is to know what we could bump into. And if we can't avoid it, let's at least catch it with both hands, in order to soften the blow...do you know what I mean?"

"Why do you want to protect me and what from?" Everyone has his fate and there's no escaping it...," Ester said slowly. "Take me, for example. I would like to travel...see the Russian steppe... that's what you were thinking about when we were burying Benny, weren't you? But that dream will never come true," she spoke quickly, not waiting for a reply. "I can hardly manage to pay for my apartment every month. I have looked for work, but when there are four million unemployed.... I used to work as a cleaner, but they don't want me now, they shoo me away from the door, they think I'll steal from them, so I went begging, a few coins for Benny; now I don't even need that..., but why did you speak to me then?"

"You know, people are like tells.... Do you know what that is? A tell is a mound with layers of soil capturing time – different cultures; it's a cross-section, in which archeologists capture the different eras.... Well, when people meet, without knowing why, the different strata in them have or don't have something to say to each other. You see, I didn't know that you were half Russian; in fact, I knew nothing about you at all, but even so you are terribly close to me, as if there was something of me in you and I can't explain it. Give me your hand, Ester."

Ester hesitantly held out her narrow hand and placed it in his large, warm palm. They both let them rest there and at that moment they fitted perfectly one in the other.

"Do you have anyone? Do you have a boyfriend?"

"No. Not now. When I was studying, there was Robert. He's a law student. We met a couple of times after as well, but when things were at their worst, when Grandma was dying, he left me all by myself at an S-Bahn station at half past ten in the evening...

and the other day he passed me in the metro and avoided me, he looked down, that hurt a lot, in short, he didn't want to know me...." Ester withdrew her hand from Leo's. "But maybe...he'll come back," she said it so quietly he could hardly hear. "I was very fond of him."

"Ester, come to my place. I'll make the tea today."

She looked at him uncertainly. Why did he want her to go with him? The fact that she talked freely, that was just her way. But here was someone who thought about what she said, added his own views, it was interesting...the first time...as if he were the father she had hardly known...and maybe something more, something with a spark...and also...an uncertain feeling that he, too, needed her....

Ester didn't know how very much he needed her in that unsteady world of anonymity and solitude. Until then he hadn't looked at it that way. People had come and gone in his life and he had not missed them, he had always been sufficient unto himself, he had been all he needed. And here...this lost, frail girl, who had made up her mind to beg, to surrender her dignity so early in life, as well as all else...to do it so thoroughly...that was what it was... and then...those layers, a tell of certain layers....

They strolled in the direction of the Rhine embankment, past Ludwig's museum. They walked beside the single track, the hopelessly lonely single track of the Holocaust monument by Dany Karavan, Leo placing one foot in front of the other, Ester behind him. When he reached the place where the single rails ran into black blocks reminiscent of an iron furnace, Leo halted and looked upwards. Ester realized there were a magic number of black blocks, arranged to obscure from this spot the sunrise and the view of the huge statue of Wilhelm on a horse. Memorials to the Holocaust cast a shadow over German history.

They went a short way along the embankment to the oldest surviving part of the town, and Leo led her up to the third floor above the Lion King Italian restaurant and opened the door into a dark, antiquated flat. He pressed the switch and a number of nooks were lit up at the same time in the large hall. Pictures of Beethoven, Liszt, Tchaikovsky....

"Where did these come from?" Ester cried out in surprise. "I thought you would have nothing but pop music. Daddy liked Beethoven. I've heard that his new wife – she buys and sells fur – now spends 500 marks a day beside the sea in Greece. He gives concerts...." She checked herself, because she didn't know why she had suddenly started on about her father of all people and about his second wife, a dealer, and then Leo had disappeared somewhere and she suddenly seemed to be alone. "Hallo," she called out quietly and went over to the first door. Leo was sitting in an armchair, looking like a ghost. In the dim light the grey strands of hair on his shoulders appeared white. Hanging on the wall above the armchair was some kind of strange native violin, made of wood and with one string, and when she looked around, she saw there were various kinds of violins on all the walls. "Ah..." was all she found to say.

Leo made a gesture and pulled himself out of his chair without a word. She followed him into the kitchen, where an ancient teapot, just like her grandmother's, was standing on the table. She sat down in a corner on a small sofa. Leo made the tea as if it were a ritual; she no longer knew how it should be done.

"How long ago did you emigrate?" she asked, watching his slow, graceful movements.

Because she had indirectly asked him how he had lived the whole of his life, and because that was just what he didn't know how to describe, his reply was about something quite different, even though it was in a way an answer to her question. "I know a Romanian here. A clever man, published a book not long ago – an anthropologist, his grandmother was German, but even so they didn't give him German nationality. A lot of people helped him. A German teacher got him an apartment and now he's doing everything possible to prolong his stay...."

"Does he have any children?" Ester asked, again thinking more about Leo than about the unknown Romanian.

"That's just the interesting thing. He has two sons. One was born back in Romania, he's about twelve years old, the other was born here, he's about six. Now the whole family has twelve years to wait, until the boy is eighteen, then they will at last be registered permanently as his parents and brother."

"The little boy will save the family. That's like a fairytale, isn't it?" smiled Ester.

"He even looks the part, like Exupéry's Little Prince – golden curls, tiny, fragile – we can go and see them sometime, if you want.... But it's like that, too. In Romania she, his wife, was someone, a good ethnographer, but she can't make a career here. He was a member of the Academy of Sciences. And here they are dependent on others, on charity, the Church. She's studying theology now, sometimes they give her work, then...all their furniture, everything they have comes from the Church."

"How did you manage to do so well?"

"I've been here a long time," Leo said, with some hesitation. "And then, mine is a completely different case. You don't know, you can't remember what Russia was like...after the war...when we were building socialism, very earnestly.... And then this

Germany...it's hard to say what it is, on the one hand they're so meticulous, on the other hand completely indifferent to their own affairs. Heine described them very well: they behave as if they'd swallowed the stick they'd been beaten with.... I'm jumping from one thing to another, but it's all connected somehow.... I'll tell you the secret of success, if you like, after all, that's really what you're asking me about...." Leo leaned back in the deep armchair and fell silent. It wasn't that easy to explain. "People choose," he continued, still thinking it over, "among the things that are dearest to them...so, let's say, they choose freedom, creative work without restrictions, they have already tried it at home, but they weren't understood, they come to a free democracy, like this one, and see that no one understands them here either, they can do it, but a different set of conventions applies here, into which they fit no better."

"You say a free democracy. Democracy doesn't exist. There are only the strong and the weak, the rich and the poor. The former can be magnanimous at best; it's only the latter who can know anything about democracy, what it should be like, because it's they who dream about it."

"America is a democracy and England...a very old democracy."

"America? You're not serious?" Ester gave a short laugh, "with the genocide of the Indians and England with its colonies?"

Leo listened thoughtfully, then he spoke up: I don't entirely agree with you. Freedom in art really does have its origins in the East, but it can be applied fully only in the West.... Our East, Ester, will never find freedom. The pyramid, controlled from the top, the patriarchal principle, that's deeply rooted in people."

"Isn't that the Balkan and oriental principle in general?" Ester asked quietly, hesitantly, crossing her legs in front of her.

Leo stared at her in surprise. Then he remembered she had studied political science: "What do you mean?" he asked her to be sure.

"I'm thinking of former Yugoslavia, what happened there, and Israel...of China, the way they sent the army and tanks into Hong Kong the day after unification.... When it comes to that, so far as Yugoslavia is concerned – Serbia today. Do you think that invasion was right?"

"You call that an invasion?" Leonard exclaimed, or almost shouted. "I see that as a turning point, that refusal to respect statehood.... What's the point of having states? At last that principle has been broken, they're giving them something to think about! After all, it was they, the heroic Serbs that started it all, the genocide in Kosovo!"

Ester stared at him dumbfounded, as he waved his arms about.

But then she said softly, but resolutely: "If I'm not mistaken, the NATO Charter declares it's there to defend, not attack, and besides.... The UN Security Council didn't agree to the bombing... war was not declared and people were dying on both sides. Are you one of those extreme liberals who doesn't recognize the sovereignty of states?"

"Of course. You've guessed right. But to return to the secret of success in art," Leonard resumed, after a few moments of silence. "When you consider, Ester, that all the motifs in art were covered in ancient times, that everything has already been said, acted, painted, then the mode of creation remains as a new...."

"When you have a good knowledge of classical laws?" Ester cut in with almost imperceptible irony.

"I'm thinking of the most individual way of expressing yourself," he continued calmly, "art grown intimate, because you won't find two people exactly the same – in that way art has sympathizers, small groups, individuals who identify with you, not entirely, but they are somehow related – tells, you know.... In this post-modern world, as the wise guys like to call it nowadays, where everything is mixed up with everything, you will find people who feel and see things in a similar way, especially if you don't try to tie them down.... The reason why this town is a pleasant place, is that it's the crossroads of many cultures. The only thing that always remains essentially the same is Nature, Ester. But let's return to the secret of success in art...Ester...you're not listening...what are you thinking about?"

"I'm thinking about Benny...," Ester said, quite frankly.

Leo gave an odd, gentle smile and seemed to move his whole body towards the girl sitting with head bent on his old sofa. Then he pulled himself together and just said, "I'd like to be your Benny."

Ester didn't lift her head, or even move. That sentence just went right to the bone, ran through her like an electric shock. "He jumped after my voice...," she said harshly and derisively.

"I know I have been talking uninterestingly and for a long time, but I'll finish replying to your question. The secret of success lies in thinking up an interesting point of view and knowing how to present it. Interesting, that means different...Ester, are you listening to me?"

"Sorry, I'm not any more, and if you want to know what I was thinking about just now," she said, as if just to be spiteful, "about well-cooled beer at the Magnus...." She got up. "Would you show me around your apartment? I'd like to know something about these instruments. But just briefly, I don't want to tire you."

Leo got up without a word, he sensed that she was retreating from him, he once more felt his age and the dark places in the flat seemed gloomy. In contrast, when the lamps were lit, all the otherwise lifeless museum pieces seemed to Ester to come alive, as if they were linked by some strange kind of dynamism and excitement. She wondered what it was as they went from room to room.

Leo suddenly spoke very little. He was silent for the most part, because each of these objects had its own long history. Only when they came to the last door did he pause and, with a Stradivarius in his hands, not looking at Ester, he said, "Stay here, Ester, the flat is big enough and I won't disturb you." At the same time he realized the uselessness of this proposal, after all, only half an hour ago Ester was somewhere else in her thoughts, she was slipping away from him, she was like the wind, yet in spite of this he hadn't felt so close to another person for a long time – in fact ever – as he did to her. He gazed at her tiny, scruffy little tennis shoes, he knew they would leave, they would not stay....

He opened the door into the last room. There was a large, wooden double bed in the middle and a music stand and score near the window, together with a violin case. The one he actually played was here. Over the bed there hung a strange-looking clock. The small wooden frame of an old cottage window, in the middle, where the crossbars meet and there is usually a handle, there was the large, black sole of a shoe, and on it the hands of a clock, which clearly served their purpose.

Ester held her breath when she realized the significance of the picture: "What's that?"

"My best friend gave me that. He said he would follow me to the end of the world, but...he never even got this far. He probably couldn't. One of the few things I brought here from Russia."

"And...this?" Ester pointed timidly to the wall, where next to the picture of Time there hung a pair of incredibly tiny, already greying ballet shoes.

"My mother was a ballet dancer...."

MARÍNA ČERETKOVÁ-GÁLLOVÁ

- prose writer, playwright;
born in Zbehy (1931)

Marína Čeretková-Gállová worked as a literary editor for the radio.

Her work is typical of women's literature. Her first publication was a collection of short novels **Koniec líšky** (*The Passing of the Fox*, 1962), in which she depicted the emotional and moral problems of young women. The world of women and the breakdown in relations between men and women, and parents and children are also dominant themes in her next works – the novels **Stokrát moje leto** (*A Hundred Times My Summer*, 1964), **Smrť červenej jarabiny** (*The Death of the Red Rowan*, 1964), **Samota pre bohov** (*Solitude for the Gods*, 1967), **Koňak pre Amáliu** (*Cognac for Amalia*, 1967), **Hriešne dievča Júlia** (*Sinful Little Julia*, 1970). Her novel **Jednooký** (*One-Eyed*, 1978) is about the life of a man in the post-war years and his vain attempts to find his place in everyday life. The fate of children from broken homes is the focus of her novella **Dlhé čakanie Anny Drozdíkovej** (*Anna Drozdíková's Long Wait*, 1982), of her book **Cudzie deti** (*Other People's Children*, 1983), from which the short story "The Actress" is taken, as well as of her prose work **Úraz** (*The Accident*, 1987). In her last works – **Anjelik** (*Little Angel*, 1994) and **Nechajte maličkých** (*Let the Little Ones Be*, 1998) – she tries in her own way to break the taboo on certain themes.

M. Čeretková-Gállová is the author of a number of radio plays for both adults and children (**Murovaný dom** – *House of Bricks and Mortar*, **Telefón** and others) and of the television play **Tereza** (1983).

In her own words:

In my women's prose works I draw attention to the possibility of an ecological catastrophe within ourselves, to the malformation of our mutual relationships. I am horrified by the demeaning model of our life together, the absence of love between us, our lack of capacity for emotional life, the demoralizing relationship between parents and children, the destructive misunderstanding of women's emancipation. The issue in my work has long been to demand a renaissance of womanhood in its fullness, the appreciation of the role of mother, its privileged position in the assessment of the importance of womanhood. It is obvious at a glance that a woman is a different being from a man; she is biologically and inherently predestined for motherhood. This difference logically leads us to conclude that different processes take place in her body and mind than in a man's.

It may seem that I am not talking about literature, but yes, I am. Especially about what is known as women's literature. All my stories should be evidence of a woman author's approach to literature, based above all on the incontestable difference between women and men and on the conviction this gives rise to, that there is little of the woman's world in art, that we must stubbornly fight for its place there, highlight and encourage it, to make the woman's world more attractive, not only in life, but above all in art.

My work is in line with this, and it is my right as an author to give my heroine a chance to be above all a woman, to participate through literature in the renaissance of womanhood and of motherhood.

(1989)

THE ACTRESS

The armchair is golden and the actress has a long robe. She holds an unread book in her lap and stares into the distance, much farther than she can possibly see in this room. The light from the chandelier shines clear and bright, she sits quietly in the patterned wallpaper and the telephone is white. The loneliness of the actress's room is disturbed only by the ticking of a small clock on the wall. The actress's hands lie helplessly one next to the other, her face is silent, her neck stretched like a bow and the room like someone forgotten, like a half-drunk glass of wine left on a table. Her knees under the unread book suddenly stiffen.

She had no longer been thinking about the betrayal when the telephone rang, which is why she started and her face turned pale. The palpitations of her heart bring back her old hurt feelings, she rests her hand on that shrieking white thing, as if calming someone's impassioned head and in a choked voice she stutters, no, don't call me, please!

24

She puts her other hand on the telephone, too, desperately covering it, as if it were her own chagrined face.

It's not natural to sit alone after a premiere, she thinks to herself. After such a successful premiere!

She laughs and gets up.

I know it's unnatural, but you don't know anything, says the actress.

She stands there in the bright, pitiless light, as if she were confronting him, she stands in the midst of the sharp ringing of the telephone, she has a black dress and she wants to tell him everything.

You don't realize how unnatural and how cruel it was to cast me in that role. For the first time in my acting career the role of a deserted old woman, a little crazy and childish.

It came off!

You can't believe it. How is it possible, where did I get it from, when I didn't have it in me?! From one day to the next, a lover transformed into an old lady, of course it took me aback, what did you expect?! I begged you, no, I need time, I don't have that woman in me, I'm frivolous and beautiful and feminine and suddenly I'm meant to be.... You knew that the world of that old woman was strange and unfamiliar to me, ah, all I felt was anguish and humiliation, I knew what it meant, who had taken my place, I was supposed to be a flop.

I packed my case, got on that train and changed at that little station, exactly according to the script.

I had no idea I would meet her.

The actress abruptly turns to the ringing phone and says: You want to congratulate me? What for?! You didn't believe I could do it. You're calling because you can't suppress your professional curiosity, you want to have me there, you want to have me beside you as always, after every premiere. This is the first time I'm missing at the celebration after the premiere, the first time, there's a first time for everything and then after that it's not the first time.

The actress's voice jams, like a key in a faulty lock, in a state of agitation she lifts the receiver and quickly replaces it, there is silence, the telephone is immobilized. The actress's knees give way beneath her.

Then I'll tell you, she whispers.

I set out on a journey, you didn't know. The weather was indifferent, not nice at all and there were hundreds of lilacs in flower everywhere, all along the track, in every garden.

When I got off, the first thing I saw was her. She's been coming to the station to meet this express for a long time, regularly, no matter what the weather. She trotted along the platform and smiled, clean, dry and crinkled as a tobacco leaf. On the other side of the rails was a house with yellow geese in the grass and the weather wasn't nice at all, very dull, it was May. She gazed through a window in the third carriage, a sprig of lilac in one hand, a handkerchief in the other – do you remember? I insisted on that white handkerchief, not just any one, a fine lawn one, edged with lace.

The express train was just disappearing around the bend, the last carriages trailing behind like a tail. She was standing very close, the cobweb of wrinkles on her little face closely entwined, merry cornflowers peeping out of her eyes, ah, she looked so innocent and so happy. She stuffed the white handkerchief into one of those shabby bags old ladies carry and looked in my direction. I'm seeing someone off, she sighed and smiled at me.

Yes? I said, smiling back. Then she told me: I never ask him to come, he comes of his own accord. I try to tell him, why do you put yourself out, why do you bother about me, an old woman, and do you think he listens to me? He says I shouldn't talk like that and can't I bear the sight of him! Well, I say, goodness me, of course that's not it. He comes again and again, tells me not to put him off, so of course I don't. He'll stop by again when he's going this way, he travels around enough, on business, duty calls. But he's not in a hurry, he doesn't insist on being driven around, because he isn't like the others, he wants to be with people. With a car, what do you have, the road ahead of you and a snooty chauffeur, or they make you go in a car full of bigwigs and that means boozing at every stop and, believe me, he doesn't drink, not a drop, he'd rather suck on candy, so I keep these hard green ones ready for him.

She gave a girlish giggle, a tinkling laugh, at that moment she seemed really shrewd. I thought to myself, how does she come to be here?! Just as if she had popped up out of my script, as if she were the old woman of my acting career, that very woman I didn't have it in me to play!

She gave me a sideways glance, sizing me up, and she smiled a little, her dry hands clasped tamely in front of her. I thought to myself, and that's supposed to be me?! It made my heart miss a beat.

Where are you going now? I asked her, and she replied, well, my dear, as you like. If you don't mind, we could even go and sit down for a while. Chat over a coffee or something sweet. Is your case heavy?

No, I said, the case is no problem.

And what is the problem? He'll get home in time, his wife won't scold him for spending a bit of time with me. And there are lots of trains, you'll be able to get one, don't worry.

I asked her, and who is your son?

Aha!

She shook her head and winked. Then she beckoned with her finger and in a little while we were entering the station restaurant. She waggled the sprig of lilac under my nose and boasted that he had brought her an enormous bunch of it. And something sweet – he always brings that, because I have a sweet tooth. I'll give you this lilac to remember me by, she said happily, and I suddenly felt light-hearted; we sat together at a table in the restaurant like two old acquaintances. She said she would tell me who he was, but I mustn't let on, what for! I was to keep it to myself, there was no need for everyone to know that it was a government minister who came to see her.

A minister? I asked in surprise, but she ignored my surprise, a minister like any other, one word like another, she called the waiter and asked him very confidentially to give her a taste of that sweet stuff and something even sweeter to go with it, a cake with cream, yes. She slowly sipped the liqueur and then licked her lips, her little finger lifted in the air on a level with those merry cornflowers – I did it at the beginning of the second act, remember, just remember what I asked for – that it should be cherry liqueur, a beautiful color and what an aroma! And Pohanka as the waiter had to make meaningful gestures and look dead bored, ah, in that restaurant I felt I was on the stage, like during the premiere today, even though at that moment I had no idea this was a true story. Then it was like a play and now like reality.

All of a sudden the old lady whispered a big secret to me – that she had once taught him. Him, the minister. He, poor boy, was clumsy, slow off the mark, but he had a good heart. She hadn't been a good teacher either, believe me, she had preferred a good heart to top marks, she never insisted on top marks. She had predicted he would go far, he just had to work hard. He should go his own way, more haste the less speed, not rush into anything. Well, he had climbed up the ladder. He had a heart as wholesome as a piece of bread. But I don't ask him to come, do you think I've ever cajoled him into it? Never. I've never complained either, or begged him, I haven't asked him for anything, not even a bigger pension, nothing at all. You mustn't think I would ask anything for myself, not for myself. I just try to tell him, well, Minister, what's the use of your good heart in such a high post, be careful or they'll even make fun of you. Better squander everything, along with your good heart, so it won't be an obstacle to you, that's what I say, that's how I test my minister. He laughs, says I'm trying to trip him up, he remembers that I used to play tricks on them during our lessons; what could I do with them all those long years I taught them?! But what tricks can you play on a minister, you tell me that?!

Then I made a mistake. I asked her: Which minister is it, what's he a minister of? And I shouldn't have. The old lady was suddenly completely different, she gave me an offended look and then burst out, I won't tell you that, you don't have to know everything! What if you go blabbing to someone about it, some women can't keep anything to themselves, they have to blab about everything! And to their men in the first place. Have you got a man? she suddenly asked me sternly, taking my breath away. I've got you and she asks me, have you got a man?!

I put my mouth to my glass, wetting my lips in the wine.

Then I asked her to forgive me. I stifled my silly, distasteful curiosity. She smiled at me and stroked my hands. I only get on with good people, she said, and you're one of them, you're like me, don't worry about him, you'll do well and you'll have a good life, that's what I wish for you and don't forget it.

I drank the rest of the wine at one gulp, my palms were moist, my fingers were trembling. Our conversation was over almost before it had begun. I realized that from the way the waiter appeared, casually propping himself on his shoulder against the door. A face peered out from behind him, plump, broad and possibly kindly, it was a womanly, mommyish face.

Of course, I should have known, this mommyish creature muttered under her breath and started off in our direction. I knew things didn't look good, but I had no idea what was coming. The mommyish face bore down on us, her purple coat unfastened, a yellow dress above her knees, she stomped along on the flat soles of her feet. The old lady was just taking a photograph out of her pitiful black bag and when she heard this, she stiffened. I glimpsed a well-known figure in the photograph, but I couldn't believe my own eyes, I couldn't believe my own ears, that mommyish creature was giving orders, get up – well, what have you been up to this time?! She grabbed the old lady by the elbow, the photograph remained face down on the table, I whispered inanely, tell me your name, address, give me your name and address, but it was too late.

Every nerve in the old lady's little body began to quiver, the cornflowers in her eyes darkened like the pavement after rain. She smiled sadly, a piece of cake with cream remained on the plate and a drop of cherry liqueur in the glass.

Come on now, said that creature, who looked mommyish, but her voice was rough.

The old lady began to sniffle and I leaped up from behind the table and said, leave that lady alone. I said it strangely and hoarsely and the mommyish figure looked at me in surprise. She's run up a bill, she laughed. How much?

She fumbled in the pocket of her purple coat and threw a crumpled ten-crown note down on the table.

When are you going to stop causing us embarrassment, woman, she shrieked, but immediately switched to a softer, mommyish tone and explained: she does this to us almost every week, we don't know what to do with her, we'll have to lock her up when this express is due, otherwise she escapes, she's terribly cunning, you've no idea.

The waiter laughed, hahaha! And the stories she makes up!

The old lady sniffled like a little child and her shoulders shook. She shuffled away towards the door of her own accord, not looking around even once.

I stood rooted to the spot, the waiter scratched behind his ear, the fun's over, he grinned, then wrote out the bill and straightened out the crumpled ten-crown note.

I took the photograph and the sprig of lilac, the waiter watching me, then he said, she's from the old-people's home, a little crazy, but otherwise harmless, you could see that for yourself.

He helped me into my coat.

She always picks someone out, but it's just a liqueur, something sweet and trumped up tales, nothing more. What story did she tell you?

I hung around on the platform, the sky was black, the trains neither came nor went, it was a time of sadness and realization. So that's how it was. But you don't know anything.

The actress slowly stirs herself, her dress rustles, the telephone begins ringing once more.

What else do you want? the actress says quietly. She takes a photograph out of the unread book and looks at it.

Don't call, please! I'd have to tell them about your mother in front of them all!

She is left breathless, but the telephone goes on ringing, on and on.

The actress chokes on her own voice.

In the name of all abandoned mothers, I'd have to tell you about her. About her and about me!

Her sob falls headlong on the ground, like an axe it cuts into the shrill ringing of the white telephone, into the loneliness of the actress's room.

ETELA FARKAŠOVÁ

- prose writer, journalist, playwright, translator;
born in Levoča (1943)

Etela Farkašová worked as a secondary school teacher and at present lectures at the Faculty of Arts, Comenius University in Bratislava.

In her first collection of short stories, **Reprodukcia** č**asu** (*The Reproduction of Time*, 1978), she reflects upon women's difficult struggle to make the most of their abilities. A related theme with an emphasis on the philosophical and psychological depiction of women's inner worlds and the search for meaningfulness in their lives is also presented in her second book of short stories, **Snívanie v tráve** (*Dreaming in the Grass*, 1983), and with certain variations also in a series of prose works: **No**č**né jazvy** (*Night Scars*, 1986), **Unikajúci portrét** (*A Disappearing Portrait*, 1989), **Nede**ľ**né fotografie** (*Sunday Photographs*, 1993) and **De**ň **za d**ň**om** (*Day After Day*, 1997). Her latest book is a collection of short stories, **Hodina zapadajúceho slnka** (*The Hour of the Setting Sun*, 1998), from which the story "A Sky Full of Migrating Birds" is taken.

She writes literary critiques and essays, and in 1998 she published a book entitled **Etudy o bolesti a iné eseje** (*Studies of Pain and Other Essays*).

In recent years she has extended her scholarly interests to include feminist philosophy. She is co-author of the book **Teória poznania** (*The Theory of Cognition*) and **Štyri poh**ľ**ady do feministickej filozofie** (*Four Views of Feminist Philosophy*, 1994).

She has written a radio play, **Rozhodnutie** (The Decision, 1981) and a number of short stories for radio (**Návraty** – *Comebacks,* **Pivnica** – *The Cellar*).

She translates from German and English.

In her own words:

For me philosophy is most interesting when it is about what happens within a person, or in the sphere of interpersonal contacts – and, similarly, literature, when it concentrates above all on "internal events," where the story takes second place to feelings, experiences, reflections. This determines my view of the relationship between the two....

As a reader and as an author I am certainly most in sympathy with the kind of short story that I would call philosophical or philosophizing, and likewise with the essay bordering on the short-story genre....

I think that in women's literature (I am aware of the need to define this traditional and rather unfortunate term in a new way) it is above all a question of the articulation of women's experience, (also with an emphasis on its everyday, tangible nature, its attention to detail and at the same time its wholeness), a question of articulating the world of feelings, experiences and imagination – in a word, a woman's inner life.

Women's literature, however, also contributes a way of looking at our common male and female – and therefore human – world and in doing so it can cast light on such strata and dimensions of human reality and experience that can escape a man's eye, or which from a man's point of view do not and indeed need not seem relevant. After all, it is well known that one's experience of life and the situation one finds oneself in have an influence on one's perspective. In this sense I understand women's writings as an enrichment of people's way of looking at the world, as an extension of it to include aspects which are important from the woman's angle of vision.

A SKY FULL OF MIGRATING BIRDS

A position which after some time makes her head spin; she mustn't straighten up too quickly; each time sparks dance before her eyes, glittering brightly on a black background; in spite of this she cannot resist the sound coming from above, still indistinct but nearer and more certain with every minute. Finally she looks up, but must quickly restore her threatened balance, propping herself up with her palm on the dampened, sun-warmed soil; she adores this touch, the warm, damp earth seems like a living organism, she thinks to herself: a soft, cosy primal mother body, on which you can always rely.

She is a little taken aback, uneasy – how had the thought of an eternal primal mother come into her mind at that moment (where in fact do our words come from and to what extent are they really *my own* words, to what extent do I speak with words and see with pictures, with whole networks of pictures that others have created before me; *(is there still any point nowadays trying to find my own words and my own pictures; can there be any such thing any longer)?*

The sounds above her grow stronger, as if they wished to speak to her from those cloudy heights, as if they wished to address her in the midst of that autumn garden. Still bent over, her outstretched hands sunk in the soil, she rests her gaze on the spot where she senses they are, though not yet visible, at least she, with her short-sighted eyes, cannot pick out against the bluish-grey background the actual shapes of birds, although their voices are growing clearer, more pronounced all the time. She shifts her weight from her right foot to her left, at which almost imperceptible movement she feels a sharp prick on her finger, an unnoticed thorn has stuck in her flesh. She straightens up carefully, brushing the soil off her hands, with the back of one hand she wipes away the thin red stream on the fingers of the other; she is standing amid the roses, in the middle of that long bed of rose bushes; that was the first thing that had occurred to her and V. when they had bought the garden: to plant roses all down the slope, Nottinghams, Eiffels, Amadeuses, but above all Eiffels, from the cottage right down to the little lake. Red, yellow, white and purple.

On the other side of the fence her neighbor is digging up old strawberry plants, rather late; they always did things after everyone else, maybe out of laziness, maybe from a kind of indifference towards time, from tiredness or resignation so far as timed duties were concerned (maybe they have already reached the point where you realize that you cannot fulfill them all anyway, and certainly not to perfection, and therefore you should not let yourself be enslaved by them); he, too, has noticed the urgent, piercing voices of the birds; in a characteristic, half-sluggish way he waves his hand towards the sky, but then immediately bends over his spade again, just pausing in between to call in the direction of the house, where his wife is sitting on a bench, slowly, as if he were chopping the sentence into separate parts: put the water on for coffee, do you hear, it's high time you put the water on for coffee.

She knows her neighbors, she knows that no answer will come from the bench; rather a strange couple, must be about sixty, shortish, roundish, slow in movement and in speech, they were rarely heard talking together; it was the kind of conversation where you have the feeling that your partner is not listening, does not want to listen, does not think what is said is of any significance, because anyway, all they needed to say has already been said, and perhaps even heard. Her neighbor slowly, slowly and too quietly calls out once more, please don't forget the coffee, and not waiting for his wife's answer – anyway, she may not have heard him – he goes on with his work: the spade cuts rhythmically into the ground, now and then clanging against a metal post in the fence, a stone in the soil; no matter how long they cultivate it, there is no shortage of stones.

The sounds above her are rapidly becoming so loud that she involuntarily turns her head once more towards the sky; this time she can already see them; at moments it looks as if the whole sky is moving, maybe they are swans, but by their voices more likely wild geese; on the fringes of her memory a recollection flutters of a fairytale, which for her in childhood had always breathed the mystery of destiny: from human to bird and once more to human, ransomed by a triple sacrifice (is it really necessary to pay for every transformation, for every return, and as a rule, with that which is most dear?); the lasting burden of experience, as revealed in a fairytale.

Her senses are now fixed entirely on the sky, her eyes, her ears, and even her nose seems aware of a strange new smell; it might be a faint smell of dry twigs burning, of smoke, but above all of far-away places; she breathes in deeply, her sense of smell does still remember it; as a child she imagined that this kind of smell accompanied something infinitely remote, almost unattainable, and for that very reason appealing, to the point of being painfully tempting. She suddenly remembered a poem by a famous Chinese poet, which had recently come her way, whose words were in the same spirit: the contrast of immobility, of being bound to a fixed point that will not let go, with, at the same time, the insistent call of distant places; pointing towards what has already been seen, experienced, known.

When wild geese fly southwards,
how I long for my cry to fly with them!
When wild geese fly from the south,
how I long them to bring the call of my land.
Yet the wild geese fly so very high
far beyond the reach of my mournful pipe…
A fearsome emptiness grips my soul.
My desolate mind…

Returning several days later to the poem, in which eighteen centuries earlier Cai Wenji had described the sorrow of a woman with a dramatic destiny, the differences in space, time and even in the story itself suddenly seemed irrelevant; the actual story really is not the most important thing, something of the feelings, older than the centuries, had entered her prefabricated room, settled on her writing table, found their way into her pen, touched her eye, her ear, the skin at the tips of her fingers; the similarity of what had been felt and also perhaps the similarity of what had been spoken, the rather confusing thought that the poet had already written it for her, for her and for all those others who one day, similarly afflicted, would pause to gaze at a sky full of migrating birds (is there any need to attempt to express what has already been expressed, attempts at less perfect variations on the same or similar themes; but can anything exist in a language without any variations whatsoever? Because language is like forming a chain, passing on and receiving, because existing in language is like taking part in a never-ending relay). As if these verses were in a sense a presentiment of her own experience, a presentiment of this late afternoon, of *this* sky full of migrating birds, the sky of *this* moment in time.

The sky in motion: with bated breath she watches the serried ranks of the flock, making regular triangles, flowing unexpectedly, as if at command, into a new formation as strictly observed as before, with only a few birds flying beyond the shared geometrical design and keeping close to one of the rear tips of the triangle, while even these formed a smaller regular pattern. The change in the angle the birds had previously assumed happened several times in such rapid succession that she couldn't even register the different phases, if she concentrated on one part of the triangle, she missed the regrouping of the other parts.

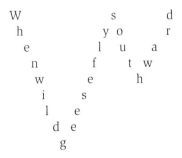

how I long for my cry to fly with them, wrote the Chinese poet (may desires and dreams fly with them too, the woman now says, dreams that may take us beyond our finality, that may help us reach, mature to transcendence); when had she last gazed with such wonder at the birds in the sky: last year, the year before, even earlier, she couldn't remember, but it was probably not in recent years; she had submerged herself too much in her work, she had let it swallow her up, from morning to late evening, fresh goals and resolutions had swarmed into her head quicker than she could fulfill the old ones; perhaps she really had thought she could help someone with her writings, that through them she could change something in the world and in others; if she had changed something, it was only herself, she had tested the limits of her own capabilities, with those writings she had measured them too: limits that in the end she had had to accept.

A sky bestrewn with birds: (migrating to distant lands, to the unknown, to memories or to presentiments?) a sky full of receding flocks...

She frowns in an effort to recall clearer outlines of vague memories, as if she has caught a glimpse of a shadow at her side, the figure of her mother going with her somewhere, talking to her, trying to convince her of something, to pass on to her a truth hard won by her own experience; she herself is protesting, she sees things from her own perspective, she is passionately arguing otherwise, when suddenly they both stop, their attention caught by the rustle of wings flapping close by (the feeling of unexpected surprise, the necessity to halt; but what had the two of them been talking about then, what truths had they been wrangling over?).

And then one more sky, submerged even further in time, a memory hard to drag up from the bottom layers of her memory, in fact only a memory of a memory, repeated over and over again by her parents, *do you remember*, began the sentences they addressed to her, *do you still remember your grandfather's kites?*

She rubs her palm, it itches, not so much from the dried soil as from the memory of touching the string, on the end of which a kite sailed in the air, an exceptionally beautiful kite, striking both in size and color, the envy of all the children in the street; kites were the speciality of her grandfather, the one who had lived in their house to the age of ninety, confined to his bed after a series of strokes, *quite unable to move, but infinitely brave and steadfast in his suffering* (words forming part of these retold memories), *no one in the neighborhood flew a kite like the ones he could make, surely you can remember something at least.*

The birds have now completely filled the space in the middle of the sky, they have showered over her like enormous black grains, she follows them with her head leaning back, the point of the triangle (an isosceles triangle, she has realized meanwhile) is just above her, an imaginary line drawn from her eyes straight upwards, a

v
e
r
t
i
c
a
l,

one of the connecting lines between heaven and earth, a special cathedral: if the bird flying at the head of the regular formation had dropped at that moment down that imaginary line, it would have fallen right at her feet, hit her shoulder, slid down her cheek, touched her face, she was certain of that, she needed that conviction, in order to assure herself of the connection between her body, her life and the formation moving across the sky, receding into infinity and tempting her to follow it, severely tempting her; correlating with the sky, with all that space up there, at least geometrically correlating (*yet the wild geese fly so very high far beyond the reach of my mournful pipe...*).

She stares at the flock of migrating birds, at the changing appearance of the pale blue sky, and it is as if the outlines of the regular formation help her to recall other memories, as if she were suddenly *somewhere there,* a part of the migrating flock. Surely these aren't the remains of an instinctive collective memory, she wonders, once more drinking in that flying closed formation, following with her eyes every change in movement up above her, only after a good while beginning to understand her strange memories of her experience of flying; in a sudden revelation she reads into the birds' triangle something about herself, her desires, her dreams, muffled by caution, by the passing years, disappointments and all the rest of it. In a flash she realizes that since her childhood she herself has stored her yearnings in images of birds, year after year, autumn after autumn, when something seemed to have come to an end, was disappearing and all that remained in her was regret for what had not been fulfilled and not retained, the first occasion being perhaps when walking hand in hand with her grandfather to a meadow to try out a gigantic kite, and then a few years later, that evening when she had tried to write her first poem, it had been a most peculiar feeling to see her *own* words on paper, at that time she had believed that those words really did belong to her and her alone, at that time she had still believed that something like that was possible. Then again when she had fallen in love for the first time, with a fifth grade classmate, who had never found out, or only later, when she had already met V. and when they were expecting a baby, when they were already a foursome, and then even later, identified with the moving sky, with a passing, whose final destination she did not know, but could only guess, for the moment it was escaping her, slipping away from her, dissolving into infinity, into the unfathomableness of every future. She grew accustomed to imagining from time to time that she herself was moving somewhere else, she imagined her life in a completely different place and wondered whether in this new location it would be much different, better, wiser, more meaningful (the moving sky has set her imagination vibrating; now it seems to her that she had on that occasion really transformed herself, or at least she had transformed her imaginings and her dreams into flocks of birds flying away; only in recent years she seemed to have forgotten them completely).

* * *

The triangle she has been following with her eyes is now slowly moving away from the middle of the sky, flying in the direction of the forest and there it is beginning to disappear from sight behind the towering tree tops, but before it can quite reach the edge of the pale blue expanse, its place is taken by another, exactly like it, which she hadn't yet noticed. Two new formations of birds appear in her field of vision, the sky looks like a huge notebook of geometrical exercises, triangles with rapidly changing angles and sides that lengthen and shorten; with wistfulness she watches the first flock disappear over the horizon, with an unbelievably acutely felt wistfulness.

The changeable and relative nature of what is usually called happiness or at least satisfaction; she has no regrets about what she has lived through, what she has done (husband, children, interesting work, surely that's enough, some would certainly think it was); on the other hand, she sometimes regrets what she has not experienced and has not done; but not to ascribe to her unfulfilled desires greater significance than they really deserve, or to those others either, simply because they have been fulfilled. Yet, even so, desires are the determining factor: I am, only so long as I desire, only so long as I know how to dream, every desire I feel is a little part of me, maybe it doesn't really matter whether one day it becomes reality, maybe the most important thing is only that tension between what is lived and what is imagined, to be always just a bit outside one's own reality: in it and at the same time outside it.

The birds in the sky are not diminishing in number; on the contrary, it's incredible so many of them have suddenly appeared;

she rubs the small of her back, heedless of her dirty fingers she runs them over her painful back, twisting her stiff neck so abruptly that the sky seems to turn in a complicated double motion, as if the whole of it were rotating with the flying triangles of birds around a vertical axis. She cannot look long enough, in spite of the sharp pricking pain in her back and the unusual giddy feeling, she is overcome with joy; in the movement of the sky and the migrating birds, she has found something half-forgotten, she has touched those distant places of her own within her, something she had considered long suppressed, not existing, that she had ceased to call to mind (as if through this contact she had denied the one-way nature of time and through the distance was again returning somewhere to her beginnings); she delights in this newly discovered feeling, she relishes it to the full, with her gaze still lifted upwards.

Only some time later is she brought back with a start, when her neighbor over the fence throws aside his spade, he has not received his coffee and has decided to go and make it for himself; for himself and for his wife as well, he doesn't show his anger or disappointment, he has learned not to demand the impossible, perhaps these flocks of birds have awoken something in him, too, or perhaps he is really only driven by a desire for coffee freshly made. Before he gets going, however, he traces a large half-circle in the air and looking upward, he says quietly, what a lot of them all at once, winter will soon be here if they're flying away in such hordes. Used to not getting a reply, he doesn't even glance in the direction of his neighbor's garden to see whether she has heard; they are standing on about the same level, only the fence and a couple of bushes shedding raspberries divide them from each other.

They're flying away, she says as quietly, and the odd tickling shiver which gripped her before is, through its surprising revival, so intense that she cannot resist it and she, too, fixes her gaze once more on the sky.

she repeats, this time not out loud, but just to herself, as if something has finished, as if something was disappearing, was completed (although not finished, not completed, again that familiar feeling of her own imperfection, of her inability to pull her weight in the world); she stands with her hands prepared to work, torn between the world of reality and the world of dreams and watches another flock flying over her head and reforming itself to continue its flight in this new formation over the edge of the forest, where it finally disappears from sight.

Now there are only two triangles left up there, she searches the sky with urgency and regret, but this time no more flocks appear; at least she faithfully accompanies these last two on their long journey, which on this late autumn evening again, after so many long years, seems at least for a brief moment (though inscribed in the journeys of others) to be her own journey through life.

ANDREJ FERKO

- prose writer, playwright, journalist, script writer;
born in Bratislava (1955)

Andrej Ferko is a lecturer in numerical mathematics and computer graphics at the Faculty of Mathematics and Physics, Comenius University, Bratislava.

His literary debut was a book of short stories, **Jemná cesta** (*The Smooth Way*, 1977), about young people in the town and in the country. In the stories of his collection entitled **Stopa** (*The Trace*, 1983) he concentrated on young people in large towns, who compensate for their feeling of unfulfilled self-realization with apparent vulgarity and brutality. The author also uses tongue-in-cheek hyperbole bordering on the absurd in other works, in **Proso** (*Millet*, 1984), a probe into the life of elderly people doomed to live in old people's homes, in **Sumaroid** (1990), a collection of experimental, humorous prose writings, from which the story "Intra muros populis" is taken, in the story of a country boy **Čobogaj** (1991), in the humorous eco-sci-fi stories in **Noha pod klobúkom** (*The Foot Under the Hat*, 1992), as well as in the book of short stories **Orbis dictus**, subtitled *Nekonečný sex* (*Endless Sex*) from 1998. Together with his father, Vladimír, he wrote a saga about the Slovak tinkers, **Ako divé husi** (*Like Wild Geese*, 1994).

He is the author of a number of books for children and young people: **Kazko Vlasko**, **O troch nezbedkoch** (*A Tale of Three Pranksters*), **Počítač Hamlet** (*Hamlet, the Computer*); he also writes plays for the theater and for television, (**Balada o doktorovi Husákovi** (*The Ballad of Doctor Husák*, 1996), as well as university textbooks. He frequently contributes articles to newspapers and magazines. In 1999 he published a book of essays called **O historickom bezvedomí** (*On Historical Unconsciousness*).

In his own words:
In some of my prose texts the critics have found "a traditionalist-cum-experimenter" and "pure delight in literature." It may be that

I am simply lucky with my choice of theme and my strategy as an author. My explanation is that I write spontaneously, that I leave the most important decisions to intuition, that I write on a given theme just when it happens to grip me. It is then that the text seems to take on a musical quality. My books are sold out in the shops and well-thumbed in the libraries, they are liked by people of all persuasions and convictions. The characters in my plays do not leave people indifferent. I really do not feel a lack of interest on the part of the reading public, nor do I feel confined by traditional genres. However, I wrote my most successful story in co-operation with my father, Vladimír. Although the novel about memory *Ako divé husi* (*Like Wild Geese*) is a two-hundred page question, a riddle so far as genre is concerned, it came out in three editions and a film version is now being made of it. Maybe I am just lucky. For which I am grateful to providence or chance. It makes me feel more humble in my approach to narration, to people, to life. Sometimes I feel very touched by people's enjoyment....

The electronic media are limiting the field of influence of books, they are opening new fields. According to the number of titles I have published, I am not a prose writer, but a drama expert and script writer. The paradox arises: the most visible part of my writing attracts the least attention. I think that the over-narrow definition of literature will soon have to be extended.

(1998)

The little girl attacked and hit me on the arm.
"Defend yourself!"
"I don't feel like it."
"Coward!"
How much stronger must I be than others, to be allowed not to want to fight.

INTRA MUROS POPULIS

Gregor suddenly had an enormous amount of time and he did not know what to do with it. His apartment was fully furnished, any additions would get in the way. He had enough money, thanks to a win in the Journalists' International Lottery, in which the only ticket of any value had found its way by some mistake to such a pitiful country as Slovakia; the large wins regularly figured in the capitals of the Czech Republic, Germany, France and elsewhere. Gregor picked out this ticket and gave the vendor the shock of his life when he immediately claimed the lottery's main attraction, a Skoda car. Gregor took the car's registration papers, got in and drove it to a place selling second-hand cars and immediately sold it for a sum just below the original price. He thus became completely independent. Earning money no longer mattered. Spending it did. He spent money on food, newspapers and the rent, he had no need for anything else. From time to time when he felt the urge, he visited Jana, a hotel prostitute, who he had once loved in the past when she was a complete amateur. Jana had retained a certain fondness for him and for herself certain illusions, since they met at times that suited her, which she considered an expression of disinterested love. Disinterested love suited Gregor financially and he was therefore more than willing to offer assurances when she was threatened by a certain diligent secret policeman, whose job it was, apart from other things, to report on any prostitutes in the hotel. On that occasion Gregor introduced himself as Jana's fiancé, which Jana found extremely touching and which saved her from the disagreeable task of explaining her high standard of living. She had, like all her colleagues, a spacious apartment with three fictitious subtenants, students who, in return for a hundred crowns, gladly provided their signatures and personal details, while unofficially living in the students' hostel. At first Gregor spent a lot of time just idling, but then he decided that here was the opportunity to listen to his inner self and choose a lifestyle that suited him, which was a particularly burning question after his long experience at the hospital with the two extremes of being punctual to the second or idling away the whole day. First he examined the trends in fashion. Style is not a world view. Bigoted idealism, though not obvious, was plentiful around him and did not appeal to him, because he could find nothing to assure him even of the possibility that something existed which, with a little fanaticism could be called God. Gregor considered all the possibilities that came into his mind and after summing them all up, he began to look for one immaterial idea. At the outset it seemed to him that an idea put forward by a wise man long ago could be immaterial, because it could both vanish into oblivion as well as grow into a real force, both of which were in any case purely physical processes, dependent on the viability and, it would seem, the good luck of each particular idea. Gregor resolved to scrutinize all human knowledge, but all the spheres of science, politics, dogmatism or culture, where one might expect to find an immaterial idea, were disappointingly historical, connected with human existence, and not only that, they were always greatly concerned with matter, or in some cases with some abstract idea, which always had material or social roots. An ordinary abstraction, such as number or beauty, always turned out to be at most a remote summary of some properties connected with the quality or quantity of matter; every concept could be marvelously pictured in n-dimensional vector space, as vectors of the necessary length, which Gregor used to substitute for an odd kind of isomorphism; he speculated no further about vectors, their real interpretation being trivial. Of course, Gregor had to overlook claims that were directly or indirectly based on the presumption of the existence of that entity or non-entity with an entity dialectically coupled with it; that way he would have gotten into the vicious circle of tautology. Apart from that, confronted by the strength of the arguments showered on him at that time by Tadeáš, an ardent debater and witness (most likely Jehovah's), who Gregor had met in the library, where they stole the latest theological findings criticized from the point of view of scientific atheism, Gregor would have had to begin believing, or to pray for many years for God's infinite mercy, which would finally give him the strength of faith. That Gregor categorically refused to do, on the grounds that if you bamboozled yourself about something, independently or externally, intensively and obdurately, over a long period of time, you would quickly succumb to it, no matter what nonsense it was. To this end Tadeáš provided Gregor with smuggled catechisms from Switzerland, Rome and God knows where, wherever the Church had printing houses prosperous enough to invest in publications in a language spoken by so few people as Slovak. These writings, under the titles of *Jesus in Reeperbahn*, *Eternal Hope*, *The History of Salvation* and *Doubting Thomas* from the pens of professional theosophists, written for sixteen-year-old readers brought up in a family of believers, only made Gregor laugh, especially when their authors ignored all the expounders of the Bible and wrapped their works up in that clever invention known as the literary form, which they used to manipulate the text in any way they liked. Gregor even found the answer to a question that had thrown Tadeáš into confusion, that is, why after the Day of Judgment it was necessary to return the elect in Paradise to that valley of tears with resurrected and imperfect bodies, if life in Paradise was so infinitely more blissful. Here the fathers did not even retreat to the over-defensive positions of the literary wrapping, which called in doubt all the gospels, but came up with a kind of new quality in the existence of the body, which is typically materialistic merchandise, in spite of all attempts to give it a spiritual dimension. The work by the Salesian priest Anton Hlinka, called *Paths to Eternity*, looked much more serious. After reading the first few words, Gregor had to admit that people who spend their lives quietly in monasteries and have enough time for deliberation can, like experienced science fiction writers, think up arguments to justify anything and everything. Our respected Hlinka also began very acceptably, that is, with the existence of religion as a historical fact in all known civilizations. Then he very abruptly marked off the sphere of the natural sciences, which he made look pitiful, since they were unable to deal with such a universal matter as, for example, gratitude. He did this on the basis of some kind of superior science, which studies the scope of the different sciences. At this point Gregor sensed ulterior motives, especially when Uncle Hlinka spurted out something about the second law of thermodynamics in connection with the thermal extinction of the universe, which he found a fascinating idea. Gregor also studied very carefully the detailed evidence for the existence of God, which consisted of Father Hlinka proving there existed something other than matter by playing around with the concept of infinity, which although he recognized, he finally defined as an infinitely large finite, but nevertheless a finite. Through similar modifications of the concepts relating to the perception of human limitations, where mathematical, physical and astronomical laws are applied to an infinity which humankind can never grasp, there suddenly emerged something vast and immaterial, which automatically had all the characteristics of God. In high spirits, Gregor dropped in on Tadeáš to return all his books on salvation and he announced that the matter was now quite clear. Tadeáš' eyes lit up with the holy fire of satisfaction. When Gregor told him that their acquaintanceship had confirmed his belief in materialism once and for all, Tadeáš broke into tears and asked God why he was trying him in this way and told Gregor that he didn't believe him. Gregor asked him if he didn't believe him, who he knew well, and when Tadeáš nodded, Gregor asked him why then he believed in God, who he didn't even know. Then he declared his opposition to any cult and any cult-like church organization, which was full of parasites who could devote their time and energy to producing other things than their own layers of fat. Tadeáš warned him that he would be punished for his blasphemy. Gregor said goodbye, expressing his trust in the infinite mercy of God, which was granted to everyone who repented in time to a degree that in this case was really infinite, in contrast to the half-hearted infinity of the priest, Hlinka, and therefore, that when he began to burn in the fires of Hell, Gregor would acknowledge his sins, repent them with bitter regret and return to the lap of the Church beyond the grave, which no doubt organized an interesting spiritual life in Paradise, Purgatory and depopulated Hell, emptied of its more repentant sinners. Gregor therefore rejected a life diversified by prayer and whispered complaints about his own weaknesses, spiced with envy towards other more successful believers and heathens. He turned to Yoga, whose roots lay in Buddhism, which as the wisest, least rapacious religion, penetrated to the essence of human meditativeness linked to physical consciousness. On account of the vague after-effects of the stressful life he had led a few years earlier, Asana postures, as an exercise in patience, did not suit him, and talk about lotus positions and nirvana, states of insensibility brought on by hunger and lax delusions suited him even less. Gregor rejected these as a useless literary wrapping, mindful of the Salesian approach to passages that did not suit them. He was charmed by the Yoga idea of cleanliness, in comparison to which the supposedly hygienic European way of life seemed absolutely infested with the barbarism of dirtiness. Gregor found this hygiene one of the more attractive aspects of Yoga, because it allowed him to feel superior and scornful of other, sinfully dirty people, whose tongues had never ever really experienced a thorough cleansing from phlegm mixed with the taste of food, from mother's milk to venison, whose intestines concealed in their folds the deposits of a lifetime's disorder, never washed out by anything except more and more digested food, whose lungs – used in their haste only to two thirds or less of their capacity – were, with their unused lobules, centers of unrest in the body, whose layers of fat from the neck to the ankles were storehouses of artificial fertilizers, sprays, radioactivity and all imaginable waste products and residues, which active and non-stockpiling muscles would never accept; in a word, sinfully dirty people, absolute storehouses of unappetizing things, untidy warehouses of old food and new tumors, were for Gregor, as for every more responsible Yogi, unattractive and inferior, which admittedly was in conflict with the Buddhist proclamation of tolerance, but in a contaminated Europe full of envy and hate cultivated and perfected through the generations, could not turn out otherwise. Gregor characterized the given state of his ennoblement as the penetration of the hygienic caste system of ancient India into the choleric rhythm of contemporary Europe, while the cleanest stratum of society was made up of those who had the most time to care for their cleanliness, who fasted regularly, in order to free themselves of fat, who breathed using the whole of their lungs, to prevent their mucous membranes from drying out, who washed out their digestive and excretory organs, in order to rid themselves of those deposits in their bowels and bladders which the organism did not manage to clean itself, who washed their eyes, noses and throats with infusions, cleaned their tongues with spatulas designed for that purpose and who did not stuff themselves with lumps of dead animal carcasses which are generally called meat. Yes, after hearing convincing arguments about the processes of putrefaction now occurring in meat, which eventually give rise to cadaveric poison and whose artificial slowing-down does nothing to prevent their commencing, Gregor switched to a milk and vegetarian diet, in which after some consideration he included freshly fertilized eggs, which carried a guarantee of self-protection, since the embryo kept the protein in a state of readiness for the birth of new life, which – according to Gregor – guaranteed a time-lapse before it decayed. Lactic fermentation as a different type of change in food producing a different and non-stinking manure predetermined milk as his supply of animal protein. When, however, in more thorough literature, especially by Belgian Lysebeth and some swami from India, whose more detailed and authoritative writings were translated privately by an association of Yogis from Rača and the surroundings, objections to cooked food, rules about rhythmical breathing and other detailed requirements began to appear, Gregor began to feel a certain antagonism. He did rid himself of a certain oral and anal flatulence when he allowed himself to swallow only thoroughly chewed food mixed with saliva to form a smooth pap, which thanks to its liquidity could not hold a single bubble, and the composition of the food guaranteed a smooth transformation and thickening of the swallowed pap into good-looking feces. He became master of his sleep and partially also of his circulation, but these advantages seemed sufficient to him; to munch raw vegetables, well-nigh ritually grown, bore a distinct similarity to the habits of the hoofed ruminants which – thanks to their laziness – are held sacred in India. When Gregor came to think about it, he discovered that Yogism leads a person to a bovine lifestyle, which was reflected in some of the Asana postures, crudely copied from patient cows. This fact, together with the discovery that an over-clean person tends to be very sensitive to dirt and easily falls prey to illnesses arising from dirt and infection, even though with an ensuing easy death, rather upset Gregor's almost firm convictions. He stopped attending Yoga meetings, whose intellectual content suddenly seemed banal and boring, unnaturally enlivened with gossip about the intimate problems of non-Yogis, for the most part actors. Immediately after coming to this important decision, Gregor felt he had made the right choice; he was once more overwhelmed by a feeling of freedom or of growing freedom, which awakens new forces in the mind, vigor in the body and appetite in the throat. He happened to learn about the beliefs of nomad tribes, who avoided cleansing processes in the hope that they would be better qualified for success in both love and battle. Science had nothing whatsoever to do with it. Gregor tried to pass a week without hygiene, but the experiment ended with an embarrassing escape under the shower, to say nothing of the way Jana turned up her nose. Jana bore the whole of Gregor's Yoga era bravely and to help her forget Gregor's embraces, she threw herself more intensively into her work, as work heals all passing disappointments. She worked so diligently that one Frenchman tried to get her to marry him, for Jana's art of contact and dialogue apparently fascinated him more than the temperament of Nigerian girls. Jana really did improve, which Gregor quickly discovered after turning his back on the asexual cleansing of the mind of base desires according to the most exacting requirements of the Rawalpindi school of some renowned swami, about whom Gregor acquired that irrefutable intuitive kind of conviction that he was incapable of desire, and that immediately after tasting the latest delicacies in Jana's progressive cuisine. This opened Gregor's very nearly healed scar of sexual passion, which festers until sensitivity is completely lost with age or injury. Jana came to Gregor's assistance with a document wrongly called pornography, although in fact it came from a certain Danish official from the Ministry of Industry. Gregor studied pornography, which was a strong impulse for the discovery of eroticism, that blind power of relaxation, which never completely disappears, successfully resisting all the snares of so-called moral people, that is, people who are driven by an envy born of their own impotence or lack of daring to persecute those who have had a sufficiently all-around education, are physically and instinctively qualified and are intelligent enough to cultivate pleasurable sensation. As mental or real eunuchs never achieve absolute rule, enabling them to carry out their icy program of sexual blindness, Gregor found plenty of partners – women partners in particular. Gregor immediately eliminated men partners, because they gave him the impression of being rivals; he took part in a group event only once, but he promptly beat a retreat, because the atmosphere seemed complete madness, which was in fact true. Here university educated people with petty-bourgeoisie tendencies, curious to discover something unusual and to see how they would react in unexpected surroundings and situations, joined in devoting themselves to love, but they were too social, too loyal to their families and partners to melt into that cohesive mass of passion which they had all promised after a secret showing of a Norwegian pornographic film, which the Italian chemist Lodoviko, the initiator of the meeting, had used as bait. Gregor went through a number of experiences before he came to the firm conclusion that human kind is still very backward. He began to lose interest in the lyrical talk of girl gymnasts determined to taste every experience, as well as the supposedly meaningful sighs of heavy mature women in search of excitement, elan and escape from the marital yoke; none of those Gregor made love to could outdo Jana, for though they were erotically enthusiastic, they were very poorly trained. In addition to this disappointment, Gregor discovered that copulation dulls one's judgement. He became so dull-witted that he no longer recognized Jana; in fact, he no longer recognized himself. During that period he occupied himself with imbecile thoughts about trivialities and it took him quite a while before he realized what had happened and why. After a short convalescence, during which he improved his experience of Yoga, he admitted, apart from other things, that he wasn't suited for such adventures. Without noticing it, he had reached the age when one woman is enough for a man. This redirection of his strength made him heavily dependent on meat-eating, spices and alcohol, that is, on vices he had already rejected on more than one occasion in the past. He had plenty of time, he didn't feel an urge to return to work, he told himself that he must solve once and for all the question of his way of life before he went back to his place of work. He tried to find a solution in entertainment, but he quickly discovered that entertainment almost always involves pouring unhealthy liquids down your gullet. After a number of hangovers and seventy-two new friendships, which after twenty minutes became completely identical in all respects, with a promise of undying loyalty and a smelly, slobbery kiss, together with loud echoes of the metabolism and collective reverse digestion, Gregor came to a sudden halt. He decided that there was no need for him to cultivate mass entertainment, that one of the very minor forms of entertainment would do perfectly well since, apart from lightning pseudo-eroticism, alcoholism and gluttony, all the other forms of entertainment were in the absolute minority. The first he came across was culture. Even this could not avoid the mark of mass entertainment; of Gregor's seventy-two friends, half of them were important, even leading, figures in the world of culture, which could not imagine life without them, as they all declared together at such moments when every word is worth its weight in gold and oaths or verifications are ridiculously superfluous. In spite of this, these friends often proved their achievements with cuttings from newspapers or portable archives containing the most valued yellowing documents. The rest of his friends were future eagles of the cultural heights, they alone knew how to recognize true art, what world culture should be like and how everyone would finally be happy with the artistic avant-garde, when their names shone out in the long lists of classics. Young poets had an odd little weakness; in spite of their different approaches to poetry and differing views of the world, they all bore scars left by unsuccessful attempts at suicide, for the burden of the poetic genius is the most onerous. Future artists and theater experts didn't have these problems, which may have had something to do with the amount of their fees. Gregor had gotten to know frail women of letters partly from the pubs, partly during his earlier, erotic period. There was only one cultural stratum that Gregor was not acquainted with – those who had something to do with music. These people devoted their time to making money, which the only one of Gregor's friends who did not regard himself as an outstanding public figure, but as a top sportsman without any intellectual ambitions whatsoever, summarized succinctly as a fear of the sudden arrival of a new trend, which he immediately undertook to prove on the ponderous example of the top centers for up-and-coming sportsmen according to the wretched German model. That is why music escaped Gregor's attention. First of all he tried cinema-going, because as the youngest, most modern, most rapidly developing art, films provided people living nowadays with the best source of inspiration. Jana didn't go to the cinema, on account of her working hours. There was little, however, that Gregor could say in favor of films. The camera kept its standpoint secret, it didn't go in search of any new views, there was nothing but worn-out clichés, the incidental music was for half-deaf simpletons, so that the more susceptible viewers could see and hear what was going to happen two minutes before the event, so that, heaven help us, their nerves would not crumple under the shock; the actors, as well as the directors, economized on ideas, the stories, if they could be called that, were sentimental, banal, transparent.... The film industry had drowned in the laziness of its creators, their age and their moldering theories of literature. Gregor told himself he was just unlucky, that it was just malicious chance that took him to transparent thrillers, interwoven with sex and brutality, without one single worthwhile thought, to tendentious trash by worn-out script writers, to naive horrors accompanied by the deep tones of organ music or to comedies with a single worn-out comedian, whose popularity had provided the only basis for the simple-minded plot – the comedy was simply an opportunity for the comedian to perform his old gags. The camera focused most often on the nondescript faces of unknown actors just watching something at that moment, while when it came to props, the competition was easily won by fast cars, as the most photogenic symbol of the four-cylinder age. Ballet, opera and drama got by with the standard performances of reliable protagonists, their repertoires stank of old junk and evergreens, thinly peppered with a small percentage of alleged progress. For relaxation Gregor read several of the best literary creations of recent years, but his melancholy did not leave him; these prose writings were full of classical descriptions, a new word appeared once in seven hundred pages. The stories were carefully worked out, but debatably credible, without a crumb of surprise. The result of skill without performance. Gregor could not decipher poems. He asked two young women poets and an old important poet to explain the only interesting poem by a young beginner from the Kremnice hills or thereabouts, but all their explanations differed – from each other, as well as from Gregor's. Gregor supposed that the important thing was the melody of the language, which was an expression of delight in the beauty of Slovak and its flexibility. He dismissed the matter by telling himself that he was not sufficiently perceptive when it came to verbal culture. He viewed several exhibitions by young and deceased artists, but he couldn't see in them the conceptions described in the accompanying catalogues. He had his own opinion about architecture; the view from his window gave him sufficient reason for continuing to omit this art for a long time from his sphere of interest; in Slovakia architecture was little short of a catastrophe. The restored historical buildings in a variety of styles on the territory of central Europe were associated with oppression and serfdom, which a priori made Gregor feel antagonistic towards the moldy old walls towering over the landscape and giving it distinctive local color as a land of mad builders of ruins. The conservationists overlooked the tiny wooden cottages sensitively set by the artist in the surrounding scenery, as if they were only concerned with preparing castles for the descendants of the feudal lords. Music was finally the only option left to Gregor. He bought a largish radio in order to have good-quality sound and so that trained people could choose the program instead of him, because he had no knowledge of this field. But it wasn't like that at all! It turned out that the music was chosen by a peculiar association of composers and of leaders of allegedly musical ensembles, all related by marriage, who usually wore Gregor's ears out with their feeble productions designed for the simple-minded. Gregor was about to sell his radio, when he noticed that it had a built-in gramophone. He bought several records and Jana lent him a few, but the results were poor. The successful producers of some originally good hit, later debased by repetition, relied in the first place on the name of the so-called star, on which they then threw the burden of commercialism. In a word, culture failed to win Gregor over, for he never considered exhibitions of products which can widen your horizons to be artistic events, on account of the strong commercial element. He regarded them rather as profitable sidelines for attracting envious petit bourgeois women and compulsory school outings, who welcomed them as a chance to miss boring lessons. Museums full of random objects, remarkable only because they were somewhat older than usual, could not capture his imagination either – for similar reasons as legends referring to times about which there existed far more detailed scholarly studies. Gregor realized that he had not included science within culture, but to get the better of his conscience, he skillfully dodged the issue by dividing up the terms of reference. He divided information into cognitive and aesthetic, thus clearly defining the sphere of culture and the sphere of science. After all these attempts, Gregor described his state of mind as one of disappointment with culture. He had found that taste can be influenced by persistent repetition, that culture was ailing in the tired routine of its already worn-out creators, in the mediocre timidity of creators on the way to becoming routinists and in the toothless revolt of post-pubescent would-be creators, that in the field of art no risks were being taken, no courage shown, that everything that should have been an unpaid expression of an inner delight in some form of beauty, was soiled with money, with competition arising from materialism and with constraining traditionalism, with the glorification of random phenomena, for feeling in culture had long succumbed to reason and reason in general to the body. It is true that this was a neat confirmation of materialism, but Gregor found this fact depressing. For comfort, he told himself that he had been unlucky, that he had been judging it disproportionately strictly with regard to the smallness of the cultural community, that he had met with the worst of what could be regarded as art, that the complimentary reviews in the cultural columns of the newspapers were right. He extended his travels in search of the beauties of architecture, to another kind of traveling. Traveling for the sake of traveling. Traveling as a hobby to fill his time. After a week of getting to know foreign countries he uncovered the great drawbacks to this manner of living. The attractiveness of the attractive places of pilgrimage lay in the presence of hordes of foreigners and a handful of natives dressed up in national costumes who dressed normally after working hours and carried the money earned by their attractiveness to the bank and then went off to the pub to drink beer. Gregor thus discovered that he was contributing to the attraction of foreign countries and after a long journey by train from Bucharest, he flopped down on his bed at home and the next morning went with Jana to Koliba hill, where he was an attraction for the foreigners who had come to lift up their chins and gaze at the television tower. They pointed to Gregor and Jana as if they were exotic animals which are attractive thanks to the place where they live. Then their attention was drawn to a lone runner, who Gregor recognized as his sportsman friend dressed up as if for a carnival. Gregor discreetly sounded him out about the possibilities for amusement arising from taking up sports, but when he learned that competition is nowhere more ruthless, that nowhere does money play a greater role, that injuries are a source of earnings, nominations the result of patronage, decisions a question of preserving familiar names and the possibilities of subsidies from clubs, he turned against this exhausting form of amusement, which, apart from other things, abolished professional qualifications and all those naive ideas about the openness of the result and the proud struggle, which the English call "fair play." Being a fan was a different kind of amusement, concluded his top sportsman friend, who was struggling to keep in a certain class of performance, so he wouldn't have to teach physical education at school. Gregor went to a football match; he discovered that being a fan was one of the most sincere amusements of henpecked fathers, enabling them to rid themselves of their complexes by yelling their malicious delight at every failure of any sportsman they didn't like from the opposing team. Thanks to the primitive rules of team ball games, these henpecked husbands, or future henpecked husbands, the sons of now henpecked husbands, felt like real experts in regaling the referee with the four most frequent and most popular Slovak words and their derivatives, in which Gregor discerned both the pleasure of escaping from work to a football match and also unmistakable traces of the inexhaustible spring of folk creativity. Those who yelled, choked by the originality of their expression of opinion, completely failed to notice that the result of the match was clear to the referee from the beginning to the end; Gregor derived pleasure from the masterly acting of this man, who had all the possibilities of deafness, blindness, unfeigned surprise as well as indignation at his command, in a word, the whole arsenal of expressive powers which he used to hide his no doubt disinterested bias (only in the interests of sport) against the visiting team. The great thrill of seeing 1:0 from a penalty kick left Gregor with the impression that the theater had escaped from the stage into the wide world, in order to fill the crowds with its humanitarian mission, since humans are the only beings in the universe equipped with such amazing bodies and minds that allow pretense of any kind and degree, actions consistently against their own convictions, in the interests of survival, the preservation of their stock. This trait strengthened Gregor's conviction that he belonged to a species of animal that is destined to control everything controllable, because thanks to its ability to simulate, it is indestructible, impossible to research and all-powerful. With this great feeling of pride, Gregor admitted his activities in the sphere of aesthetic information had reached their climax. The result of this activity cost Gregor much melancholy meditation, characteristic of the broad-minded Slav soul, always close to tears, self-destruction, profound sorrow and other tones in the minor key. The only kind of art he considered genuine were the efforts of amateurs and naive artists, whose pure, though poor, work was indisputably not inspired by the most primitive material considerations. Otherwise he considered artistic culture as a whole to be the production of unrealistic, or realistic but not contemporary, illusions drawn from the sphere of the combinatorial analysis of means of expression according to verified algorithms of the undemanding taste of the general public brought up on just such production, the inaudible echo of the enthusiastic delight of the spectator, reader or listener. The foundations in which these illusions were rooted, real material life, the whirl of changes and their development in time with short intervals for leaps in quality, did seem a little chaotic to Gregor. The creation and development of imagination and the process whereby reality gradually adapted itself according to its instructions, as the resistance of matter to voracious time, gave Gregor a little hope, although imagination itself as an impulse to progress looked very much like an illusion, a promise made by a secret shaman which was impossible to fulfill. The result of Gregor's systematic endeavors to find the assurance of a view and way of life was a feeling of distaste. By considering the negative sides, which were always more striking than the norm, he had soured every possibility, he had rejected – in many cases even when only at the stage of a passing thought – anything that could provide a solution for him, as being impossible, crazy or beyond his capabilities. It seemed to him that one source of happiness was not having enough time to think about the purpose and aims of illusions and realities, in other words, work and a busy life, the usual cure for all doubts, as common as a punctured ball or as aspirin at the doctor's. However, he did not feel like going to work, because the hedonism of unproductiveness and a personal, irregular timetable were pleasant. Gregor saw that he had eliminated all possible lifestyles through his continual doubts and insufficient devotion to any of them, which had protected him from having to accept them as a permanent part of his life and from identifying himself with their instructions and opinions, but had left him on the sideline. Around him he sensed the presence of a large number of gentle people, happy in their limitations, absorbed with just one thing, not attempting to gain a general overview and a universal modus vivendi. Moreover, he despondently realized that there was nothing unusual in his latest experiences; in fact, there existed a scientific method dating back to the end of the Middle Ages, which perfectly described his passive state of mind, and that was nihilism. Methodical scepticism had very nearly brought him to a total negation of one of life's certainties, the illusion that there is sense in trying. He also recognized the cause for this state. He had involved himself in over-daring experiments without a solid basis, without knowing himself and his expectations of his surroundings, his habitat, historically determined and predestined through education, environment and genotype. Such an initiation could help him to find humility in Yoga, to lose his scornful and reserved attitude, accept the peace of the consumer society or of meditative discussions with himself. Concentrating on a single field would make him a specialist, which would bring him the feeling of success and of making progress, the first essential stimulus for acknowledgement of himself by himself. He would be happy in the limiting enthusiasm for one direction; all the others would inevitably become stunted. In spite of all his certainty on this point, which concerned the period following his choice of a way of life, Gregor was not sure about how to choose, from that tangle of alternatives which stretched out before him on all sides, all of them almost equally probable, their probability only slightly weakened or strengthened by Gregor's distaste or sympathy. The only strictly logically suitable, though trivial, solution was suicide. This method of solving the question of how to provide for his material needs to a ripe old age, as well as relief from the need to be a genius or to make decisions, was not in accord with Gregor's idea of an honorable approach to fundamental questions, one of which was his demise. The law of custom had so far left this to chance, or to the deliberately heightened wonder of the gregarious way of dying known as war, which humankind has never managed to do without for more than a century. In this respect Gregor considered himself a sufficiently zealous supporter of the law of custom, especially as it suited him. At the present time, at this beginning in time, he was conscious of one thing: he wanted to live. The question remained the starting point for this obligatory functioning of the metabolism, for this stimulation, this preservation of himself and his descendants, and the directions they should take. For this purpose, however, he needed the company of a partner. Gregor tried to make Jana pregnant, but she just laughed. Gregor made a serious attempt to produce an offspring and turned to Jana for assistance in questions which he had to accept he could not resolve by himself. Jana told him something about old wives tales concerning polyandrous women, which asserted that when there was uncertainty about the father, such a body defended itself against new life, in order to protect it from material want, since a flock of fathers scatters faster than any other of the quick-moving animals, which Gregor had no reason to disagree with. Jana trusted him and so she missed work for two months, to give motherhood a chance of success. Gregor tried harder than ever before, but the algorithm diverged at some point. The input data was all right, which the appropriate doctor confirmed, but the desired result was not achieved. Gregor thus met for the second time with the treachery of nature, hidden in the body and mind of a woman. He was convinced that Jana was not sufficiently committed to her desire for a child, that she didn't really believe in the possibility, although she did not let it be known in any way. After two months they both gave up, which was the beginning of the break-up of their relationship. It was not long before Jana got married, as is the custom with the more self-confident of Slovak women, to the oil son of one of the Arabian drilling towers, who, after nine years of successful study, graduated from one of the four-year faculties. Gregor told himself that he had been let off lightly, which, however, was little relief for his loneliness and his thin savings book, which, after two fertilizing months in the Tatra Mountains' Arena of Dreams, full of Hungarian and German tourists in tennis shoes and, in Jana's opinion, on the edge of insolvency, had lost most of its interesting columns. Thanks to the postal charges for a wedding present – an extortionist custom, which has spread from Slovakia to other continents as well – Gregor was forced to close his savings account. He had twelve crowns and thirty hellers, the very least he had ever had over all the years worth remembering. Exactly like his age – he was now thirty years and twelve days old.

ALEXANDER HALVONÍK

- prose writer, literary critic, journalist;
born in Nová Bystrica (1945)

Alexander Halvoník worked as an editor for Veda, the publishing house of the Slovak Academy of Sciences, then at the Ministry of Culture of the Slovak Republic. He was editor-in-chief and publisher of the journal *Knižná revue* (*Book Review*) and after the establishment of the National Literary Center, he became head of the department of literary criticism and editor-in-chief of the journal *Literika*. At present he is the director of the Slovak Writers Society Publishing House.

In addition to his editorial and organizational work in book publishing, he devotes much of his time to literary criticism, showing particular interest in original Slovak works; he publishes synthesizing views in journals and frequently contributes to literary programs on Slovak radio.

His first book was an original retelling of old stories from **Rozprávky z Tisíc a jednej noci** (*Tales from a Thousand and One Nights*). Apart from short stories published in magazines (of which "Strach" – "Fear" is one), he published a short novel, **Svrbenie krvi** (*The Itch of the Blood*), in which through the fate of his "antihero" he depicts the complicated times of transition from socialism to the new social situation, raising the question of conscience and compliance and offering a picture of people at a crossroads in history.

He translates from French (M. Butor, *Mýty a legendy*, *Myths and Legends*).

In his own words:
Our literature is predominantly serious, philosophical, searching and digressive. A characteristic feature is that there is very little joy in it. What is more important for me is whether Slovak prose really reflects our existence. Here I must say – with all the risks of generalization – that it does. It could even be said that it is too conscientious and thorough in this respect. At the same time, I think it has

really had no other choice. Yes, we have lived a much too serious life, and literature has taken on itself the role of an ambulance train: it has tried to carry us through all these battlefields and take us off elsewhere.

(1992)

What use is a writer who has nothing to lean on, has no one to send his messages to and whose messages are of interest to no one? Writing only makes sense if it communicates and a presupposition for communication is a cultural background. A cultural background exists when people read a lot of books, not just one – after all, we all remember what happened with Mao. So, I want to be a writer, but I can only be one if my thoughts as a writer interact with those of others. That is why I think the most important thing is that new books should be written and that together they should form a source of inspiration on which I can draw in my cultural life and to which I can also make my modest contribution. Culture must be created and its foundations built bit by bit. That is why I try to publish the best works that are written. If they are not all that, allow me to doubt the purpose of writing, and therefore of my own writing, too.

(2000)

FEAR

Just as Paul Eluard was once overcome by sorrow, Ivan Imelo was overcome by fear. Hello, fear! "Tu es inscrit dans les lignes du plafond. Tu es inscrit dans les yeux, qui j'aime. Tu n'es pas tout à fait la misère, car les lèvres les plus pauvres te dénoncent avec un sourire." Hello, fear.

Fear is the most ridiculous thing that can happen to a brave man. There was not the slightest doubt about Ivan Imelo's bravery. He had often risked his neck, often behaved like a madman who thinks nothing can happen to him. He dealt with case after case, but not even a routine approach to his job prevented him from getting to the bottom of those that others would have laid aside in that storeroom of inexplicable, unsolved cases, by turning a blind eye or even two, of course. Because every case is different, just as every murderer is different. There are never two the same. That applies to justice, too. If justice blossomed, it would have an admirably beautiful, but very dry flower, as if it had come from a museum. The driving force of all change, however, can be found in ridiculous things.

It is only in detective stories that the murderer is always found. In life some murderers are simply uncatchable. As if they were loved by some omnipotent God. And since God hasn't time to bother with trivialities, the professional approach of Ivan Imelo had plenty of scope. His successes eventually brought him so much fame that he had enough to give away. But because he was no fool, he considered it impolite to give away gifts bestowed by the Almighty. Modest as he was, he began to consider himself his chosen representative on Earth. As some cases went beyond his terms of reference, he simply dropped them. The Almighty seemed satisfied, and he was, too. He liked this kind of celestial communication, since it helped him solve all, literally all, the other cases that appeared on his desk at his private detective agency, which on occasion even the state would entrust with its most embarrassing failures.

Investigating murders, robbery with violence, blackmail, rape, kidnappings and other crimes was, however, slowly beginning to bore Ivan Imelo. So much banality! Yes, yes, everything bad begins with boredom. Boredom is the secret enemy of truth. For truth never lasts a short enough time to avoid being boring. Moreover, at the same time as boredom, anger for the elusive protégés of the omnipotent, who no law could pin down, was beginning to eat away at the serenity of his criminologist's soul. At night he raged, in the day he was bored.

Yet all of a sudden the boredom was over. Ivan Imelo was confronted with a case of cold-blooded triple murder, and if he had had any hair, he would certainly have gone around with it bristling like iron filings in a magnetic field. He had four suspects in detention cells, none of whom had the feeblest alibi. He had victims: a 37-year-old geography teacher, murdered on Friday the thirteenth at 1 p.m. at one of a cluster of chalets at Tomky with an automatic pistol; her lover, a 33-year-old HZDS member of the Slovak National Council; and a 63-year-old mushroom picker, who had clearly just happened to be there. The same weapon had dispatched them all from this world. He had suspects: the 43-year-old husband, a successful and exceptionally jealous psychiatrist; his lover, a 23-year-old student in her last year of Business School, who had attempted suicide because of him; the half-brother of the murdered woman, three times champion of Slovakia in clay-pigeon shooting, whose half-sister had done him out of all his restitution rights and, as if to make fun of him, had left him only their father's silver pocket watch with a broken hour hand, which had been found somewhere in Jáchymov's prison camp stores; and a family friend, who had gone bust doing business with some trustworthy-looking Swiss Jews and on account of his three-million-crown debt was under threat of bankruptcy or even worse – the uncompromising fists of debt collectors working for a certain specialized firm. During an inspection of the scene of the crime they found not only the footprints of all the possible suspects, which confirmed that each of them could be the murderer, but even the sperm and vaginal secretions of most of the murdered and of the detained. But only one person could have been the murderer. At least that is what is recorded in the genes of this civilization, which has always known how to use this simple rule to its own advantage. All four stubbornly denied their guilt, but that was just the same as if they had confessed. One of them had wanted to murder one of the dead, but circumstances had forced him or her to murder the other one, too, as well as an innocent mushroom picker, who could have been a witness. People nowadays kill for any reason, but they do the job properly. Killing is not a problem; punishment, however, is, because whatever way you look at it, killing concerns the individual, while society alone has the right to punish. Yet when it comes to punishment, society likes to remind itself that it is superior to some misguided individual, although for the most part it only punishes the helpless. It was logical, it was clear as daylight. That, however, didn't particularly worry Ivan Imelo. What worried him far more was that in spite of the facts, he didn't believe that any of the four suspects was really the murderer. If he wanted to understand, he simply had to ignore the facts: if three murders can have four murderers, they needn't have even one. If they had one, what were they to do with the rest, who hadn't gotten around to being murderers? The crime hung over the heads of each of them like an ominous augury. After all, they had all been in the same place and even at the same time, and it was only chance, or only a cluster of chances not understood, which we presumptuously call laws, that made just one of them shoot.

That is why, more than by the facts, he was worried by the figure three, which appeared in some form in association with each of the murdered as well as each of the suspects. Hello, fear! The mathematical precision of deduction could not be applied here, but this experienced trail blazer in the sphere of crime was thrown off the track by a coincidental figure three, which overwhelmed him with more fear than all the murders he had or had not investigated so far. What if it should be the angry finger of that benevolent God? Hello, fear!

At first he wanted to release all the suspects, but the prosecutor wouldn't hear of it.

"We'd be releasing at least three innocent people and one murderer. The risk is one to three. What is one murderer nowadays? Havel released hundreds of them and nothing very dreadful happened," he argued with the prosecutor.

"Of course," said the prosecutor. "Of course, nothing would happen. I'm afraid for you, though, sir. You have been a pillar of society and you'll become...its gutter. You will flow like...like sewage-water! Forgive me, I don't usually use such vulgar language, but...."

"But if we don't release them, Slovakia will lose face, don't you realize that? Its bladder will burst. It will get sunstroke. They won't let it join the European Union or something even worse. Let's release them, sir. We've no other choice."

"No one will be released!" shouted the prosecutor. "If we had the death sentence, I'd be scared, too. But we haven't. There's nothing to fear. Choose a murderer and make him confess. You've got plenty of proof!"

Ivan Imelo left the prosecutor's office with an uneasy feeling in his bowels. Those words resounded in his ears. He knew very well what the prosecutor meant, but he knew equally well that he mustn't obey him. After all, that would be more or less the same as the ancient law of the underworld: there's no such thing as a friend among thieves. He would leave the four suspects alone and set about investigating on his own initiative. No doubt it would be a simple matter to convict one or another of those under suspicion, but he must look for a murderer who could free him of his own fear.

It was a couple of hours after noon and he was surprised to find himself thinking of the massage parlour SHAMHAI PRODUC-TION. At other times it came into his mind when he was already in bed, and on happier days when it was still only getting dark.

He banged the antique knocker and a rustling sound could be heard immediately on the other side of the door. The eunuch shouted, "Just a minute," and hurried off to inform his bosses.

"Hello, Captain!" The fat, bearded owner in a dark purple jacket and yellow flowered tie flashed a dazzling set of teeth at him through the open door a few seconds later. "I hope you haven't come on business."

"Cut that out, you wimp!" he growled at him.

The bearded owner retreated and followed him at a respectful distance up the winding staircase leading to the dance hall. Ivan Imelo paused in the doorway and ran his eyes over its occupants, counting. Eleven people all together. Eleven possible murderers. He looked around, searching for a twelfth and thirteenth, but there were no more there. But the twelfth could be the owner and he the thirteenth! This thought gripped him like a steel band, whose chill he could feel somewhere near his heart. In the middle of the room on an oval table decorated with artificial flowers an attractive woman he recognized from previous business calls lay like Goya's Maja propped up on her elbow, one breast bared, as she listened to a shrivelled fifty-year-old. The staff and guests were standing around the table with glasses of champagne in their hands and stupid smiles on their faces. Who knows why, when he saw them like this, a vague memory of Rembrandt's picture *The Anatomy Lesson of Dr. Tulp* flashed through his mind, even though these Majas and criminals were quite different. A long-haired youth was kneeling at the lady's head, most likely smoking grass at this warming-up stage, and a mist seemed to swirl before his girlishly widened eyes fixed on the dark pink nipple. Ivan Imelo later found out that he was a successful poet, who had just invested his fee for a series of spots advertising TURQUOISE cosmetics. He knew the fifty-year-old like the back of his hand: it was Maro, a well-known loafer, a pal of the famous Kajt, who some years earlier had been torn by the wind from a noose fixed to the doorframe of one of the last ruins along the notorious Vydrica stream. He was the darling of the underworld, a harmless narrator of tales from a million and one nights.

"And then I said to that snake who wanted to be Minister of Culture: Maria Theresa's there. You know – Maria Theresa. The same one who did the dirty on the Hungarian Diet, when she dragged herself over there with her kid. That same one who stood in Šturovo Square before the Commies took over. I sunk her there with my pals when we found her in some boiler room. I ain't been able to sleep ever since. I keep gettin' this crazy idea that I gotta pull her out! And that prick, when he was gonna be minister, hired a boat – he did really – and he used to go out at night 'n try and fish Theresa out. Of course he couldn't give a shit about me. He wanted to fish that bit of Austro-Hungarian history out for himself, poor bastard. He would've hired the whole of the Danube fleet to get her, but fast-thinking Maro got the better of him. One day, when all those idiots were cuttin' barbed wire at the border crossing, he and his chums took a tow boat and pulled Mary out. Then I slept with her, but I tell you, she wasn't soft like Izidorka here, was she, Izidorka?"

Maro reached out to touch the nipple, but first he looked bashfully around him and his eye fell straight on Ivan Imelo.

"Ah, inspector, my humble respects."

"Enough of that, you angelic sissy! Go on with your story. Have you lost your tongue?"

Maro looked at him, his lower jaw still hanging open and both astonishment and respect appearing in his narrow eyes; you had to admit it was impossible not to understand that kind of language.

"If it's your expressed wish, Captain, why not?"

Everyone stared in surprise at Ivan Imelo. The Maja turned up her eyes, as if she was about to fall into a rapturous faint.

"Gettin' on for fifty and Maro wanted some of the easy life. Freedom came, too, so why not loaf around a bit? I wanted to unload Theresa on someone, but in the whole of central Europe, even in Vienna, I couldn't find anyone suitable. Some wanted to make money out of her, others didn't have the dough. There was no shortage of customers, but I had my conditions. One wrangling old fart wanted to put her in his cottage, at Tomky, I think. The bastard offered me thirty thousand in cash, but he got zip. He was scared of Hungarians and Austrians, but the Slovaks weren't much to his liking either. In the end I got a pal of mine with a truck to take the statue to Salzburg and give it to Karol Kryl. I thought he'd put it in his garden near the villa he inherited from Mozart, but that idiot doesn't have a garden or a villa – when it comes to it, I don't think he even lived there at all, so my pal pawns it off on some builders and they cut it up into blocks and build it into some high rise or something of the kind. That's how my patron ended up."

Maro took a sip from his champagne and looked inquiringly at Ivan Imelo. The rest of them stared at the floor. The poet sighed. The Maja took Maro's cigarette out of his mouth and said, "Well, I never, Maro!"

Ivan Imelo nodded his head in Maro's direction. The darling of the underworld shrugged resignedly and said, "It can't be helped."

"Don't take him away, boss, we'll be bored without him," said one of the beauties, but Ivan Imelo was already walking determinedly towards the door and Maro followed him shamefacedly. Someone sniffed.

Ivan Imelo waited just outside the entrance for Maro, who was evidently saying goodbye to the eunuch.

"So what's up, Captain?" inquired the darling of the underworld.

"I'm not Captain to you! And own up where you were on Friday the thirteenth."

"Friday the thirteenth? I'm too old for things like that, Captain. I probably snoozed all day on Friday the thirteenth."

"By yourself, of course. And in the evening? Say between six and nine?"

"I was probably snoozing, too. Captain, snoozing's the only thing I like doing nowadays."

"But Tomky means something to you, doesn't it. I'll tell you straight. After all, we're old buddies. I've decided to arrange your retirement for you. You yourself say you get no enjoyment out of life. I'm not surprised. Even I can't stand listening to your claptrap any more. You must admit, it was different at one time. We needed each other like the earth and the sky. I think I was even fond of you. Maybe you won't believe me, but all of a sudden your stories somehow mean nothing to me. You yourself know how many people they've helped into prison, but now it's all over. My secret sympathy for people like you has gone. You're finished, you bottom feeder! You're just a pitiful amateur, Maro. You can't make a living from that. No social net is going to save you."

"How many, then, Captain?"

"How many what?"

"Years of retirement?"

"Life, of course. For three murders you can get as many as a hundred and twenty years."

"Three murders? You're not serious, Captain. I've never even thought of murder in my whole life."

"Because you were a weakling. If you hadn't been, you really would've killed someone. And you wouldn't be such a write-off as you are now. I wouldn't have a right to you."

"That's true, Captain. But what about proof?"

"Don't talk trash, Maro. It's less probable that someone didn't kill than that they did. I need a murderer now and I can assure you that there's nothing easier than to find one. This isn't socialism. I'm richer and meaner now. And you're still an artist, aren't you?"

"Where are those times, Captain.... I got the boot. Thanks for giving me a chance."

"I knew we'd come to some agreement. So be outside my house at seven tomorrow. Do you know where it is? Uhlárova 99.... See you!"

Ivan Imelo shook hands with Maro and strode off down the street. After a while he looked back and saw that Maro was still standing there with his hand held out, as if he had turned to stone. The darling of the underworld suddenly snapped out of his trance and waved jovially.

"And don't forget to take your walkman. I'll arrange for them to let you listen to it."

The streets were beginning to empty, teenage chatter spilled over from the backyards. He didn't feel like going home, but against his own will he quickened his pace. He even had to break into a run, because he was almost taken short.

He got there just in time. He sat down on the toilet, but suddenly he didn't need to go after all. Instead, he felt a drop on his face. At first, he thought it was sweat, but tears were spilling from his eyes and running down his cheeks faster than he could wipe them away. He tore off a piece of toilet paper, but that was soon saturated. He threw it into the toilet in disgust and tore off another. But that was soaked immediately, too. He had perhaps seen more blood in his life than water, but tears? Involuntarily, Freud's tales of self-punishing crime came into his mind, but they belonged irretrievably to the last century, not one of them could be applied to his tears. He pulled up his trousers and went to stand in front of the bathroom mirror. He gazed into his grey eyes. They were calm and expressionless, but streams of real tears were flowing from them. Real? He tasted them. Yes, they were salty. They pushed their way out from under his eyelids and ran in a continuous stream down into the washbasin. Ivan Imelo pressed his fingers on his eyelids, but it didn't help.

"The body is wiser than the mind," he told himself and went to lie down on the sofa. He put a thick towel under his head, which was, nonetheless, soon soaking wet.

About an hour and a half later he heard the sound of a key scraping in the lock. His wife entered the apartment.

"Ivan? You're home already? You can tell that immediately. What are these wet spots? You've been watering the flowers again? Your beloved white coffee color! The carpet's got spots all over it. You really can't be left at home alone!"

"Hi, Blanka!" Ivan Imelo called from the sofa. "Must be from these tears."

"What tears? Have you been drinking again? Heavens, what a life I have."

His faithful and compassionate wife entered the living-room and when she saw her husband lying on the sofa with a towel under his head, she hesitated at first and then immediately let him have it: "I should have known. He hasn't even taken his shoes off. You never consider me – sometimes I could cry."

"Don't you cry, one of us is enough," said Ivan Imelo, feeling ashamed. At the same time, he was glad it had slipped out of him and that solved everything. He didn't have to explain.

His wife looked puzzled, she stood in the doorway looking as if she couldn't believe her eyes, but then she hurried over to him and began to pull the towel away from under his head.

"Your head hurts, does it? You've even had time to get sober. Yuck!"

But Ivan Imelo didn't even move. He remained lying where he was, so she couldn't fail to notice the wet smudges on his face. His eyes were smarting from the salt, but he could feel fresh little streams trickling down his temples.

"Blanka, something has happened to me," he murmured.

His wife sat up. She was beginning to suspect some kind of betrayal. She realized that out of habit she had gone too far.

"Look, my eyes are simply watering. Watering, you understand. You don't – because I don't either. I'm producing tears. When I open my eyes, the tears come out, and when I close them, it's the same. Who can understand that?"

His good wife looked in disbelief at the wet towel, then at her husband's face. It seemed quite incredible. She would have expected anything, but not that her husband would soak a towel with his tears.

"And...why are you crying? Has something happened?"

"Nothing. That is...I don't know. I'm not crying. The tears are just running out of my eyes. How do I know? Don't worry, I'm not in pain." He shrugged his shoulders.

"But why?!"

She bent over him and touched his cheek with her finger.

"Ivan, look at me."

He opened his eyes. He saw her bending over his face and felt her nearness. Any other time, he would have drawn her to him. Now, however, he quickly turned over on his stomach and pressed his palms to his temples.

"I'll call the doctor," his wife said uneasily.

"No," Ivan Imelo growled between clenched teeth. "Don't you know me?"

His body! He had carried on a relentless struggle with it the whole of his life and suddenly it had let him down. It was cynically making fun of him. With tear-filled eyes he was good for nothing. He couldn't even let Maro see him, let alone prove someone was a triple murderer. He thought it would pass by the morning, but it didn't, even the next day. He used the intercom to tell Maro, who, after waiting a polite quarter of an hour, had obediently reported his presence by ringing the doorbell, that the arrest was being postponed indefinitely. When he called the director of operations at police headquarters and told him that he had injured his knee and couldn't walk, he had no idea that his tears would still be flowing even a week later. He really was seriously ill and he couldn't show himself in public. By then he had stopped thinking about murders and he had learned that a wet feeling under your head can be a lot worse. He felt as if he were naked. However, this kind of nakedness seemed monstrously perverse to him. He was most worried about his solicitous wife. She had requested unpaid leave and tactfully watched him through the glass in the door. From time to time she offered him something in a hushed voice, before discreetly retreating. After a few days he even got used to the screeching of the trams and the morning revving up of cars under the windows. He spent the whole day lying down with his eyes closed, because everything seemed to look unnecessarily large through his tears. At times he even thought he had died.

On the seventh day, behind his closed eyelids, he once more sensed the presence of his wife's body. He drew her towards him and made love to her from behind. He didn't let his wife look at his face. When he pressed up to her warm back, as he used to do, he did not feel any intimate warmth. He only felt the soaking wet towel under his head.

"Blanka? Have you ever been unfaithful to me?" he asked her.

He felt the body in front of him start, but then relax immediately.

"You've never asked that," she whispered. There was something romantic in her voice.

"Well, have you, or haven't you?!"

"Only once. Just once," she said, in the glow of intimacy.

Ivan Imelo's fingers wound themselves round the fattening nape of her neck and he strangled his wife. A little stream of blood trickled from the corner of her mouth and mixed with his tears. Then he pulled his revolver out of a bedside drawer and was about to shoot himself. Just as he was going to pull the trigger, his attention was attracted by a shout in the street. A voice shrieked: "Look at that!" Ivan Imelo leaped out of bed and flung himself towards the window. At the very least, he expected to see a flying saucer or a UFO landing in the little square of his home town. Or perhaps a killer poised with a machine gun pointed in the direction of his windows. All his tear-filled eyes could see, however, was his own wife in a dress slit down from her breasts to her thighs. She was standing bent backwards, legs apart, on the plinth of the statue of a forgotten politician, which had survived at least five regimes, her hands at her crotch holding her torn panties wide. She looked really magnificent and unattainable. Goodbye fear....

PETER HOLKA

– prose writer, journalist, playwright;
born in Považská Bystrica (1950)

As a journalist Peter Holka has worked for a number of editorial offices, most recently for *Literárny týdenník* (*Literary Weekly*) as editor-in-chief.

His first book was a short novel, **Ústie riečok** (*The Mouth of the Stream*, 1983), in which he confronts a young couple with the opinions of people from a doomed village. The book **Leto na furmanskom koni** (*Summer on a Wagoner's Horse*, 1986) contains the adventures of a schoolboy and his mischievous grandfather. The novella **Pretekár v džínsach** (*Competitor in Jeans*, 1990) is a harsh picture of the life and first love of a secondary schoolboy. The book **Piráti z Marka Twaina** (*Pirates from Mark Twain*, 1993) is again about children and for children. **Normálny cvok** (*A Real Nutcase*, 1993) is a realistically harsh novel, in part about love between young people, but also about the dangers posed by drugs. A book of short stories **Škára (do trinástej komnaty)** (*A Chink (in the Forbidden Chamber)*) from 1994 considers various modifications of the relationship between a man and a woman (it also includes the story "Láska ako zločin" – "Love as a Crime"). A year later he published the prose work **Neha** (*Tenderness*). In **Sen o sne** (*A Dream about a Dream*, 1998) a contemporary man looks back on his fifty years in this world spent "in a bed full of dreams." **Nezabudnuteľná vôňa zrelej pšenice** (*The Unforgettable Smell of Ripe Wheat*, 1999) is about growing up and trying to find one's place in the family.

Peter Holka has contributed many articles to newspapers and magazines. He published a collection of interviews with the writer Vladimír Mináč (**V košeli zo žihľavy** – *In a Shirt of Nettles*, 1992). He writes plays for radio (**Reťaz** – *The Chain*, **Jazva** – *The Scar*).

In his own words:
A literary voodoo saying exists: "Writing is exorcism, a shamanis-

tic exorcism of fate, so this or that will never happen, so that by writing we shall chase away evil spirits, and at the same time bring good and happiness to those close to us, to those we love." I must confess I like this idea very much and a possible response comes to my mind: Yes, yes indeed, writing can be used to exorcise: to call on all the gods, spirits, all natural, spiritual and supernatural forces to help me live, experience and write as I want and as I like. This is because in the recent past I happened to write something and some time later it actually took place. It was sad and disheartening....

What about love and eroticism? I think that without love, in the widest sense of the word, the rule of evil would take over and the Earth's atmosphere would suddenly become a lot cooler. Life would be sad and dull, it would lose its taste, color and smell; I for one would not want to vegetate without love. I consider eroticism, if it is also brightened with that love, to be a natural and beautiful part of human culture; maybe it is hardly more intimate than writing a good prose work or good poem....

I write every book for a particular inner cause, for a particular personal reason or in reply to an exterior stimulus or problem, which, however, then becomes my problem, too. I deliberately write it as my own most subjective confession and response. As I change, like everyone, that is I grow older, so does my experience change, and with it my texts, which are really in part reports on a particular experience of life.

(1998)

LOVE AS A CRIME

There *is* such a thing as the perfect crime; it is possible to think it through to the smallest detail, then carry out the plan and leave the criminologists to fry in the flames of their own inadequacy. After months and years of futile investigations, they will file the case away under the title of *ad acta.* I was obsessed by this idea, it soaked into my nervous system, it flowed in my veins along with my blood.

In my mind I used to compare my trip with Dora to the perfect crime. Although in fact it was not like that at all.

Dora burst into our editorial office with the wonderful strength of spring that enthralls everything living. I say this in spite of the fact that we were just at the beginning of the long, dirty, and therefore cheerless town winter, permeated with dampness like an old forgotten mattress in an abandoned shack. It was as if after those depressingly grey days the sun and fresh spring rain had moved into the office, as if new energy had whinnied within the walls of the century-old building and sap had begun to flow through them.

"I'm Dora. I'm new here," I heard, as I sat head bent over an inferior contribution. I was crossing out words and even whole sentences, changing the order of paragraphs, just to make the future article more or less readable.

"Fine," I muttered and went on correcting.

"I'm going to meddle in ecology – I hope you won't mind."

Why should I mind, when I had been working for years in the cultural section?! At last I looked up at her and at that moment I sensed that aura of spring. She came up to me and offered her hand, repeating:

"I'm Dora."

"Glad to meet you, Dorka, I'm Marek."

I clasped her hand firmly and life-giving energy flowed through her long fingers into me, flooding my whole body.

"I'm not Dorka, my name's Dora!"

"As you like, Dora."

She smiled, her eyes shining with the blue of the sky and the brightness of the sun.

"First names?"

"Of course – we're colleagues," I nodded in agreement. She stood on tiptoe and gave me a light kiss.

"You smoke too much, Marek," she commented. "If I need any advice, can I come to you? You know, I like your articles."

"I'm at your disposal. Any time...."

I put particular stress on the *any time.*

With a smile she freed her hand, which I was still clasping, and swung around.

"Bye then, Marek!" she chimed from the doorway.

At forty, you can't talk about love at first sight. It would be banal and untrue. When he has just reached forty, a man is mature, he has a stable and untroubled family life, he knows he will not conquer all the peaks, or even the foothills and caves of this world, and that is why he at last devotes all his energies to his work. There is hardly any room here for emotional adventures and digressions: either on account of emotional aridity or fatigue, or as a result of a rational approach to life, when he realizes that new emotions would be a disturbing element, that they would be inappropriate at his age and in his position. This was the image I had created of myself and I really did devote my energies to the newspaper. I no longer expected any great surprises in life; I did not even allow myself to consider the possibility. One failed marriage was quite enough for me; I was trying to maintain and enhance the second, as a good householder does his garden. For a long time after the divorce I couldn't concentrate properly on my work. I was haunted by the idea that I was a perpetual destroyer, that I always ruined the lives of others as well as my own. Morning after morning I used to wake up tired, and the moment I opened my eyes the thought would throb through my head: "How pitiful you are!" That's why I was trying to get the better of my conscience in a second marriage; I was trying to avoid the mistakes that led to the previous flop. No, I was not an exemplary, and certainly not an ideal husband, but I didn't provoke unnecessary conflicts, either.

But at the moment when Dora stepped into my life, my image of myself collapsed. I felt a real physical need to gaze at her, touch her, embrace her and to breathe in her natural freshness.

I also noticed a marked change in the behavior of my office colleagues: forever frowning, occupied with themselves and their problems, unshaven and often in sweat-soaked shirts after boozing all night, they suddenly competed with each other in the latest men's fashions, gallantry and charm. Of course, in front of Dora, in relation to Dora and with the transparent aim of maneuvering Dora into bed. Inveterate stay-at-homes suddenly felt like traveling all over Slovakia – with Dora. Hangers-around in coffee bars and taverns were willing to desert their kingdoms and go for walks in the dirty, stinking town, and what quite shocked me – they even endured the afflictions of trekking in the mountains. Our editor-in-chief was sincerely delighted by the metamorphosis of the male members, that is, the majority, of the editorial staff, because the ambitions of these roosters led to an improvement in the quality of their journalistic work. As if we had turned into lovesick schoolboys longing for praise from an attractive school teacher....

Dora was everywhere. The office and very soon the newspaper, too, seemed full of her. To my surprise, she learned quickly, her articles made sense and what was hard to believe, considering she was a woman, they had their own special style, with gently ironic overtones, so it wasn't long before the readers began to respond to her contributions. Dora sounded earnest when she wrote, you could feel the spark of personal conviction and involvement in her texts, and what really left me at a loss, was that she actually believed what she wrote, she was deadly serious about it, she even supposed her articles could help set to rights the wrongs done to the environment.

"Marek, look!" she cried triumphantly and with unconcealed enthusiasm as she burst into my office and thrust into my hand her very first response from a reader. Some forester had said Dora was right when she claimed that wolves are really necessary in our forests and even essential for the healthy development of the fauna there.

"You see, you'll soon be a great star," I teased her.

"Do you think so?"

"Of course, but since we're a serious paper, it will involve you in more work, because you'll have to reply to every letter you get. You thank them politely, express your pleasure that they share your views, add a few courteous phrases and remain yours sincerely, Dora!"

"You're a cynic!" she declared.

"No, I'm speaking from experience."

"Really? But you can't call that work! I'll be glad to do it, even if I have to write letters like that night after night."

"Night after night?" I grinned. "That's hardly...."

"Marek – you, too?!"

"I didn't mean anything, I just think the night's for sleeping and not for writing silly letters."

"Really?"

"Of course. That's all I meant...."

"OK then." She kissed me lightly on the cheek and ran off to write back to her dear forester and his wolves. With her spontaneity and sincerity Dora really swept me off my feet. She stopped by in my office for a while every day. We talked about her articles, but I was careful not to reveal my inner suffering. I tormented myself with fantasies or illusions – delusions to be more precise – of a relationship consummated with mad passion; I would wake up in the night completely soaked in sweat, I could feel her skin beneath me. I usually got up, had a cold shower and smoked, leaning out of the window. I would stare into the night, as if I expected her to appear out of the shadows cast by the birch and willow trees that grow in the little park in front of our house. She didn't appear. No, I couldn't let Dora know how I felt. She would have considered me an old fool, whose head she had turned; she could have played with me like a cat with a mouse. No, I couldn't let that happen. However, I'm ashamed to say that I secretly spied on her, that I was jealous of my colleagues, who were always trying to win her attention, inviting her to the cafeteria for coffee, and even on business trips lasting several days. I would suffer in silence while I awaited their return. Then I would anxiously watch her and the editor concerned, to see whether I could sense any change in their behavior, the slightest sign of intimacy, or the touch of a hand. Anyway, nothing could stay a secret for long in the office, rumors soon spread about every intimacy, every relationship, however casual, and for a few days it would be food for whispers in the corridor.

Where Dora was concerned, all was quiet. Like the quiet before the storm. When even the office playboy Žaketský had no success, after being with her in the High Tatras for three days and complaining to me on their return that that woman was either frigid or a crazy virgin, I was as thrilled as a child at Christmas. I even invited Žaketský for a glass of cognac, which turned out to be eight large ones, but at least it loosened his tongue. He claimed he had used all his reliable old tricks, which would have worked on the Virgin Mary, but not on Dora.

"Man, I was kind, sweet, irresistible, but she acted like she had never heard of sex, as if she was from another planet, where they reproduce somehow in a laboratory. So I told her straight out that I wanted to have it with her," Žaketský complained.

"And, then?" I couldn't resist asking. "How did she react?"

"Silly cow, she pretended she didn't know what I was talking about. I was in her room in the hotel, so I was tempted to thrust it into her hand, to teach her. Christ, it almost flew out of my pants. She just stood there, looking innocent. That's never happened to me before....I tell you, she's either frigid or a crazy virgin and she doesn't know what it's for. Or she's a lesbian!" the thought slipped out. "Why didn't I think of that before...man, she's a lesbian – that's it!"

That I didn't believe. However, I forged a diabolical plan, as if I was preparing for the perfect crime, a flawless and undetectable crime. It dawned on me: Dora had such a mania about nature that she identified herself with it; nature had become an integral part of her personality, as if she was just simply a female in the animal kingdom, which had mistakenly mingled with people and had not yet become one of them, had not yet been civilized. So her sexual, or rather her reproductive instinct was controlled by natural biorhythms. I got this idea when I was at the zoo with my son.

Dusk was falling, it was just before closing time and the zoo was almost deserted. Little Peter still wanted to go and see the monkeys. I gave in and it was a good thing I did, because there in front of the cage of macaques stood Dora, her fascinated gaze fixed on a robust male, who was at that very moment mating with a female. A little way off a younger male was sitting among a pile of cabbage leaves, grasping his long, thin red penis in his tiny black fingers while he masturbated.

"Daddy, why is that monkey pulling at his willy?" he asked me.

He had caught me off guard. I didn't want to say anything silly in front of Dora. I searched for some acceptable explanation which would satisfy his curiosity.

"Look at those two over there," Dora bent over to Peter. "You see, they are mating, so they can have little monkeys."

"Yes, but why is he pulling at his willy?" little Peter wouldn't be put off.

"They're mating, because their time has come, or to be more exact, her time has come, nature has told her," Dora stuck to her tune. "It's the strongest male who is mating, so they'll have strong baby monkeys. The smaller male doesn't have the right to mate yet, but he would like to mate. Do you understand?"

My son shook his head.

"When he's bigger and stronger, he'll mate as well. Now he's only trying it out, that's why he's pulling at his willy."

"Aha," Peter brightened up. I brightened up, too.

It occurred to me that I was already a sufficiently mature and strong male to mate with Dora. Maybe even too mature. All I needed was to catch the moment when nature awakened in her, then I'd take her to a suitable place, where no one and nothing would disturb us, the most suitable would be somewhere in a lush nature reserve. I only hoped nature wouldn't awaken in her when it was freezing cold. Anyway, even that needn't put an end to my plan. I prepared an alternative for the harshest winter. I know of a wonderful spot: quite high up in the mountains there is a little hut used by spelunkers and it leads directly into a deep cave – a ravine. A splendid place for our love. I telephoned the spelunkers' boss.

"Marek, is that really you?!" he yelled into the receiver. "I haven't heard from you for ages.... Of course you can come, any time. You can rest there for as long as you like...."

Ah, the news business, cursed a thousand times and yet loved. You have friends and acquaintances in every corner of Slovakia. It's the result of the semi-nomadic way of life: from town to town and village, from hotel to hotel; human faces, hundreds and hundreds of faces, which sometimes merge into a faceless mass with a thousand eyes, noses and mouths....

When spring broke into summer, a friend invited me to go fishing with him.

"Marek, I can't understand why you don't go fishing. Well, you'll see what you're missing," Jano assured me.

I did see. We drove to a place about seventy kilometers from Bratislava, near that unfortunate super-gigantic dam Dora wrote about so often with such bias. Jano turned his old Skoda off the asphalt road onto a dirt track, we drove a short way along the dike and then we lost ourselves in a jungle of willows, poplars and alder trees. We came to a halt in the middle of an earthly paradise – a peninsula washed on two sides by arms of the river and on the third by the main stream of the Danube. Fine Danubian sand under our feet, lush greenery all around, stunning birdsong and in the shallow water fish which we grilled in the twilight. Sensational.

This and nowhere else was where I would bring Dora.

When we were driving back to Bratislava three days later, I asked Jano to reset his trip mileage recorder and I made a note of every turn in the road, along with the distance and some conspicuous natural feature, which should lead me safely to my destination. I also repeated in my head what Jano had told me about fish.

Later I borrowed a tent from Jano, together with a double inflatable mattress and two sleeping bags. I stored them in the trunk of the car to await the time when Nature would awaken in Dora. The following weekend I retraced the route and reached that garden of Eden even without Jano's map. A week later I drove yet again to the place where I was going to spent a heavenly night full of bliss and passion. Every time I went there, I put up and took down the tent, in order to get the knack of it. I could have done it on the darkest of nights; that reassured me and added to my self-confidence.

All I had to do was determine the right time. Dora's time.

Day after day I watched her, waiting for some slight change in her appearance and behavior. Perhaps I was mistaken, perhaps my diagnosis of the natural woman was not correct; I began to have my doubts, because summer was in full bloom and Nature still slumbered in Dora, it just didn't want to awaken. I knew that in this case there was nothing I could do to speed it up. No superfluous references to her beauty and attractiveness, nothing that would give her the idea that I was crazy about her. Involuntarily, I abandoned the picture I had gradually built up of myself of a firmly settled and emotionally stable man in his forties, who devoted all his energy to his work.

I was beginning to give up hope, when what had to happen, did happen. One morning Dora came to see me in my office, just as I was sipping my first coffee and smoking my I-don't-know-how-manyth cigarette, and my practised, professional eye immediately noted a change: her eyes, usually home to the sun, sparkled darkly with the blackness of night. I focused my attention. I was not mistaken. She came up behind me and leaned her whole weight on me, her breasts burning like red-hot daggers into my shoulder blades. I almost cried out. She had never done that before!

"Ah, Marek...," she groaned. "I'm not myself.... I think I might be coming down with the flu...."

Not flu, dear girl, I thought to myself. Soon you'll be going down under me. But I controlled myself. Not yet. What if I should be mistaken?! It would be a tragic mistake and all my efforts would be wasted. I laid a tender hand on her forehead.

"You don't have a temperature," I reassured her.

A strange aroma hit my nose. Dora was saturated with it through and through. If I hadn't been smoking, I would have realized earlier: the musky odor of a female in heat rose from her in the enticing cloud that sends any male mad who catches a whiff of it.

"Would you like to get out of the office?" I suggested in a strangled voice.

"Where to?"

"I know a wonderful place where cormorants nest, where silver salmon a meter long plunder the Danube backwaters at dusk and when they are full, they just kill for the fun of it or for their own pleasure, because they're real brutes, albeit beautiful brutes. I know a place where time has stopped and that wretched dam of yours hasn't changed anything so far. The water seethes there while passionate fish rub up against each other with unspeakable ecstasy, in order to produce their offspring. I've seen a magnificent sheatfish two meters long protect its young while risking its own life in a pool left there after a flood...." I poured out at random anything I could remember of what Jano had told me. "I'll take you to a place where there are not only whitefish, I mean dace, roach, bream and other riff-raff, but also fascinatingly slim and lightning-quick predators with teeth that can bite through a plank of wood. Dora, you must see it! I've been wanting to take you there for a long time, so you know what you're really fighting for when you write about that wretched dam. When you see it, you'll write the best copy in the world; the whole government will be bowled over and will admit you're right. They'll admit they can't destroy the last oases of paradise on earth just for that cursed electricity. And the cormorants.... Dora have you ever seen cormorants?"

Dora gave a deep sigh, groaned as if making love, her eyes stared absently into some bottomless void. She ran her hand through my hair like a child.

"Let's go! Marek, we'll go there right now!"

Ah, there are times when love really is like a crime. I congratulated my cool intellect for its perfect preparation; I congratulated my intuition, which led me along secret wicked paths; I congratulated myself on my own perseverance, patience and strength of will, which had kept me from scaring Dora off with some ill-judged act. All I had to do now was to get up and say, "Come on!"

A short while later we were sitting in my car with a tank full of gas and a tent in the trunk. I started the engine and we set off to act out the fantasies that had haunted my dreams. Dora sat in a kind of stunned silence, her face suffused with a mysterious smile full of expectation. Although I was impatient, I took care to keep to the rules of the road. I kept punctiliously within the speed limit, so that nothing could hold us up or disturb our journey towards love. I sarcastically realized that I could easily become a cold-blooded criminal. After driving exactly seventy-three kilometers, I turned off onto the dirt track which took us to the dike. The tires bumped regularly over the seams in the concrete road and four kilometers on I turned into the undergrowth.

"We're here," I announced.

I got out of the car and immediately discovered that the place had changed somehow since my last visit. It was narrower, more confined. The Danube roared threateningly and its waters were a murky brown. Never mind – it was still a paradise on earth, and even more wild now than before. Dora sat in the car and stared in front of her, wide-eyed. I opened the trunk and took out the tent. I carried it to a higher piece of ground I had picked out earlier, where the sand was mixed with clay. Thanks to my thorough preparation, I was soon tightening the outer cords. The cloth was so taut that when I flicked a nail at it, it let out a ringing sound.

"I'm thirsty," Dora's voice came from behind me.

"Wine, mineral water, beer or fruit juice?" I offered her.

She frowned. It was clear she had suddenly become suspicious. Perhaps she had realized that I had prepared for this trip down to the last detail ages ago.

"I often come fishing here with a friend, so I like to be ready when he calls."

She smiled and stroked my cheek.

"Give me whatever you like. I'll have the same as you. But quickly, my mouth is so dry I can hardly speak."

I opened a bottle of wine and mineral water and mixed two tall drinks. Meanwhile Dora had disappeared somewhere. I presumed she was roaming among the alders and willows, looking for a nest of cormorants in their branches. I sat down on the grass and sipped my drink. I was quite contented. I had oodles of time and so far everything was going according to plan. I just had to be careful not to spoil anything, not to be in too much of a hurry.

At that moment I caught sight of something that took my breath away. Dora stepped out of the tent completely naked. Or rather, she didn't step out, she crawled out on her knees like a child that hasn't yet learned to walk. She shook her mane of pitch-black hair and swayed along on all fours in the direction of one of the branches of the Danube. From time to time she stopped, stretched her back like a cat, until her flat tummy was touching the sand, while she slowly waved her buttocks high in the air. I stared at this live pear, whose roundness narrowed into a thin waist, I stared at her fuzzy genitals, opening between her thighs. Dora lifted her face to the blue sky and howled like a wolf.

I thought I was seeing things. In a second I was covered in sweat, drops of perspiration trickled from my forehead and flowed in streams from my armpits, flooding my chest. I blinked to keep the sweat from stinging my eyes and in frenzied haste I tore off my shirt, trousers and the rest of my clothes. When I was naked, I leaped, bellowed like an orangutan, scaring all the birds in the trees and sending them flying, and I beat my sweating chest with my fists. I lost control of myself. I, too, threw myself down on my knees and chased after Dora on all fours, showering dry sand behind me. Dora spun around and bit into my right shoulder. Her teeth penetrated the tight skin, and when she let go, large drops of blood oozed to the surface. They soon spread out and Dora licked them hungrily. The burning pain in my shoulder receded and changed into bliss. Our foreheads bumped together and from close up I saw her misty eyes, heard her hoarse breathing, felt her nose rubbing my face, while she gently nibbled my ears. Then she rolled over on her back, rubbed it in the rough sand and lifted up her arms and legs. I crawled around her and thrust my head between her thighs. I lost contact with this world, I wandered in the dark depths of humankind's early years, until I felt Dora's fingers tugging at my hair, pulling my head higher and higher. I licked her and bit her tummy, her breasts and throat. Little shrieks and deep groans broke from her wide-open mouth.

"Not yet, not yet, not yet," she whispered, squirming seductively under me.

She slipped away from beneath me, again crouching cat-like on all fours. She turned to look at me and beckoned me with her gaze. I didn't keep her waiting long. I knelt behind Dora, I saw her buttocks, waist and arching back, I saw her head bent low. I entered her from behind and while making love, we imperceptibly moved forward until we fell sweating into the backwater. Fortunately the water was shallow and warm, the river bed covered with slimy mud. Dora dipped her face into the murky stream, shouted into it, letting out boiling bubbles. When we emerged from the water, inflated greyish-white clouds were colliding with each other in the sky. I felt terribly tired, as if life was slipping away from me with every breath. I crawled into the tent and flopped down on the mattress. I fell asleep from exhaustion, but the thought throbbed in my mind: it was worth it, all my preparations had paid off a thousandfold, my patience had borne fruit of hitherto unknown succulence. Dora flopped down beside me and in a moment we were both fast asleep.

I was awakened by a roll of thunder. Overhead strong gusts of wind were sending old alder trees crashing against each other, long green strands of hair were torn from the willows and the poplars bent almost to the ground. The dark night sky was rent by lightning, which could be seen even through the tent. Large drops drummed on the cloth. Dora woke up, too. She huddled up against me, clearly gripped by fear, for the tumultuous roaring of the trees, the antics of the lightning, wind and rain filled us with dread.

"I want to make love," she whispered in my ear. A second later she was crawling hurriedly out into the pouring rain. I followed her. We made love in the soaking grass and damp sand, branches and bits of trees torn off old trunks by the wind falling all around us and others flying over our writhing wet bodies, which clung together to withstand the destructive elements.

Completely exhausted, I dragged myself back into the tent on my knees and in spite of the rolling thunder I fell into the world of dreams. I don't know how long I was lost in the depths of sleep, but I was awakened by the blare of a loudspeaker calling. I emerged from the tent and was horrified by what I saw. The peninsula had changed into a tiny little island. Murky water was rushing past all around. Only the roof of my car stuck out of the water. Thank goodness I had pitched the tent on high ground. It was the only bit that had not yet surrendered to the wild waters. A little way off I could hear the roar of the engine of a river police boat. They pulled me aboard and wrapped me up in a blanket, because my clothes had been carried away by the raging Danube.

"Where is Dora?" I asked a young lieutenant.

"You weren't here alone?"

The lieutenant used his transmitter to speak to his colleagues in Bratislava and Komárno and asked for assistance. I described Dora to the last little detail.

"So you were more than colleagues...," the lieutenant grinned.

"Definitely more, we were linked by a mysterious force...."

"Really?" he rejoined, unconvinced.

A month later the lieutenant came to visit me at the mental home where I had been hospitalized, because I kept insisting that Dora had been with me and that they must find her. But they didn't find anyone. They didn't pull her out of the waters of the Danube, even though they notified their colleagues in Hungary. In the end the editor-in-chief confirmed their false presupposition that no Dora had ever worked in the office. They said I was the only one ever to have seen her.

So even the editor-in-chief played into my hand and without realizing it covered up my perfect crime. What is more, the only evidence – the wounds on my right shoulder left by Dora's teeth – had already healed over. All that remained was a little chain of tiny scars.

IVAN HUDEC
- prose writer, playwright, journalist;
born in Nitra (1947)

For a long time Ivan Hudec worked as a medical doctor. From 1994-98 he was Minister of Culture of the Slovak Republic.

His literary beginnings are associated with Bratislava's student theater U Rolanda (1970), for which he wrote a number of plays (e.g. **Ostrovy** – *Islands*, 1974).

His first book was a novella entitled **Hriešne lásky osamotených mužov** (*The Sinful Loves of Lone Men*, 1979) about broken marriages. The short stories in the book **Bozk uličníka** (*Kiss of an Urchin*, 1981) are absurd tales taken from the lives of his contemporaries, often with grotesque overtones. In his novel **Ako chutí zakázané ovocie** (*The Taste of Forbidden Fruit*, 1981), he examines the interpersonal relations of medical specialists in the course of their work. **Pangharty** (*Bastards*, 1985) is a historical novel set in the Kysuce region, where he worked for some time. The short novel **Čierne diery** (*Black Holes*, 1985) looks at human greed. His book of short stories **Záhadný úsmev štrbavého anjela** (*The Mysterious Smile of the Gap-toothed Angel*, 1987) explores the difference between human perceptions and reality; it includes the prose work "Neodtajiteľná podoba dvojčiat" ("The Undeniable Likeness of Twins"). The short novel **Experiment Eva** (1989) tells of the great strength of motherhood. In **Báje a mýty starých Slovanov** (1994) he retells the fables and myths of the Old Slavs.

He is also co-author of history plays for the theater from the period of the Great Moravian Empire – **Knieža**, **Bratia** and **Kráľ Svätopluk** (The Prince, Brothers, King Svätopluk, 1986-90).

In his own words:

Slovakia is rich in dialects, which is extremely fortunate for the Slovak language. It is in these dialects that the future of our mother tongue lies. I am greatly envious of future generations of writers, for I believe that when they have learned these dialects, they will have at their disposal an extremely valuable literary tool.

With the establishment of the Slovak Republic new possibilities have arisen for the development of our language. Slovakia, which, until then, Europe and the world had regarded (if they were at all aware of its existence) as a region, suddenly had the chance to show the world that it had its own highly structured regions. This could be demonstrated through examples from the long-established cultural and historical regions, such as Orava, Spiš, Záhorie, Kysuce and Zemplín. Each of these regions, these true regions, can be described in terms of its art, music, dances and, of course, its literature. That is why I have also decided to make a small tangible contribution to this mill of Slovak emancipation, which has happily been put in motion. I have initiated a series of dialect dictionaries. I believe that this is one way natural patriotism can be strengthened. For he who does not love his family, who knows nothing about his descent, who has no family tree, who does not love his birthplace, his village, will never love his nation. And it is also true that he who does not love his nation, does not love humankind either.

(1997)

THE UNDENIABLE LIKENESS OF TWINS

Without any hesitation whatsoever, I openly declare: my brother was a real bastard!

He sent me a letter asking me to meet him without delay. Was his conscience pricking him? Did he want to atone for his sins?

If anyone tells you that identical twins are alike in character, send them to.... A year from now I will be celebrating my sixtieth birthday (I had just been wondering whether to contact my badly brought up identical twin, my brother Cyril, to suggest that we organize our celebrations together, since it would be cheaper that way and who knows when we would meet again this side of the grave), and I have experienced for myself how deceptive this popular belief can be. Written records, my memories, will convince you sooner than any scientific treatise.

He liked poppyseed cake and I preferred chocolate cake. Since poppyseed grew well in my mother's garden, he had his way. When we were at Brezno, firing away at German tanks, he was given an antitank gun, it didn't matter that I'd asked the commander first! In fact, only one thing was true – in face and build we looked like each other's reflection in the mirror. But that was as far as it went. Cyril was cantankerous and stubborn, and whenever he could, he played nasty tricks on me. He would have wiped me off the face of the earth if he had had half a chance. When the shooting began, we always separated. "So we don't both fall in battle at once – it would be a pity to lose me, if you'd already bitten the dust," he would say, sending me as far away from him as possible, but I kept a watch out in case the antitank gun should fall from his hands.

We were both good shots – but that doesn't mean anything, does it? The same could be said of about seven of us in our company and we were no septuplets.

It infuriated me that when I got a medal, they soon gave the same one to Cyril, too. Of course, I wasn't going to let myself be pushed aside either, so as soon as they'd pinned one on him, I had to earn one too, no matter what it cost. Anyway, they usually gave Cyril a decoration after giving me one only because they were determined to see us as twins. That's easy when you're in uniform. Thank goodness as partisans we didn't have regulation uniforms. I'd rather have gone over to another division.

The war came to an end, my thumb was sawn off by a circular saw and my Katka married Cyro. As if misfortunes grew like mushrooms, never alone. I didn't go to the wedding, the whole day and night I sat staring at my hand in its bandage. Why had the Huns' bullets spared me, but the circular saw had not? Cyro had ten fingers, I nine – and my Katka could count.

Even then they told me it wasn't right to call my brother a bastard. A sensible person like you, however, must surely understand and agree I can't do otherwise.

OK, I'd replied.

For thirty-seven years we hadn't seen or heard from each other. We had both moved, I here to Prešov, and Cyril, I was told, to Nitra – at least that was the rumor I heard, even though I turned a deaf ear – what did Cyro and my Kaťuša, as everyone called her when the war broke out, have to do with me.

At first I made plans. I spent a while writing an angry letter. You this and that – curse after curse, as many as I could stuff into the envelope. I didn't even mention Katka – no need for her to get big-headed. But I agreed to the meeting, as I've already said, because it would be cheaper that way and who knew when we'd meet again this side of the grave.

Then I wrote an aloof letter. Terse, only three lines. It even shrunk to a telegram.

What happened in the end was that I got all emotional, like an old woman about a bride, and my shaky, thumbless hand began to write screeds of sorrow, memories and regrets, expressions of joy that I would see him and meet him, the rat!

He answered my letter with a telegram, saying OK, at our sister's home in Orlová, next Sunday morning.

Not at his family's house! So I sent him back a telegram, too. No sister, no special meals, no witnesses. There was an old bar and a new restaurant in Orlová. In the bar at nine, before it was full of people coming out of church, at the corner table, mark of identification – the latest issue of *100+1*. I wondered how he'd get ahold of it. I subscribe to it, let him make the effort.

Silence gives consent, so I got into a taxi – I'd show him – and off I went to Orlová.

I was holding my copy of *100+1* and wearing a white rainproof coat, spotlessly clean, thanks to Miss Božena, who had washed and ironed it so lovingly for me (eh, plump Božena, if only she weren't so keen to get married!), a light grey suit and a dark purple – mysterious-looking, according to Božena – tie. I hesitated whether or not to put a white lace handkerchief in my jacket pocket, because Cyro was also fond of that type of elegant trick. First of all, I concluded, his habits had completely changed, secondly, it was the right finishing touch to my perfection – so I did stuff it in my pocket after all.

I reached Orlová at half past eight, so I got the driver to take me to the cemetery outside the village, from where Orlová was spread out at my feet. My fellow countrymen were in church, clearing their throats with a dragging hymn.

Cyril hadn't yet arrived in the bar. I was just ordering coffee with rum when he entered.

What a good thing I had taken off my dark glasses! Unsmiling Cyro in a pale grey woolen suit, dark glasses on his nose, a copy of *100+1* in his right hand with its un-sawn-off thumb, a white rainproof coat slung over his forearm and a dark purple tie around his neck! But in the middle it had a horrible pink stripe – ha!

"Have you been waiting long?" Cyro asks indifferently and sits down. We shake hands, as if we had last seen each other in the bar only the evening before.

"I've just arrived," I lie, just in case Cyro should suffer from an overdose of pride and smugness.

"I can see you have good taste," Cyro feels the sleeve of my suit, as if he hadn't noticed that he was facing an image that could have stepped out of a mirror.

"I have," I said, "and your wife has, too. But you bought your tie yourself!"

"Pity, they only had this one with a stripe," he replies, and when he catches sight of mine, he quickly adds, "I was looking for one with a little maroon pattern in the middle. This tie should not be just plain...."

"Why not?" I retort, startling the waiter and making the cup of coffee rattle on the tray he is carrying.

"Bring me the same," Cyril tells him, and when he catches sight of the dram of rum, he sniffs it and turns up his nose: "You're drinking rum? I'll have cognac."

"We only have rum," the waiter says.

"Good quality cognac, I'll buy a whole bottle if necessary," Cyro begins boastfully. "Won't you have cognac instead of rum?" he asks me, although he can see I have already tipped the rum into my coffee.

"We don't have cognac. We only have rum," the waiter chants mechanically.

"Well rum, then," Cyril rolls his eyes up to the ceiling and goes on, "I wanted to arrive on time, so I took a taxi," he announces casually, longing to see whether he's knocked me out.... When I don't react, he begins talking more to the point: "I thought that since we have the good fortune," I grin ironically, "to have been born on the same day and at the same hour...."

"But not at the same time, one after the other," I correct Cyro, who grits his teeth.

"Even then you made sure you were everywhere first," Cyro comments with feigned magnanimity and indifference, although I know very well that envy is clutching at his heart, "but let's not get off the point. I thought it would be cheaper and anyway, who knows...."

"Who knows what?" I pry out of Cyro, who is fumbling angrily for lost words. He won't admit that he had wanted to meet me, too.

"I said, who knows?" Cyro asks, looking surprised. "I said it would be cheaper that way."

"And then you said who knows," I won't let him get away with it.

"I was probably thinking that in fact it might not be cheaper – which is true," he argues crossly. Life hadn't mellowed him one little bit, he hadn't improved at all.

"No, that would have sounded different. You were beginning the second half of a compound sentence, a different argument; in fact, I would say you were beginning a different thought. You said, I thought it would be cheaper anyway, and who knows.... Can you hear that change of melody? And who knows. You'd already put the conjunction and there."

"I sometimes have problems with hearing, too," Cyro comments bitingly, and I could have socked him one there and then.

"We haven't seen each other for thirty...," I pretend to be considering the matter, in case Cyro should think I've been counting the years since we last saw each other, "thirty-six years," I deliberately make a mistake, "that's why I'll forgive you for trying to be smart. OK. You have never ever said who knows in your life. Go on."

"Of course I have!" my brothermost brother Cyro protests indignantly. Our poor dead mother used to say, "You're more than brothers, I thought it'd be a pity to give you each a different name, you're brothermost brothers."

"Then you said," I wave my hand crossly, "because it might not be cheaper."

"Precisely," Cyro agrees. "And anyway, who knows when you'll see me again this side of the grave."

He could drive me crazy!

"And who are you – Lev Tolstoy? Werich or some other legendary figure?" I grope for the nitro-glycerine pills in my pocket.

"I'm your brother," he answers back, really satisfied that he has got my goat.

"Younger brother," I snap.

"Still as petty-minded as ever?" he takes my hand in a fatherly way.

"Me, petty-minded? Me? Why then do you doubt that the celebration would be cheaper for us? Do you think I'd drink or eat more than you?"

"For heaven's sake, Metod!" he reassures me, and my name grates on me. Both our names – after the saints Cyril and Methodius – had been forced on us by the priest at our christening. What ridicule we had had to put up with on that account. That was the only time we would join forces like brothers and beat up those who laughed at us. "I wasn't thinking of you or of your family. On such rare occasions someone might plan something, how should I know?"

"You're the one with a family, not me," I retort, not without bitterness.

"Do you live by yourself?"

"Well, that depends on how you look at it," I don't want to be insincere, "most of the time."

"Most of the time?" Cyro inquires.

"Oh, by myself." Why should I explain to him? Božena is no exhibition piece. But she is good, and cuddly.

"Well, I am too, if I don't count girlfriends and acquaintances," he smiles guiltily.

"You've left Kaťuša?" I exclaim, horrified.

"She left me, and this world, too. Fifteen years ago."

"Katka died and you didn't let me know?"

"She didn't want me to. Sorry, I promised her."

"What?"

"That's how it was. They treated her for leukemia for half a year. She suffered a lot. She thought it was enough to make me sad; that's why she asked me not to invite you to the funeral."

"Can you understand that?"

He can't.

We fall silent and I suddenly feel sorry for Cyro. He isn't as happy as I supposed, after all.

"What about children?" I ask him, to change the subject from our sadness.

"We only had one son. She gave him your name."

"Such an awful name," I protest.

Cyro shrugs his shoulders. I know he doesn't like his own name much either.

"I've heard you're well off," Cyro begins suddenly, finishing his coffee. He sips the last drop of rum from his glass.

"I haven't spent much and I was lucky. Twelve different countries bought my patent, the Americans included."

"You mean the one for firing the subsoil under houses being built on marshy land? How much did that bring in?"

"I have a house in Prešov and something saved up. I have enough."

"Hm."

"What's that supposed to mean?"

"Nothing," he reassures me and nods to the waiter, "The same again."

"I shouldn't, I'm taking heart pills."

"Come on, half the people our age take them! Have another rum."

"Well, just one," I agree. "Where does your son live?"

"In Prague. The firm building the metro persuaded him to go and work for them. Less work and more pay. He has to make money. He's paying off a debt."

"What debt?"

"Got himself into a bit of trouble." He doesn't want to say what. In the end he confesses: "He was sentenced for fraud. He has to pay back two hundred thousand." I feel somehow annoyed that Cyro has lost his manly air. Here is a poor old man sitting in front of me.

"If you could help him," he begs shamelessly. "I've given him everything and I don't ever want to see him again! I'll keep my word."

However, it's a promise made with an old man's last scrap of pride.

Of course, we got drunk. I promised to help Cyro. Come and see me and we'll sort things out. We didn't know when to stop, and the waiter began to smile at us when at one point we couldn't help ourselves and we burst into tears. That's when I gave Cyro my savings book. There was only a hundred thousand in it, but that was some help, wasn't it?

I woke up at my sister Marka's house. She was vexed with me, but I didn't care a dam, because I had a worse hangover than I had ever had before. The last time I got that drunk was at my father's funeral, which Cyro hadn't managed to get to.

"You should be ashamed of yourself," Marka, said, doing her duty, "the driver brought you home. Do you travel around by taxi?"

"Where is it?" I asked in alarm, thinking of the enormous bill I was running up while the taxi waited.

"Back at home. You paid him in advance, don't you know that?"

"No."

"Metod, Metod! When will you get some sense into your head?!"

"I won't. Good sense didn't divide when my mother's egg did. Cyro got it all."

"Where's my wallet?" I foolishly asked Marka.

"You gave it to Cyro."

"...?"

"Why are you staring at me like that? You told him to send it to that crook, Jožo."

"Jožo. What Jožo?"

"His son. He lives in Prague." Marka was losing her temper, but I could no longer care less.

"But his son's name is Metod, like mine!"

"Who told you that? Goodness, you are a fool. Sorry – so that's how Cyro trapped you! Just like he snatched Kata away from you! He told her you were sick, that you had caught some venereal disease in the army, he even told her the name of the woman soldier you got it from!"

"What woman soldier? What disease?"

Marka just made an impatient gesture.

"The whole village was laughing behind your back! Cyro used to howl with laughter in the bar about it. He forecast a terrible epidemic in Prešov...."

I was suddenly more sober than I had ever been. My reactions weakened, I wasn't even able to defend myself any more.

"I hope you didn't promise him any money," Marka called from the hall. "He owes me twelve thousand for the past six years. I can't get it out of him, I don't have any money to fix the roof with."

What can you say to that?

I borrowed the money for the journey home from Marka.

Can anyone reproach me if I say my brother was a real bastard?

Two weeks later I received a package. From Cyro. He had sent me my savings book, wallet and a note: "If Mara told you I owe her money and she can't repair the roof, don't believe her. Did she mention the six thousand she owes me? Before our brother-in-law left her, he came to get the money. I have a receipt showing I paid it – and six thousand extra. Is it my fault that he was killed in the mine? She gets a pension.

"You're a good man, but stupid – sorry! Carrying a savings book around with you and giving away your wallet when you're drunk! When will you get some sense into your head?" Cyril with an ornamental C and a beautiful flourish; only he knew how to sign his name like that.

That all happened less than a month ago.

I stood over his open grave with five or six coffin-bearers sobbing and sniffing behind me and I repeated to myself – my brother was a real bastard! I didn't even stay for the wake, even though his son had invited me.

Only when I was in the train did I open the unfinished letter stuffed in an envelope bearing my name. Cyro's son Jožo claimed he had written it with his left hand, hardly a week after his stroke.

The letter was made up of random thoughts thrown together, which without the ending made no sense. There was just one thing I did understand. The aim of this letter was to fool me into believing he hadn't snatched Kata away from me, or invented that story about venereal disease and the girlfriend – he said the gossip had mixed me up with Franck from Skalica, who was an orphan and had been a servant in our house.

I didn't tear the letter up, for the simple reason that it would have made me even madder at Cyro's last deception. I mustn't get excited, according to my doctor; my veins and my blood pressure are my ever-watchful enemies. Be careful you don't get a heart attack or a stroke, the young doctor would raise a warning finger.

I wouldn't choose to have a heart attack now, even though I ought to have one, thanks to Cyro.

ANTON HYKISCH

– prose writer, playwright, journalist;
born in Banská Štiavnica (1932)

Originally an economist by profession, he worked as an editor for radio and held various posts at the Central Library of the Slovak Academy of Sciences, in the firm *Dielo* and the *Mladé letá* publishing house. From 1993–97 he was Slovak ambassador to Canada.

His first literary work was the short novel **Sen vchádza do stanice** (*A Dream Enters the Station*, 1961). Together with other authors of his generation, he created what is known as "the literature of every day." Contemporary life is also reflected in his collection of short stories **Stretol som ťa** (*I Met You*, 1963) – from which the story "Slobodné kráľovské mesto" ("A Free Royal Town") is taken – and in the novel **Krok do neznáma** (*A Step into the Unknown*, 1963). The novella **Naďa** (1964) is a love story about a university student. He portrays the lives of people from the post-war generation in the novel **Námestie v Mähringu** (*The Square in Mähring*, 1965). In his short novels **Vzťahy** (*Relations*, 1978) and **Túžba** (*Desire*, 1980) he returns to the present. The book **Dobre utajený mozog** (*A Well-Concealed Brain*, 1979) contains science-fiction stories. The short stories on a historical theme in **Obrana tajomstiev** (*The Defense of Secrets*, 1990) probe the possibilities of human thought. The historical novel **Čas majstrov** (*The Time of the Masters*, 1977) is set in his birthplace, Banská Štiavnica, and **Milujte kráľovnú** (*Love the Queen*, 1984) is about Maria Theresa.

He also wrote a book of articles (**Kanada nie je kanada** – *Canada Is No Joke*, 1968), and he is the author of popular science publications (**Budúcnosť už dnes** – *The Future Already Now*, 1987) and a number of radio plays.

In his own words:
(about writing and his novel Milujte kráľovnú – Love the Queen):
Above all, the book is a reflection on the responsibility of rulers. It

begins with an epilogue – with the death of Maria Theresa, who in the hour of her death looks back on her achievements and failures, while having various visions. As a firm believer, she knows she will be called to account. I have tried to write the story as a contemporary novel about power and the responsibility of those who wield it.

Even after my experience with politics, I don't think that politics can be separated from morals. Politics is not governed by different rules, and all rulers, whether kings or presidents, must be responsible to the public for their behavior. Even Maria Theresa says, "I shall be judged; therefore, I must act in such a way that I shall measure up...."

Slovak national history cannot be understood in isolation, only in the European context. One of the characters in the novel is a Slovak scholar, Adam František Kollár, who was director of the library at the Vienna court and who was elevated to the aristocracy by Maria Theresa. It was he who understood the sovereign's efforts to gradually introduce democracy into society, in which an important role was played by Slovakia – at that time officially called Upper Hungary.

I tried to imagine and understand Maria Theresa as a person of her period with her difficulties, needs and also weaknesses, but my further endeavor was to point out the ties between nations in Europe. I can see a lot of similarities with the situation today, because the question of Slovakia's further orientation is still a topical one. I hope that the direction chosen is the right one at last....

(1998)

A FREE ROYAL TOWN

1.

It was a lonely holiday, and since for a young person loneliness is a state of want, it was a holiday for want of anything better.

It's possible he felt rather uncomfortable when he realized this. It's ungrateful to claim that summer days spent in one's home town are a holiday for want of anything better.

Everything went as he had expected. He had known the town from his childhood years, and for the first few days he was thrilled to be walking through the streets with long pants and a university degree and a full wallet in his pocket. He spent a lot of time sleeping – a lonely holiday can be shortened by sleep – then for the rest of the morning he strolled along the main street, gazing with the unconcealed wonder of the naturalized citizen on a sightseeing trip.

Then he got through the family lunch and visits to several aunts, which he achieved with the stamina provided by his afternoon swim. That was the only way he could manage a walk in the cemetery with a third aunt, tripping over fallen tombstones and eagerly fetching water to revive the wilting asters. On such occasions he felt very young.

In the evening he returned to the town with his wet trunks in his hand and without the smart of chlorine in his eyes. He was tired, it was cool inside the town walls and beer was not something he ever longed for. He always spent an hour thinking that he was bored and that it was silly to spend the evening without the company of a woman, but by half past eight the main square was deserted and the two coffee bars were occupied by men drinking beer and playing cards, along with a few tourists.

This was a free royal town even before the Tartar invasion, and though it now had street lamps, the plaster was still falling off the walls and there was plenty of it for another thousand years to come.

He would then return to the house, where the walls between the rooms were an average of ninety centimeters thick and the outer wall over a meter. He tried not to think about this and half-closed his eyes, so he could picture the open-air swimming pool with its sun-tanned bodies, which weren't on average ninety centimeters thick; they were alive and breathing, simply made you think you were on holiday, which was really what it was all about.

He carefully shut the heavy reinforced door behind him and hung the key on its nail, which had been there for at least twenty years. His uncle was no longer alive and he was the only one he could have asked how long that nail had been there. He couldn't ask the old folks in the house where he was born; they were dozing on their chairs, as an overture to sleep. Exactly five minutes after half past nine.

2.

He woke up a little after midnight; the room was lit by a brilliant moon smiling back from the Empire style mirror; it was enough to give you a shock, because the mirror was only two steps away from the wide divan.

It doesn't happen in literature, but it does in real life. His tooth ached.

It didn't surprise him at all, which doesn't mean it didn't trouble him. He always carried Sedolor around with him; he didn't switch on the bedside lamp, but soon fished the pills out of his pants pocket by the light of the moon. The water left in the cup was as lukewarm as the wide halo around the moon.

He swallowed and nothing changed.

He got right out of bed and leaned on the creaking window. Outside there was a breeze and below him the trees, which he couldn't see, were rustling and the lamps on the slope opposite, which he could see, were silent. The pill would begin to work in an hour's time. He hitched up his pajama bottoms, leaned out of the window, damaging a geranium in the flower box which he tried to straighten; if he had felt like going to the table to get the matches, he could have propped it up – life consists of a series of proppings-up, well-intentioned, of course.

Two more days and he would travel back to Bratislava. All this would be gone, and the rest of the summer would be the Golden Sands lake, his colleagues, the drawing board and his new boss, who hadn't yet shown what he was really like. Holiday over, did you have rain? I went to Mamaia, it's out of this world, you must go there, you're single, for heaven's sake, it's no problem for you, don't tell me, and the project must be ready for signing by the twentieth. Yes, Mrs. Benková, the drawings will be done by the twentieth.

His tooth ached and at that same moment the counts who had owned the mines were hanging on the walls below the vaults of the castle museum, and who knows whether the moon was shining on them, too, and whether those people had really lived and whether their teeth had ached, those waxen faces in golden frames, whose wrinkles concealed clean, respectable dust.

The outer walls of the house where I'm sleeping are over a meter thick – as a construction engineer, he couldn't shake off this thought. It hadn't troubled him when he was a child, but now he pondered it and his tooth ached. The house was wonderful, it was cool inside even now in August and behind these walls you didn't even have to think about hot August nights.

Outside, beyond the windows, the scene was like a striking stage set with a net curtain in the proscenium.

Two castles – they made it a town to be proud of. It offered tourists plenty of brochures, and the visitors admired their glossy paper, but he had grown up here and only now did he realize what a luxury it was to have two castles overlooking the town and both of them visible from that very window.

Below the house stretched the terraced streets interspersed with steep, miniature gardens and roofs scattered like cards on trampled sand, which he feared might be scratched by the brittle file of the moon's rays.

The free royal town hadn't had an urban planner and it had taken centuries to build. It sounds high-flown, but it was a fact that his tooth was aching above a wall about three hundred years old, which in a Slovakia of new housing developments was rare enough to inspire you even with a painful nerve in the root of your tooth.

He didn't smoke, but now he longed for a cigarette whose smoke could scare away not only the pain, but also the silver moon. He wanted to drive it out of the mirror, because now the light had thrown its arms around the statue of Cleopatra, a statue in very bad taste – after all, Cleopatra had been beautiful and she hadn't had deformed thighs and breasts, which a green snake was crawling towards, but, thank goodness, never reached. When he had been fourteen that statue had excited him and he had wished it was bigger, but now he could be on the brink of marriage and the statue seemed very small.

He looked at his watch. Outside, everything looked as if it were in a state of suspended animation, not a voice or a step anywhere, it was a wonderfully hard-working mining town, in the night they slept and only occasionally made love, during the day they slogged away and in the afternoon they criticized the tourists.

How many holidays he had spent here like this, not having to struggle over his books and with well-toned muscles from so much swimming. And now everyone was asleep. No doubt about it – this wasn't a big city, where you could imagine strange and interesting things going on at night; one person counting, another dispatching a train, making love to a woman or guarding the army barracks, recording a radio program or working the night shift, building a block of apartments in a new housing development.   Here they would be asleep. No doubt about that. Fast asleep.

Maybe it would take him another two weeks to make up for it. In this town even young women sleep an awful lot. Saving their strength. And he thought despairingly: For whom?

3.

There was no beer in the house, only warm mineral water that had gone flat and the day before yesterday even the evening had been exceptionally hot.

So he had gone to sit on the terrace of the coffee bar and there was music playing below. Around the edge of the dance floor were small groups of tourists and local bigwigs talking over the district building contractors' plans and the scandal of Mikulčička caught in her slip with the brewers' accountant, here in this very hotel, I ask you.

The beer was cooled, thank you very much, better than in Bratislava, here was at least something he could praise in this former royal town. Thank you, the waiter replied respectfully; we're not even a district town any more, but we maintain the standards we were used to. It was said seriously, and it's possible the waiter said it to everyone who didn't give the impression of being the chairman of the Local National Committee or who looked like an outsider.

Of course, the waiter was mistaken, but on that occasion it went down well with our guest sipping his beer.

Then he carefully picked out a tall black-haired woman in a close-fitting white dress. He could see everything from the terrace above, the beautiful cleavage included. He smiled to himself and made up his mind to dance with her, because a fellow in a checked shirt was pestering her. Flushed and drunk. He could not stand drunks either, unless he was in that state himself.

Of course she was a well-bred, good-looking lady, almost like out of a fairytale; to his short-sighted eyes she seemed to move gracefully and she was here in this town on a trip of some kind, because there were just two of them sitting in an alcove, wearily dancing with drunken former royal burghers.

So he had gone down to sit two tables away from the battlefield, ordered a glass of red wine, which this time had not been cooled, when fat Jano Marčák came over to him, slapped him on the shoulder and bellowed, "Welcome back, Pip, you bastard. Come and join us."

He couldn't go and join them, because Marčák was drunk and he was sitting with Checkshirt. That was clearly out.

"Sit down, Jano," he pulled him down onto a chair, gave him a gulp of his wine and Jano Marčák said nice to meet an old schoolmate, I couldn't finish my studies, so I'm a fitter, I've put on fat (he patted his twenty-five-year-old paunch and began to stroke it, then spilled the remains of the wine on the tablecloth) and I've an appetite for women, but there aren't many here and I know all of them, damn them, don't be stuck up, pal, if you don't move your ass and join us I'll be very pissed.

"Thanks," he answered quietly, "I hope you strike it rich as a fitter, I've heard you want to sell your motorbike. You'll have a car – the latest model – in no time. If you're not happy just now, don't let that worry you, I'm not either."

There was nothing left to drink to each other's health, so Jano staggered away and, gripping Checkshirt's shoulder, made a threatening gesture in his school mate's direction. Then he saw Checkshirt cringing under Marčák's fist and he stepped out in the direction of the woman in white.

That's just how it was, a white dress like a Sedolor pill.

4.

In spite of all the efforts of handbooks on the social graces and ballroom dancing courses in the local hall, a dance is always, from the very first moment, an eloquent interview.

She clung to him and he put it down to them both being outsiders. Two lonely people in a strange town can safely get to know each other, physically as well. It was an infantile conversation, which dispersed all the illusions her elegant dress had created:

"Are you here for long?"

"I'm leaving in two days' time."

"On holiday...? Let's try it a bit quicker."

He nodded, but he didn't know in answer to what. She had magnificent hair and it was well styled. His sister was a hairdresser and he was a good judge.

"Are you here on a trip...?" he asked.

"Should I let on?"

Of course, they had stopped playing meanwhile.

"That man, the one in the checked shirt...he was pestering you...."

"Thank you, kind sir, you rescued me."

Any time, he thought to himself, staring into the overturned glass, which had spilled over along with Jano Marčák's anger.

After the break they were the first on the dance floor and continued.

"Just imagine, young man, I know you."

"I'm not...famous. Do you know how to draw a ground plan?"

"Let's not talk about work this evening...I know you. You were ten years old and...."

"Weren't we in love with each other?"

He realized that was a stupid and tactless remark. It was a very small town and he now began to rack his brains, trying to imagine those grubby little school girls with ribbons, god, how beautiful her hair smelled and what an excellent dancer she was.

"I know your parents, too, and I even remember your uncle."

"I can't volley back that information."

"You can dance instead. Do you like me? You really don't remember me?"

Then again. When are you leaving? In four days' time? Only four more days and you've already been here for ten. She almost let slip, what a pity.

He was disappointed. She isn't a tourist. No doubt everyone knows her here and these townsfolk have awfully good memories. Tomorrow they'll be pairing me off with someone...but he smiled at her, because he felt good and she knew it.

He couldn't remember any more about the dance. A Sedolor dress and hair. All very familiar.

5.

Everything finishes before midnight, because the waiters live in the hills above the town and one of them even has to catch the bus to the next village.

He stood outside, in front of the hotel and thought with surprise how simple life had suddenly become.

"My sister-in-law," she introduced a tall, older woman. He stared at her under the lamp. Her name wasn't Twiggy, but appearance is not always the same thing as essence.

Twiggy strode along beside them, she didn't giggle and she took everything seriously, and their hands touched unnoticed. It was an ordinary summer night with a touch of a breeze, which ruffled their hair, and with Twiggy there he couldn't think of love or even anything like it.

With a feeling of boredom, he waited as they walked down that endless main street; when they reached her home that Sedolor dress would ask him to hold her handbag while she opened the door, no doubt one of those enormous doors leading to impenetrable castles. Thank you, it was wonderful, what a pity you are leaving, remember us when you're back in Bratislava. Bye.... And, with a rumbling and clanking of rusty chains, the drawbridge to the woman's castle would be lifted against the August night.

Twiggy unexpectedly left them and they went on alone for about five minutes up a steep street, and if she hadn't asked whether he could remember from his childhood where a certain cleaner's had been, they would have remained hopelessly silent, in the grip of an excitement they could not discuss.

The former royal town was deserted and for the first time he was glad he was wearing sandals with rubber soles. If you went by the sound, he did not exist, she was alone, her pretty shoes clacking on the medieval paving stones, those huge smooth round cobbles.

"Do you really not remember now where our laundry was? Mom used to work there sixteen hours a day."

She stopped in front of a two-story house, which also had outside walls about a meter thick or more and a round-arch door. She didn't ask him to hold her handbag, but she deftly opened the huge door, which did not creak. At that moment he seemed to be six years old and he could smell, he was sure he could smell beyond the door that special smell of a laundry and cleaner's, and in the yard he could see a lot of wooden barrels with chemicals and that caustic substance used to bleach linen and blouses.

She was standing near him and he realized that what he could smell was her hair.

6.

He stirred in the window and he sensed the Sedolor was beginning to work, but there was no question of falling asleep, because the moon was shining outside and the town was like something from a fairytale.

Somewhere up there, below the castle, he had smelled that hair.

He had grasped her hand, squeezed her fingers and wondered what those hands did during the day, yesterday, today, in two days' time, when he wouldn't be there.

She closed the door and they were standing under the arching roof of the long gateway leading to the former cleaner's. He walked beside her, because her hand was in his palm, and he peered beyond the arch into the wide, square courtyard with heavy balconies running along the walls.

He was on the alert and then she leaned up against him.

"Are we going to take our time to say goodbye?" he whispered. He was sure they would kiss and she would disappear somewhere in that passage.

He was surprised to sense she wouldn't leave, and nor would he.

Over her sun-tanned shoulder he gazed around the courtyard, feebly embraced by a modest lamp in the opposite corner, and he waited to see who would emerge from their midnight shelter. He, too, ought to go home, he'd wake the old folks when he crept through their bedroom, once more knocking over the bottle of mineral water beside his father's bed.

He loosened his embrace, intending to walk slowly back towards the door. He wanted her to go with him, so they could lean on its warm wood.

"Come and have coffee.... But you won't tell on me?"

His eyes opened wide, she stroked him, took his hand and, feeling her way in the dark, opened a glass door at the side of the passage, which led to a winding staircase.

"Please...be very quiet," they passed through something which, seen from behind the blinds, could have been a kitchen the size of a dance hall. She closed the door behind her very carefully, turning the key. He squeezed her a lot tighter and he felt on his cheek a huge wave of shame that washed over him, so the only way of drying it was by a visible expression of affection and unexpected familiarity.

A few seconds later he was sitting beside her on the wide divan in the light of a little lamp, and he sat tensely aware of the glass door with a cretonne curtain, beyond which her mother was sleeping.

"Welcome," she said out loud and noisily opened the drinks cabinet, took out an old carafe with a decorative cork stopper and poured drinks into old-fashioned stemmed glasses. He didn't ask what it was, he just drank, his hand shook and he spilt a drop on her dress, she laughed, it's wrinkled anyway, don't worry, tomorrow I'll put it in the wash, cheers, to the most beautiful day of my life.

He drank two glasses in quick succession, furtively glancing at the low door with its cretonne curtain, and he turned his eyes away from her dress, because he was afraid of losing control.

There was an absolute (but not frosty) silence in the room, the windows were more or less covered and the only sound was their breathing, which could be seen rather than heard, her breasts were rising and falling regularly and awfully, he stopped drinking.

"What do you think of me?" she asked.

He didn't say what he thought, but moved closer to her, she was now enfolded in his arms, she was heavier, heavier than she looked in her dress. This can't have been my classmate, she is like a ripe fruit in September and she could never have worn ribbons in her hair.

"You're beautiful.... I've never seen a woman like you, never felt...," he added very quietly and slowly, but he meant it. He felt giddy and he sensed he must get a grip on himself or he might faint.

She stroked his face, you don't know anything, every year I looked forward to seeing you boys come back from the universities in Bratislava, Košice...here I was, the only one without an education, pure as a lily, losing my fragrance in the shadow of the laundry, drink, darling, drink as much as you like, if you're not fibbing when you say I am the most beautiful, drink an ocean and then I'll be waiting for you. It doesn't matter what you think, if you can feel me and can't think straight.

"I can't."

Now he tried to capture with his senses everything around him, he wanted to let out a whoop of joy and they fondly played with names like little children. The most beautiful woman. The most beautiful woman. Beyond the windows all was quiet. The most beautiful woman.

It was an hour after midnight and they had both stopped watching the door with its cretonne curtain. They stood up, looked each other up and down, one minute sitting, the next standing, touching each other and whispering sweet nothings.

"Don't talk about what I was like as a schoolboy, OK?"

"What a good thing you don't remember me. Now you like me very much.... Say after me...I like you very much.... Repeat it!"

They lay beside each other, unaware of the frayed pillows. She was like a modern vase with a narrow throat and shapes no one could identify, but anyway the shapes were there and they were unchangeable, incorruptible, they were there and they were his, without prudery, lamentation or giggles, he suddenly wanted to smoke, it may have brought them to their senses, but they hadn't the strength.

She sat up straight on the patterned pillow....

"What'll happen tomorrow?"

She had a frightened look, but then the rings of fear dispersed over the surface and once more she lay down, closed her eyes and they talked some more and they knew the climax was very near.

"Will you come and see me in Bratislava?" he pulled out a notebook and tore off a piece of paper, intending to scribble down his office number, fourth floor, to the right, last door but one, it's easy to find."

"You won't leave. You won't leave," she kept saying and there was nothing, not even Sedolor, they existed and all that was nothing.

"How old are you?"

"Twenty-five."

He didn't ask her in turn. She was strong and at the same time she was taking on the fragility of a vase that future mothers have.

"I'm twenty-six. Do you mind?"

He pulled her up and once more they stood next to each other. She slowly opened the door leading into the kitchen, they both felt that darkness was their friend; they tiptoed out and didn't know who was where, then they sat down on a kind of wooden chest, and the cloth slipped off it and his keys fell out of his pocket; in the courtyard beyond the window there was a lamp and silent arches, crumbling pillars and the sleeping twentieth century.

Then all they saw was their arching eyebrows and they called them arcades, nothing else shone beyond the curtains, which sharpened their other senses, and they were more clearly aware of each other in this half-darkness than ever before. He felt he would never ever love anyone like this again in safety and bright light – light would be a miracle for physicists, you could warm yourself by it, drive machines and solve equations.

He had her beside him and he sensed that she too was wondering what a moment meant and why the world was made up of a long river of vast time and of unexpected moments, which pause and no one ponders. Where do people live, how do they live? Who lives and when do they live? In that great flow? In those little moments? In that great flow, of course, he knew he had to believe that, but here was her hair and the kind of unreserved devotion that is not given to cattle, only to people, and if you don't want to put yourself to shame, you must deserve it and be ever indebted, until you have given everything you have in this world. What I have in this world, and what I can give does not depend on brains, education or clothes, on walls and on time....

He felt he was too weak for this great task, everything had suddenly become unexpectedly complicated, because it wasn't just a question of sleeping with someone and then quietly leaving, wondering whether it had been good and whether she had enjoyed it, too.

A silence, in which the outlines of the kitchen table loom out of the darkness, yet the universe might be breaking up. At least in this town at this moment. A universe without a shining moon. Did she feel that, too? Was she thinking about that? Could she sleep now, tell me, could she?

7.

They both knew that the minutes would bring an ebb and they stopped dreading it. It was all over and then they would straighten their hair and crumpled clothes. He fumbled around until he found his fallen keys and she suddenly said quietly:

"Would you marry me? What a good thing you can't, because in December.... Yes, really, I'm getting married. Before Christmas. I won't send you an invitation, will you mind?"

They threw their arms around each other and kissed again and they may have sobbed, if it hadn't been for real, it would have been banal, but that's what toothache and a lonely holiday do for you.

"I'm not getting married," he said needlessly and wanted to smile even more. "Why don't such people wait?"

"For you? Until the time you condescend to notice village girls? Mr. University Graduate."

He caught her in his arms and covered her mouth. You're a silly fool. For four years we used to come back here for the holidays and we were scared of you girls, you had changed so much, you're stately and majestic, we were scared of you, the future wives of the town's big shots, directors of factories, deputy directors, National Committee secretaries, officials, professors, head physicians.

"Shut up."

She caught his head in her hands. We dreamed about you,

you're from these parts and you don't come back to live here and something's rotten here, people with cars come here and they have to transfer people here, young people come to work in this back of beyond at the Party's orders, because these walls would fall to pieces without normal people.

"Is he a good person?"

"He's a normal person. He wants a lot and he's tough.... You'll look down your nose at me because I'll have a car and a dowry from the remains of my mother's hardworking hands...," she laughed, "...remember this cleaner's."

"Here I've experienced the most beautiful...."

"Shh!

She wiped his mouth with her handkerchief, wetting it under the wheezy tap, whose rattling awoke the centuries-old house and vibrated the arching pillars below.

"Where do you work? Tomorrow...."

"Bürger's House below the New Castle. The pay office of the Local National Committee's public services.

"Does he work there, too?"

"No, but they're in the middle of an audit. Come, if you like! You won't startle me."

They kissed and maybe it was for the last time.

The stairs were worn out, smoothly rounded in the middle, descending steeply. He was in her hands and it seemed to him that she was making too much noise with the keys.

The gateway was very long, maybe as much as ten meters and he couldn't see what kind of vaulting there was, but they didn't hurry, it took them perhaps an hour to cover those ten meters, it didn't matter and you'll see, I'll come tomorrow.

"I'm going on holiday. The day after tomorrow, to the lakes."

But tomorrow she would be there. Tomorrow.

8.

He had to shut the window, because it had begun to rain and the geraniums were shivering.

Cleopatra had a botched-up figure and the snake was like a shriveled cucumber.

It would clear up by the morning and he hoped he would know why it was worth living at the age of twenty-five.

Maybe even those walls a hundred centimeters thick were no more than a little town's innocent toy.

He slowly got into bed and amused himself by thinking hard of her, and he was convinced he would succeed in pursuing her through telepathy. After all, it wasn't so far to below the castle. Any television antenna could manage that.

No, it really wasn't a holiday for want of anything better in that free royal town.

At last he could smile. Sedolor was white and wonderful, his teeth were white and were falling asleep in a stupor which emanated the kind of strange, wanton delight of those in love.

ANDREJ CHUDOBA

– prose writer, poet, script writer;
born in Malé Krškany (1927)

Andrej Chudoba worked as a teacher, draftsman, account-ant, administrative officer and again as a teacher in Pukanec, where he lives now.

His literary debut took the form of a collection of lyrics about love and nature, **Letokruh srdca** (*A Growth Ring of the Heart*, 1958). Relationships between men and women are the main theme in his prose works **Kde pijú dúhy** (*Where Rainbows Drink*, 1962), **Pustý dvor** (*A Deserted Yard*, 1965), **Miesto pre dvoch** (*Room for Two*, 1966) and **Leto s pehavou pannou** (*Summer with a Freckled Virgin*, 1970). His book of short stories **Zbohom, Cyrano** (*Goodbye, Cyrano*, 1973) focuses on people involved in tragic events. The psy-chological novella **Obkľúčenie** (*Siege*, 1976) tells of people's resist-ance to fascism. In the stories in **Hlinené husle** (*The Earthen Fiddle*, 1977) the author portrays people formed by social events. The short novels in the collection **Konečne bude mier** (*Peace at Last*, 1979) draw on themes from post-war life. With the novel **Nákaza** (*Infection*, 1982) he returned to a rural setting, as he did in the short stories in **Krv nie je voda** (*Blood is not Water*, 1985). The novel **Stopárka** (*The Hitchhiker*, 1986) speaks of the complicated emo-tional relations between young people. In the autobiographical novel **Zázrak na konci sveta** (*A Miracle at the End of the World*, 1993) he again returns to the post-war period. The short story **"Sneh a havrany"** ("Snow and Rooks") is taken from an unpub-lished manuscript.

His book of Slovak legends, **Sedemdesiatsedem povestí spod Slovenskej brány** (*Seventy-Seven Tales from below the Slovak Gate*, 1974) was written mainly for young people. Andrej Chuboba is the author of the film scripts **Most na tú stranu** (*This Side of the Bridge*) and **Pustý dvor** (*A Deserted Yard*).

In his own words:

I am fascinated by the actual, as well as metaphorical closeness of the region I come from, its many-faceted significance, its multi-dimensional nature, the way it is imbued with deep feeling, becoming a word in confidence, a whisper reminiscent of the mother, woman and fairy godmother who so generously bestowed on me this lovely region.

This region is my daily bread, it is my human and literary livelihood. Deep down in my heart I am a daydreaming country boy and I shall stay that way.

It is often only when we find ourselves in a situation that we call extreme, only during such a trial in life do we realize the existence of conscience as the basic element in human morality; we come to know not only the severity of its judgement, but also its liberating, purifying force. It is often only then that we become aware of conscience as an inseparable part of the moral code, which amazed not only such renowned people as Kant, Tolstoy and Aitmatov, but also so-called "ordinary people," who have more intuitively (through faith) than consciously understood that the universal moral code and the phenomena of conscience incorporated within it, are the *sine qua non* of human existence, that if a person wishes to retain his identity, they must live in harmony with their conscience and with truth. But to live with conscience, to submit to its incorruptible judgement on a daily basis is a supernatural task. For conscience, unfortunately, does not recognize such words as "compromise," "strategy," "tactics" – it is mercilessly unequivocal and almost inhumanly absolute. Only a perfect soul can stand the test of its judgement. But does such a soul exist?

(1989)

SNOW AND ROOKS

An Epiphany blizzard whistled across the land in the night, but the morning was calm and clear and the snow-covered yard was half swept clean. Uncle stood in the doorway, his fur hat on his head, staring at the pink woolly clouds and breathing in deeply the spacious white silence, in which voices seemed to freeze, when all of a sudden from the nearby snowbound village came a muffled sound, as if from under a layer of ice, the melancholy tolling of the death bell.

"There's a rook swinging on the bell again," muttered Uncle, kicking away the tabby cat that was rubbing up against his felt boots. Uncle, a stocky, red-cheeked sixty-year-old, couldn't stand cats and women, maybe partly because he had been living for years under the same roof with two sisters-in-law and three nieces, that is, with my sister and two of my cousins. Uncle regarded rooks as the harbingers of death, and whenever he heard the death bell he would come out with the same remark. He believed in all kinds of mumbo jumbo, signs and illusions, and he would claim by all things holy that crows and rooks announced bad luck and death, because when one rainy autumn one of his four brothers (all alcoholics) drowned in a flooded grave, those "black devils" had flown down a few days before and one of them had settled on the roof top and Uncle swore it had cawed his brother's name three times over.

My aunt, the drowned man's widow, who was out in the snow cleaning the bottom of a copper cauldron, threw Uncle a sidelong glance and pursed her lips scornfully.

"Been sucking at the bottle again, you old blabberer?!"

"And on an empty stomach, so his breakfast won't do him any harm," joined in his other sister-in-law, my mother, dark-haired with large brown eyes and strikingly thick lips, also a widow, who was mixing the pigswill in a bucket.

At that moment – as if someone had blown hard from above – the snow on the roof whirled up in a sparkling cloud and fell in a shower on the two widows, transforming them in a flash into statues of old silver.

Both women let out squeals. One of them cried, "The witches are going wild up there!"

The shower of snow hit my uncle as well. He shook it off his sheepskin hat and, squinting, he examined the sky.

"That's not a good sign. The wind will be back."

Inside the house my sister, dressed in dark clothes, with the sleeves of her indigo print blouse rolled up and her hands covered in flour, bent to look out of the window, her attention caught not by the snow shower, but by the soldiers who were marching through the yard in close formation, their tin mugs clanging as they strode down to the village for breakfast. They were led by a greying first lieutenant with glasses, but the rest of them were for the most part seventeen to eighteen-year-old lads, slim and close-cropped, their cheeks pinched red by the frost. Their grey-green caps were pulled down over their ears and those marching at the back smiled at my sister. They were two platoons of mountain riflemen and they had arrived in these parts before Christmas. They probably didn't trust us much, because they took their machine guns with them wherever they went, and the first lieutenant, who was billeted in our house, usually slept with his boots on, and he no doubt had reason to, because even the blizzard in the night had been drowned out occasionally by a sinister rumbling, like a distant summer storm. The soldiers had found accommodation in the deserted herdsman's hut up the hill from us; they would come to our house for water, because there was no well on the hill, they kept a fire burning in the old stove, their smoke mixed with our smoke, as our lives did with theirs. At least ten times a day the first lieutenant covered those two hundred meters to the thatched cottage along the path past the old nut tree, part of which leaned over the snow-covered garden, in the middle of which stood two scarecrows with stuffed rag heads.

When the officer came into the kitchen with his adjutant and interpreter the first time, my aunt happened to be sitting at the loom and my sister, a seventeen-year-old well-developed girl, was kneading bread dough in a wooden trough supported on a stand. The officer greeted us in a terse, military manner, shook hands with everyone present, even me, a fifteen-year-old boy, then inspected the room in which he was to live and nodded his head in agreement. On the way back, he ducked to avoid the lamp hanging from the ceiling and came to a halt in the middle of the kitchen. He stood there, a tall, forty-year-old man in a short coat lined with cat fur, glasses, cheeks shaven pink and white, a long oval face and pale, straight, narrow lips, a real Nordic type, a German officer, like those we later saw in war films. His interest was suddenly caught by something, maybe something unusual for him, but we couldn't read anything from his expressionless face and glassy-blue eyes. We only noticed a strange twitch puckered his cheek with something like a wrinkle running from his right eye down to the furrow above his mouth, revealing an old, long-healed scar. Maybe there had been no scar, maybe it was only a narrow strip of reflected light, maybe it was only an involuntary facial movement, but it expressed something profoundly intimate, concealed, unfathomable. The only thing that was clear to us was the direction in which he was looking. He was staring at my sister mixing the dough, at her white neck above the dark, wide collar, at her rolled-up sleeves and her powerful floury hands, deftly and unremittingly kneading the dough, at her shoulders rising and falling as she breathed deeply, almost panting, blowing the pink flour dust around her, which settled on the bright red scarf tied around her head. We could not help noticing that look, but none of us could really understand it. It could have been a sudden interest in unfamiliar work or a peace-time picture long not seen, the play of colors and light on a flushed girlish face or a peaceful, homely scene conjuring up the atmosphere before Christmas. The unfathomable silence, disturbed only by the creaking of the wooden stand and the squelchy sound of the kneaded dough, was broken at last by a kind of transparent flying shadow – a layer of snow slid off the roof, glittering in the sunlight like a meteor shower.... Immediately the suspended scene resumed movement and sound, I continued taking nuts out of a sack and putting them into straw bowls, Uncle went on splitting logs beside the stove and Mother offered the officer a coarse linen towel and grey, home-made soap. Only then did the officer seem to come down to earth. He took the offered towel, and when he noticed the shapeless soap the color of a three-day corpse, that odd twitch furrowed his right cheek again and he said, "Ja, ja...das ist der Krieg."

He looked at me, as if I should say something to this, then he went into his room and we didn't see him again until late that morning. Whether he was sleeping or working none of us knew. Meanwhile everything went on as before. The little soldiers – because they were not yet real soldiers – carried rye straw down from the loft (at one time Granddad had sold it in Štiavnica); they hung around the snow-covered yard, admiring the way my mother deftly put the dough into the oven and grinning at my sister in a provocative way when she went outside to get some water. The bell had already chimed twice in the village, when they brought a thermos can on a sled with a late lunch for the soldiers, and two of the older ones in helmets stretched telephone wires to the window of the first lieutenant's room. It seemed almost an idyll: sparkling white snow reaching endlessly as far as the eye could see, blinding whiteness making visible both happy and bitter memories, purity spanning all those pits and abysses of the soul, dazzling whiteness as part of the brightness of the universe, like a drop in the sea of light, with which we will one day merge. The hardened soldier, who had no doubt looked death in the face more than once, may have caught sight of this in my sister's eyes and for a few moments he may have forgotten that chilling darkness of Death's vacant eyes.... My uncle, a soldier in the First World War, for many years the village bell-ringer, saw death as a rook that swings on a bell as its sound fades away, because he said that one autumn evening, when he was summoning the congregation to church, a rook flew in through the open window and gripped the swaying bell tight with its claws. A day or two later the old bell-ringer, Uncle's predecessor, died.

"It's a black angel, a harbinger of death, no one's going to tell me otherwise," he used to stress with both hands, when my mother smiled ironically and shook her head, clearly unconvinced, because her brother-in-law told this mysterious story only when he had downed quite a few, and on Christmas Eve he added another tale, about how one night somewhere beyond the Ural

Mountains he had heard the Christmas bells ringing in his own village. This memory of my uncle's was part of our Christmas Eve and came as a climax to the recollection of events that had happened a long time before in our family, in addition to my mother's remark that everyone has two souls – one for every day and one for Christmas day....

The first lieutenant spent Christmas Eve with his own folk and when he returned in the morning, he wished us a peaceful Christmas, and then he reached into his haversack and presented my astonished sister with a bar of white toilet soap stamped with a picture of a flying bird. My sister first tried to make all kinds of excuses to wriggle out of it, but in the end she took this tempting perfumed gift. The officer smiled, perhaps for the first time, and we were so astonished that no one thanked him for the gift, no doubt also because his smile was suddenly crossed by that strange twitch, once more furrowing his cheek with the deep wrinkle, which penetrated somewhere deep beneath his skin, maybe to where in every human being there exists something like a Christmas soul....

Uncle sat on the bench beside the window, carving teeth for a rake and watching uneasily as from time to time sparkling clouds of snow blew off the roof. After a while his hands paused, he turned around and muttered, "I don't like the look of it one little bit. Those big black devils will fly in again. You can take my word for it they will."

When he saw our skeptical expressions, he added for good measure, "You'll see!"

He was right. Two days later, just before Epiphany, the snow unexpectedly began to melt and they arrived. In fact I think it was their cawing that woke us up. First they cawed somewhere in the fields, but soon warm smells lured them right into the village. A flock of maybe as many as fifty flew onto the barn and the trees around. One fat old rook settled on the very top of an old walnut tree as if it was an observation post and seemed to be directing the arrival of his companions with his harsh cawing. The village in its white hollow was veiled in a light mist. The sky looked as still as a frozen lake. Uncle had already taken his morning "medicine" and wherever he went, he declared, "There was rumbling again in the night. It's that rumbling that chased these devils here. They caught a whiff of carrion, the bloodsuckers."

His sister-in-law snapped at him, "It's you that stinks, as if you'd come from the pub. You'd do better to take yourself off and relieve Ďuro at Lazisko.

It was at Lazisko, a remote cluster of cottages beyond the village, that we had hidden the horses, so they wouldn't be requisitioned. Uncle objected. "What d'ye mean, I should go? It's his turn," he pointed in my direction, "our first young lad should go."

"No, he won't. I want him here at hand. You've been swilling it down ever since you got out of bed and the soldiers...look, they're all over the yard."

"You call those soldiers, sister?" Uncle drawled scornfully. "They're no more than boys and the officer keeps them on a short leash, strict, SS style. I heard he was supposed to have had leave from his regiment over Christmas, but he got into some kind of trouble, which is why he had to go back to the front with these boys and lead them to a certain death."

His sister-in-law thrust her knife vigorously into a fresh loaf of bread: "You can see you've been drinking from the way you blather on."

"Huh? That one little swig of...?"

"One, you say...! You...you...."

His sister-in-law was about to give him a piece of her mind, but she suddenly threw down her knife and ran to save the milk which was boiling over. Just then two shots were heard outside. My fourteen-year-old cousin rushed into the house, her face flushed, to announce that the soldiers were shooting at the crows, and she giggled that the dog had hidden in its kennel out of fright and the scared chickens had flown out of the hen-house.

"Those aren't crows, they're rooks," I retorted.

"Rooks?! D'you think I don't have eyes?!"

"Well, you don't, because they're rooks."

"They're not."

We began to quarrel childishly. Two more shots were heard.

It seemed the first lieutenant's adjutant was doing the shooting and a couple of soldiers were staring up into the sky. The first lieutenant emerged from his room, and as he bent his head to step through the low doorway, he gave my sister and me a searching look, as if we had something to do with the shooting. There was a clean new bandage on his hand, his glasses glittered with a bluish tint, something had clearly annoyed him, but I didn't know whether it was the screeching of the rooks or the shooting. He went outside and a second later Uncle came in and predicted ominously, "Those rooks didn't come swarming in here for nothing. It's not a good sign. Something's going to happen. In a few days they're going to break through the front. The rooks can sense it, the scavengers."

His sister-in-law – my mother – put some more wood in the stove. A shower of sparks shot out of the iron door and my mother instinctively jumped aside.

"See, just as I say. That flame is trying to tell us something, too."

My mother banged the little door shut.

"Stop that, think what you're saying, you'll only frighten the children."

My curious sister ran out into the yard and a moment later rushed in all out of breath.

"The SS man is going to shoot at the crows. Come and look. He says he'll kill the biggest one with one shot.

"With that bandaged hand?" Uncle said doubtfully, but he followed my sister into the yard.

Perched at the very top of the old spreading walnut tree, on two branches facing each other, were two rooks. The largest was sitting on the highest branch, turning its head in all directions and cawing, as if it were sending agreed-on signals to the distant flock. The other was huddled up in its puffed-out feathers and it seemed to be dozing. The first lieutenant took the short carbine from the adjutant, propped it up on his shoulder with his healthy left hand, moved one leg back a step, straightened himself up, took aim and in a split second the rook on the walnut tree changed into a bunch of flying feathers. The boy soldiers applauded as if at a concert. The first lieutenant turned towards them with the carbine pointing into the snow and something suddenly appeared in the glassy blue eyes behind his spectacles that imprinted itself on my memory forever, that very strange twitch in his face and that deep, slanting wrinkle penetrating far beneath the skin, to some inaccessible place inside. That moment was just like the one when he had presented my sister with the round, white bar of soap with its stamped picture of a flying bird. It was once more a short, but visible spasm, a tremor of some inner pain, unspoken regret mixed with scorn, which perhaps was like his scorn of death, and at the same time was so near love, that I couldn't tell one from the other. Only later, when I was older did it seem to me that I had after all, for just a second, understood him.... The first lieutenant briefly inspected the carbine, as if he were looking for something on it and handed it back to the adjutant. Only then, at a hardly noticeable sign, did the soldiers run up the yard, in the direction of the distant forest where the flock of rooks had taken shelter. It looked as if the echo of the shot had driven them to flee for good.

The fading cawing and curiosity drew me towards the walnut tree.

The black bird, or rather its torn body, lay in the snow among its scattered feathers and its large blue and, I suppose, still living eye, gazed at me so unbearably sternly and reproachfully, that

110

I looked away and stepped around the bloody remains of the bird with bowed head. The first lieutenant didn't wait for the dead bird, he went inside, into his room and didn't come out until his usual early evening inspection of the guards. Grey-green young lads in peaked caps threw the dead rook away on the compost heap, where the snow was quickly melting. Uncle didn't leave him there, however. As soon as the soldiers had gone, he buried it deep in the manure. When he was cleaning his rubber boots on the grate in front of the door, I heard him muttering, "I've buried him, so they won't find him when they come back."

But they didn't come back. By morning the sky had cleared once more, there was a hard frost and the rooks had probably flown away to their winter habitats.

I slept very uneasily that night, the rook's eyes appeared to me even in my dreams, so I spent more time awake than asleep, and that's why throughout the night I could hear that disturbing mumbling rumbling so much like a distant summer storm.... Just before dawn, however, I had a short, vivid dream. I saw my sister in her Sunday-best snow-white outfit and, curious as I was, I asked her, "Why are you dressed up like that – there won't be any Epiphany celebrations this year." "But there will be, there will, whatever you say!" my sister stamped her boot obstinately, large tears shining in her eyes.

In the morning I was awakened by the clatter of pails, the stomping of boots and excited voices in the first lieutenant's room. Through the half-open door the adjutant could be seen shaking the Bakelite telephone box and shouting into the mouthpiece at someone who couldn't hear or understand him properly. About half an hour later a light four-wheeled buggy came racing into the yard. Two officers in peaked caps stepped out of it. One older, rather small one in a bright green coat with a lot of buttons fastened up to the neck, and the other a head taller in a short rabbit-fur coat, who from quite close up looked so much like our lieutenant that at first we thought it was him. The older man immediately went in the direction of the shepherd's cottage and the younger hurriedly followed the adjutant into the first lieutenant's room without so much as a greeting. No sooner had these two shut the door behind them than the banging of the loom stopped, unspoken questions could be seen in the expressions on our faces, we realized that something had happened, something serious, but we didn't know what, and in that helpless, unknowing silence we tensely concentrated on the foreign voices coming from behind the door in unpleasant tones reminiscent of the unusually sharp exchange of opinions between the first lieutenant and his subordinates that had taken place at Christmas.

About ten minutes later our motionless tension relaxed as both men emerged from the room. The one in the peaked cap was carrying the first lieutenant's haversack and with an eloquent gesture the adjutant indicated we were to go on with our work. Only when he got to the doorway did the man in the peaked cap turn around and nod at my uncle to accompany him outside.

When Uncle came back indoors, he gave us all a mysterious glance and said almost in a whisper, "Something stinks here, folks."

He cast a look in the direction of the first lieutenant's room and went on, "He asked me about him. When had I seen him last?"

"I saw him come out when the clock struck two," cried my sister, who slept on the floor next to the loom.

"Shh! Not a word about it!" Uncle silenced her. "If anyone wants to know, you didn't see anything or hear anything. That'll be best."

Uncle was relishing our dumb show, which he concluded with the declaration of one in the know and a gesture that was easy to understand: "He's deserted. There's a bullet for that."

But that's not how it was at all. The buggy returned from up the hill with something that could have been a human body, covered with a brown-green-yellow piece of tenting. We only saw it from a distance, because the buggy didn't halt in front of our windows.

Once more the man in the peaked cap went into the first lieutenant's room with the adjutant and when they came out a moment later, I noticed that the adjutant didn't have a pistol. His pistol was carried by the man in the peaked cap. The adjutant went out in front of him, and through the window we saw him climb into the seat beside the coachman. The man in the peaked cap paused in the doorway (in height and attire the first lieutenant's double), weighing up the pistol in its holster and looking us over with an unpleasant, scrutinizing gaze, until his narrowed eyes fell on my sister, dressed in her Sunday-best snow-white dress, and against that blinding whiteness, quite involuntarily, I suddenly saw the large bluish eye of the dead rook.

The man in the peaked cap stared at my sister for hardly a moment, but that moment seemed to have no end.

However, there was nothing rough or military in his eyes. It was just the scornful gaze of a tired man.

PETER JAROŠ
- prose writer, playwright, script writer;
born in Hybe (1940)

Peter Jaroš has worked as an editor and film script writer. He has been on the staff of the National Literary Center and now of the National Cultural Center.

His first literary works were two short novels, **Popoludnie na terase** (*Afternoon on the Terrace*, 1963) and **Urob mi more** (*Make Me a Sea*, 1964) about people living in town. In his novels **Zdesenie** (*Horror*, 1965), **Váhy** (*Scales*, 1966) and a novella in two parts **Putovanie k nehybnosti** (*Journey to Immobility*, 1967), he showed his inclination towards the philosophy of existentialism and the style of the anti-novel. He wrote about his youthful adventures in the books **Menuet** (*Minuet*, 1967) and **Návrat so sochou** (*Return with a Statue*, 1967), **Krvaviny** (*Blood Stains*, 1970), in his prose memoirs for young people **Až dobehneš psa** (*When You Catch Up With the Dog*, 1971) and the novella in two parts **Pýr** (*Couch Grass*, 1971), also in his novel **Trojúsmevový miláčik** (*The Thrice Smiling Darling*, 1973) as well as in the books of short stories **Pradeno** (*Skein*, 1975*)*, **Telo v herbári** (*The Body in the Herbarium*, 1979) and **Parádny výlet** (*The Wonderful Trip*, 1982). In these he often makes use of elements of absurdity, slapstick comedy, the detective story and horror. The story in this anthology, "Grimasy" ("Making Faces") is taken from *Krvaviny*.

In his long novel **Tisícročná včela** (*The Millennium Bee*, 1972), he depicts the lives of Slovaks from the end of the last century until after the foundation of the Czechoslovak Republic. **Nemé ucho, hluché oko** (*Mute Ear, Deaf Eye*, 1984) is a loose sequel to this novel. In the novels **Lásky hmat** (*Love Touch*, 1988), **Psy sa ženia** (*Dogs Marry*, 1990) and **Milodar slučka** (*The Donated Noose*, 1991) he portrays a crisis in human relations.

He writes radio plays and is the author of film scripts (**Pacho, hybský zbojník** – *Pacho, the Outlaw from Hybe*, 1973; **Tisícročná včela** – *The Millennium Bee*, 1983).

In his own words:

The writer's memory works in such a way, that at least in some of my writings I have returned to my childhood and the region of my birth, to the people I once knew well. I am most interested in stories about people, which need not be original, so long as there is something dramatic, something unusual or special in their lives....

Art is a synthesis of fiction and documentary evidence, a synthesis of the subjective and objective. I look at documentary material in art from the perspective of someone living nowadays, the fictive really enriches me. It is therefore the fictive in art that is of supreme importance to me, because it allows me to reflect on people, but also on the times in which they lived or live, from the point of view of their significance for me personally, but also for the present time in general.

I realize that my attitude to art is the attitude of a poetic sensualist. This is, however, my reaction to the loss of sensual richness in the perception of reality.

Apart from literature and films, I am also interested nowadays in Buddhism.... If I were to sum up for myself its essence, it is love and goodness. That is probably the most difficult thing, to be loving and good; we learn it all our lives.... Love and goodness! These two concepts are common to all the great religions, including Christianity, in which I was brought up and which still has a deciding influence on me. Love and goodness also offer themselves to people as that which make life worth living....

Culture and art are a kind of ecology of the human soul. Without them the human soul becomes barren and insensitive, and people themselves destroy the very essence of what has enabled them to live and develop so far, for just to have a full stomach is not enough....

(2000)

MAKING FACES

I now have a stick to lean on and I am walking along a dusty path. I have reconciled myself to the chaos of the physical world, although I have not yet managed to become completely indifferent to it, and that is why I am walking. I don't even know where I am going and I am trying not to let it interest me. I am not trying to reach any particular goal, although I often used to say that any goal was better than none. Now I am just walking.... Yes, I have tried to learn and I have read the Bible, Homer, Socrates, Aristotle, Indian epics and the Upanishads, Kant, Hegel,

Feuerbach, Marx, Lenin, Engels, Bakunin, Mao Tse-tung, Lukács, Lev Tolstoy, de Sade, Kierkegaard, Dostoyevsky, Nietzsche, Janko Kráľ, Makovicky, Schopenhauer, Husserl, Freud, Kafka, Heidegger, Jaspers, Camus, Sartre, Thomas Aquinas, Spenser, Mickiewicz, Soloviev, Herder, Pushkin, Griboyedov, Belinsky, Škarvan, Masaryk, Teige, Croce, Bucharin, Bergson, Kosmas, Radhakrishnan, Joyce, Khlebnikov.... But I'm probably a fool, because I have stopped asking: who am I? why am I? and where am I going?... I have stopped thinking these questions are important, because I haven't found a satisfactory answer to them either in books or in myself. It's enough for me to know that I am and that I am walking along with a gnarled stick in my hand. The road is long enough for me not to reach its end. I don't know whether it is sensible or silly, but the quality of my actions doesn't interest me. Nor do I ask: what do I know? Although, as some people claim, a question like that is more thoroughly sceptical than the statement: I know that I know nothing....

As I go along, I make faces and amuse myself imagining what I must look like. I let the corners of my mouth drop and I have the impression I look like a miller's-thumb, but when I also narrow my eyes, I immediately become a fox. I open my mouth wide, I stick out my tongue and I am a panting dog. I open my eyes, lower my neck and I moo like a cow.... No, this is not an attempt at metempsychosis, I am just trying to make myself look the way I sometimes see myself.... However, I don't stop walking, I tread quietly on the soft dust, stirring it up with the soles of my shoes.... And although I don't ask: what do I know? and although I don't claim: I know that I know nothing! nevertheless, there are times when I cannot rid myself of the suspicion: I am a fool! and that one thing sometimes spoils the pleasure I get from my own grimaces....

Even though natural religion, the religion of the law and the religion of the spirit, have tried to get the better of me ever since I was little, I forget fairly quickly, and that is a good thing.... Of course, even things I have forgotten often come back to me, but not for long.... I am always saved by these grimaces, which I can't even see, because I have no mirror, I just imagine them....

I have no idea what went before the legendary history of humankind, what went before archeology, alchemy, chemistry, astrology and astronomy, or where mythology, poetry, philosophy or science are leading, but I have discovered that grimaces can be made with your whole body or part of it.... I simply have to crouch and hop on both feet to be a sparrow. It's a rather exaggerated grimace, perhaps, but it's good enough. Playing at being charitable looks less forced. It's enough to take a piece of bread to the square and feed the pigeons, who could manage without it anyway.

At times it has been possible to use the rights of the state to abolish the rights of the individual, or to benefit a dictator by oppression, but it was probably not of much service to the order of the world, which is said to derive from Cain. Not even of such service as my latest face, "the Philanthropist," which was my only companion on at least one quiet evening when the mist was so low it almost touched my head. I lie under a tree on a tuft of sweet-smelling straw and I tell myself: I'll take off my shoes, let my feet rest; then I will get up barefoot and before I fall asleep, I'll taste those strawberries nearby.... But I don't do anything; my unreliability no longer grieves me. Laziness is the only aspect of my character on which I can always rely.

I am thinking, I only think when I make faces, and at that moment I am not myself and I'm not too happy about it. What I feel even more sorry about is that my thinking lags so far behind my intuition, which does me the favor of visiting me only on exceptional occasions.... I'm probably fated to remain a fool, although fate is not exactly what I believe in....

But in the morning, when I wake up and have a drink of water, I take my stick, breathe in the damp air and move on once more. I walk, supporting myself with my stick and making faces until I meet someone. At such times I have to restrain myself and take an equal part in the meeting....

I see a hay wagon standing in a sloping meadow of cut grass. On either side of it there are about fifteen cocks of dry hay. The cows have been unyoked and are tied to the shaft. They are waving their tails, shaking their heads, driving off the bluebottles and gad flies. The farmer, a robust-looking man, thrusts his long fork into a pile of hay and swings it into the wagon over the hay rack. The handle creaks and cracks in his hands, but it doesn't break. The pole to weigh down the hay is lying a little way off. I sum up the situation at a glance: the farmer can't cart away the hay all at once by himself, and so I go towards him. He stops loading when he catches sight of me, sticks the fork in the ground in front of him and stands there, legs apart.

"Where now, where to?" he asks me before I have a chance to greet him. He is still smiling when he pushes his hat higher up his forehead with his index finger.

"To the river, fishing, good morning," I say. In fact we are not unlike: we both have pants, unbuttoned shirts, tanned chests and hats on our heads. Only I have a coat slung over my shoulder and a gnarled stick in my hand.

"It's going to be hot and sticky," says the farmer, "and there may be a shower before evening," he looks up and his face immediately seems to reflect the blue of the sky.

"I see you're getting the hay in," I keep up the conversation.

"Aaa, it's already dry," he points to the hay, "it's started to snap."

I look at the hay, too. Most of the haycocks are all heath grass, but two above the wagon are bristly fescue; they come from the very top of the meadow, where it is driest. In such places the sun burns the sparse grass yellow. However, I can also discern two haycocks of bur-reed, that must have grown at the lower end of the meadow, near the ditch. It is long and sharp, it has turned brown in the sun and it'll be for the sheep.

"I'll help you," I offer. He hesitates a moment, rests his arms on the handle of the fork and looks at the cows, which have begun to ruminate. Saliva is dripping from their mouths and they are taking no notice of us.

"As you like," he says finally. I quickly throw aside my stick and put my coat down beside it. I roll up the sleeves of my shirt and wait. He is staring at me, but kindly, he's weighing me up.

"You could get up into the wagon," he says, "it needs pressing down...."

I nod and scramble up into the cart from the shaft end. I wade into the hay, pushing it down. The farmer begins to throw whole forkfuls in my direction. He sticks the fork into a haycock and lifts half of it at one time, without so much as a groan. He just breathes out, blowing away the dust that has settled under his nose. The hay is dry and flies all over the place. I have my work cut out to keep up with him as I spread out the hay and press it down well. I shove it under the front and rear poles, push it out into the chains at the sides, but it is soon on a level with the hay rack. Now I begin to arrange the first layer from the front. One forkful to the right, the second to the left, the third in the middle, I cross them over so they hold together.... When I glance down, I see there are three more haycocks in the meadow. There'll be enough for another layer....

Now the wagon is full, the meadow empty. The farmer uses his rake to tidy up the wagon from all sides and he hands me the pole to keep the hay in place. We pull it really tight. He then throws the hay fork and rake up to me and I stick them firmly in the hay, so they won't get lost on the way, and I can jump down. I take a critical look at the cart. It seems a bit fat, I've put a bit too much on the sides. Otherwise....

"As if you'd been doing it all your life," the farmer remarks with a smile.

"You learn all kinds of things in your life...."

"Let's have a smoke."

We sit down side by side on the grassy stubble, at a distance from the wagon. The farmer pulls out his cigarettes, offers me one and immediately lights it for me. I have been sweating, and the dust and specks of hay are beginning to prick my skin. But I feel fine. I blow the black snot out of my nose, squeezing it between two fingers and I feel even better.

"On holiday?" the farmer asks me.

"Yes, sort of," I say.

"Not too many come here yet," he says, meaning tourists. "There are more fish here, too...."

"I don't know, I haven't tried catching them here."

"Where's your fishing line?" he inquires, turning towards me.

"I haven't got one, I can manage with my hands."

He nods his head approvingly. I watch him as he unhurriedly presses his cigarette stub into the soil with his sinewy hand. He looks around at the cows and gets up.

"I must hitch them up," he says. I follow him over to the wagon and hold the yoke for him. The cows are quiet, they don't twist and turn, even though the insects keep worrying them. The farmer takes another look around the cart and then retrieves his knapsack from the shaft.

"Here you are, you helped me," he says and hands me a large bit of fat and a slice of bread wrapped in a greasy piece of paper.

"Thank you!"

"Enjoy it!" he says and cracks his whip. The cows strain at the creaking yoke and the wagon moves forward.

"Don't you need me to hold on to it?" I ask.

"No, the path goes uphill here," he replies. "Goodbye!" he calls out and then he doesn't look around again until much later.

I remain standing where I am for a while, watching the wagon move away. Then I bend down, pick up my stick and sling my coat over my shoulder. I feel sadder than I did in the morning, but I then think of the water and the fish. I step out....

I am alone once more. Once more I occupy myself by making faces. I pull out my lips, stick out my teeth and maybe I look as if I am smiling. When I sniff, I must move my mouth and so I smack my lips at the same time. I walk on and it is like groping my way. Do you know the four vedas? Rigveda, Yajurveda, Samaveda and Atharvaveda. The most important of all is Rigveda. The Indo-Europeans brought these songs to India from their previous home as their most precious treasure. Someone called on people or ordered them to collect them, in order to preserve them. They did it when in their new homeland they came into contact with a large number of worshippers of other gods. That's what they

118

say. This suddenly struck a chord with my recollection of the farmer. The farmer, his cows, his wagon, his hay. Did it happen long ago? Did it happen at all? Am I not repeating to myself an old fairytale? When I walk along, I make faces, I imagine and then all kinds of things occur to me. Have I invented a fairytale farmer, or did I really meet him? I've got nothing to point to, nothing to prove it, even my own conscience has often betrayed me...!

Like Epicurus, I tell myself: don't worry about your funeral, and so I walk on to the waterside. I don't worry about things that are finite. But even so, the water is cold, especially at altitudes like these, and in that water I will throttle a fish. I will catch it by its fins, pull it out on to the bank and hit its head on a rock. Or I'll break its spine. I can't say to the fish: "Don't be afraid, nothing terrible awaits you when you are no longer alive," or: "Death does not concern us, because when we are, death is not, and when death is, we are not," because the fish doesn't understand. The fish is dumb, it suffers, if it suffers....

Something bumps against the small of my back. I fumble around for my coat pocket and discover a lump. I pull it out and, goodness me, its the fat and slice of bread. I feel pleased in spite of myself; I bless the farmer for his gift, because it is now the only proof not only of his kindness, but also of his existence. I hunt around among the odds and ends in my pants pocket and I pull out a knife. A cheap pocket knife, but sharp. I am not, or at least I think I am not, an egoist, a pleasure-seeker or a cynic, but the moment has come when I can think only of myself. I sit down on my coat in the grass and begin to eat. I nibble at the fat, the bread, I chew, masticate, smack my lips. My free moment, my moment for taking in food. I wallow in the intense enjoyment it gives me, as if it were the goal of a blissful life. I relish the pleasure so much, that in the end I feel ashamed. If Epicurus were here, he would tell me: "Ugh, you wretch! Happiness in life cannot be found in constant drinking and nightly reveling, nor in intercourse with boys and women, nor in eating fish and other things offered by a rich table, but sober judgement, which seeks reasons for every choice and for every refusal and repudiates deceptive suppositions, which fill the soul with the utmost chaos." I am even more ashamed when I realize that just a moment before I had longed for fresh fish far more than anything else. In fact I'm horrified, shivers run down my back, at moments when I.... I am he who wants nothing, neither a meaning, nor an aim, who does not want to be either good or bad, who doesn't want to stay anywhere or get anywhere, and a moment ago I had wanted nothing more than to get to the water and to the fish.... This confirms once again that, although I desire nothing in my mind, in fact

I long for everything I want to give up, even a good rest beside the cool waters.... But what can be done, I have already betrayed myself so often, that all that remains is for me to quickly forget. It really is impossible to live with contradictions like these, especially if one is afraid to take one's own life, and so I don't throw away the fat, but I finish eating it and I don't even relinquish the idea of resting at the waterside.

The valley above me runs into a ravine. The valley below me descends to a river. There are the marshy places, there are the soft damp spots overgrown with dock leaves. There the willows have grown strong and their supple canes criss-cross each other in all directions. Only there does the ground squelch under your soles and only there can drunken consciousness, a part of mystical consciousness, find a cool place to rest. And maybe just there it is possible to achieve with James that divine physical rapture. I focus my gaze on that place, I shout out loud (and insanely), I just can't wait....

But first, what torment it is to enter this oasis.... And perhaps it only seems an oasis. Happiness demands suffering as its condition. I am setting out on a journey, I am delirious. I would like to get from the unreal to the real, from the darkness to the light, from death to immortality.... As if in my imagination I were already reaching for the absolute....

And here is a little beetle! He is traveling in the opposite direction from me. I bend over him, I tell him: come with me, because I want to have a companion. He trots on stubbornly. I turn him around, poke him with my thumb, but he traces a half circle and returns the same way. He doesn't want to! I have to lift him up with a handful of earth and shove him in my pocket. He may bite his way through the material to my thigh, but by then we will already be beside the water, among the dock leaves.

The absolute? I am taken aback. Not long ago I didn't want anything, and now I want everything. Is it really only possible to long for extremes? I am forgetting, however, because I want to, I am forgetting the beetle in my pocket. Is it really so easy, only thirty steps and I will be beside the water. Look at my grimaces.... I make the journey more difficult by crawling, I tear my trousers, dirty my shirt, graze my palms and knees until they bleed. What does it matter, after all, I am going to the water and there I will wash. Who knows, maybe the water has the power to heal!

The dock leaf hides the sun, but cannot stop it shining. When it waves in the breeze, it fans my face. When it dips, bent by the wind, it strokes me. The ground is soft, the water rises. A person longs for nothing more than for himself....

Here is the bank already! The reflection in the water can be seen, its coolness felt, its fragrance smelled. On the bank is a dead fish with a dead eye. I crawl over to it as to a mirror. I want to see myself in it, my grimace.... I bend over it, searching for an image, and I see nothing more, only death.... My head drops, the fish eye penetrates mine. What will it be like to breathe one's last?

ĽUBOŠ JURÍK

- prose writer, journalist, playwright;
born in Nové Zámky (1947)

Ľuboš Jurík has worked as a journalist and from 1992–97 he was spokesman for the Speaker of the National Council of the Slovak Republic.

His literary debut, **Na Poľnej ulici** (*In Poľná Street*, 1973), was a collection of short stories set in the outskirts of Bratislava, as were those in his second book **Dlhá namáhavá cesta** (*A Long, Tiring Journey*, 1976). In the novel **Emigranti** (*Emigrants*, 1977), he reflected on the difficult lives of emigrants after August 1968. The novel **Novinári** (*Journalists*, 1984) is about the complicated life of an editorial office. With the short stories in **Už o tom nehovorme** (*Let's Say No More About It*, 1986) he returned to Poľná Street. The novel **Spravodliví** (*The Just*, 1989) looks at the judiciary in the final period of the totalitarian regime. In the short stories of **Keď sa raz nahnevám** (*When One Day I Lose My Temper*, 1991) – from which the story "Smetiar" ("The Road Sweeper", 1991) is taken – he depicts complicated interpersonal relations in the post-communist period of transformation. **Tri detektívne prípady reportéra AZ** (*Three Detective Cases of Reporter AZ*, 1992) and **3 x reportér AZ** (*Three Times Reporter AZ*, 1993) are crime stories set in the old part of Bratislava.

Interviews form the main part of his journalistic work. He published the collection **Rozhovory** (Interviews, 1975) and **Rozhovory o literatúre** (*Interviews about Literature*, 1986) containing interviews with Slovak artists, **Nepokojné dialógy** (*Troubled Dialogues*, 1984) with European artists, **Pražské rozhovory** (*Prague Interviews*, 1987) with Czech artists and **Americké dialógy** (1993) with American artists. He writes radio plays and he has used his political experience in a book of essays entitled **Eurochaos** (1997).

In his own words:
Slovak writers become involved in politics far too often. I would

even say that it is sometimes difficult to see the border between their literary and social – or even actually political – activities. It is a strong tradition, which dates right back to the times of Kollár and Štúr [19th century] and is not only a Slovak speciality. I am in favor of writers being involved in politics and the life of society, speaking up for the needs of the nation, struggling to reveal the truth – but at the same time they should try to achieve an overview, reach a timeless dimension, be above things. The writer leaves his work behind him, it is a measurable criterion, of spiritual value, but nothing remains after the politician, not even a bad smell. When I was offered the chance to work in the highest political circles, I saw it as a logical continuation of my efforts to help realize the state and national ambitions of the Slovaks, to contribute to the establishment of a modern democratic state. At the same time, it was an ideal opportunity to gain unique information for future literary work. The period between 1992 and 1997 was so full of events, that it seems reasonable to me to choose to write non-fiction and leave a testimony to this complicated, contradictory time....

In our century alone historical hurricanes have swept through this country. They have devastated the nation, left towns and villages in ruin, overturned values, killed men and women. The Slovak nation has always found enough strength within to pull itself together again and renew its inner source of energy.

(1997)

THE ROAD SWEEPER

Violence frightens me.

I wake up in the middle of the night. I can see my son dying. He was beaten to death during the war. I feel I'm suffocating from fear and powerlessness. I would like to forget. After so many years! I can't.

During the day I'm tired from lack of sleep. I have dreams in which I am sweeping an enormous square with a huge broom. I myself am a giant. I am driving before me the trash the town spits out. The houses shake from the blows of my gigantic broom.

In real life I am an old road sweeper; I have an orange jacket and a cart with wooden wheels. On Poľná Street, next to the wall of Ondrej Cemetery, there is a small park and that is where our wooden trailer stands. Here we keep our tools and we rest on the dilapidated benches: deaf-mute Juliška, Vratko and I. I'm the oldest; I retired ages ago, and they did discharge me, they wrote out the papers, bought me a watch, but I returned to the trailer: I'll work for free, I said, just let me stay here. I'll die without work. So they agreed. Vratko is what they call simple-minded; otherwise, he's very good-hearted. I'm a little afraid of him: when he shakes your hand, you can feel your bones cracking. He means well, though.

There aren't many road sweepers. The streets are swept by machines with silly suckers, like huge bees. When we emerge from the trailer early in the morning, we must look like apparitions; our carts rattle over the paving stones and we are lost wanderers. At the corner of Poľná Street we go our different ways to our own patches.

I have been sweeping this area on the outskirts of town for almost half a century; I can see how little has changed – there's only more trash. Unassuming little houses huddled up together, blocks of apartments with connecting balconies on each floor housing workers' families, two bars, Ondrej Cemetery on one side, the Medical Faculty's gardens on the other. In the morning people leave for work with vague hopes, longing for a change, drunk with the wine of impossibility; after knocking off, the men stop for a drink in The Horse and the women hurry off to do the shopping. Young lads sit around on the patch of grass near our trailer, strumming guitars and occasionally breaking into a tobacconist's. I feel sorry for them; they all look like my son. Sometimes Vratko chases them away, when they are too rowdy. I keep quiet; I'm afraid they might beat me up.

I begin to sweep Poľná, driving the trash ahead of me: fallen leaves, scraps of paper, cigarette butts, dust, tiny stones, apple cores and God knows what else. I sweep slowly and thoroughly, so as to leave the edge of the road and the pavements quite clean: an upward swing, downward pull, backward bend, forward movement, the broom pushes against the litter and moves it on. I sweep the little pile onto the shovel and tip it into the cart. It takes some time for the cart to fill up, so I go down three, sometimes even four streets before making for the nearest dumpster and tipping the trash in.

I like rummaging in the trash: it stinks of extinction. Garbage can tell you more about people than words. If I could send something into space to show what our civilization is like, I would send a dustbin. There you can find everything that has turned monkeys into men – above all, vanity.

The trash on Poľná Street is like its inhabitants: they pretend. They'd like to have more than they can afford. I'm rummaging among the potato peelings, bits of stale bread, shabby clothes, worn-out shoes, bottles of inexpensive alcohol, sardine cans and cheap meat paste, when suddenly in the midst of all these no longer needed essentials, there glitters a pot that once held the most expensive face cream (still smelling sweetly of the smooth complexions of young women), an empty bottle of cognac, I suppose too tempting to be drunk, you just swill it around your mouth, or a plastic bag that had contained some kind of spotlessly clean underwear. Poľná Street rebels against the monotony and mediocrity of life: a gesture which solves nothing, but offers an opportunity to forget.

I live on Poľná Street. Just like the others, I, too, pretend. I pick all kinds of showy things out of the dumpsters: bottles that contained expensive spirits, little boxes and pots; I wash them, polish them and restore their former dignity. I have an old dresser in my kitchen, where I keep a collection of things I've found. I gaze at them and imagine how shiny and sweet-smelling the world could be. It gives me pleasure.

Newspapers spoil my mood. I don't have a radio or a television, so I take the newspapers out of the dumpsters. People wrap their garbage up in them, or just throw them away. They are torn and damp, but I don't care. I smooth them out, dry them and then I can begin to read. I read everything, even though I don't understand it all. I'm horrified by the violence described by the printed letters, which crawl like insects into all the crevices of my body, and neither the sweat of fear, nor the urine of anxiety will wash them out. Wars and murders. Corpses. Demonstrations.

Blood everywhere.

I'm afraid of newspapers, but I can't stop myself from taking them out of their stinking burial grounds. They revive the horror printed on their pages. The horror is different each time, although it is the same. Blood is blood. The blood of my son was bright red, luminous like the protective jackets we road sweepers wear; only when it dried did it turn dark and black.

I go through the streets, emptying two or three cartfuls, rummaging in several dumpsters, and when it's getting on to noon, I go back to the trailer. We sit on the narrow benches and eat our lunch in silence. I chew a slice of bread and dripping and wash it down with lukewarm tea from my thermos bottle. I'd like to say something about the horrible things in the newspapers, but who to? A deaf woman, a lunatic? I keep my anxiety to myself; they have their own protection against it. They are happy in their own way.

We finish eating and Juliška nods her head: it's time to go. This skinny and withered spinster is our leader. They didn't have much of a choice with us three, but I don't mind. Someone has to be the one to obey. I've got other things to think about.

I trundle along the streets once more and after lunch the cart always seems heavier. I have less energy than before. I trace the same route as in the morning; litter has accumulated again in the streets, although there isn't too much of it. I sweep slower, my movements are lazy and my broom scrapes sleepily along the paving stones. My arms and legs ache, my breathing is painful. Every few meters I have to pause and get some air into my lungs. I can feel the blood pulsing even in my eyes; when I close my eyelids tight, I can see wriggling purple and black snakes, they are crawling up from my swollen belly. I feel a sharp pain in my side. After a while my body calms down, so I move on a few meters, dragging my broom behind me like the white flag of someone come to negotiate a truce. When I've dragged my feet as far as the bar, all is well; I leave my cart in the parking lot alongside the cars, and I can go and drink a small glass of beer.

I've been coming here for years and the bar has always been the same: a long, narrow room with a beer counter at the end, a few tables covered with dirty tablecloths, a wooden floor painted with creosote and spattered with sticky beer spit. The dusty windows peer into the busy street, over the road there is a railway line and then a factory. My buddies sit in the corner near the window; it seems to me that over the years they have become permanent fixtures there, reminiscent of bronze statues covered with a layer of shiny mud. They sip their beers and philosophize. A deaf train driver, a postman, a bent grave-digger, a tram worker, a chimney-sweep. My buddies from Poľná Street.

When my wife gave birth, I bet a barrel of wine it would be a son. I won my bet; we rolled a barrel into the bar and got drunk. The whole bar drank with us. The men danced on the tables and slept on the floor. We had a great time; we talk about it to this very day.

After the birth my wife died and I brought up the boy by myself. He was a good boy, he was just unlucky that they beat him to death in the war.

I order a small beer and join my friends. They're talking about something, but I don't listen to them; I take a sip, swill the liquid around in my mouth and then I let it run gently down my gullet, washing away the dust. I feel better, my eyes focus, my tongue softens. After a while I can join in the conversation.

Everything we need to say has already been said, and so our words are freed of any burden; they fly as they like. We are not irritated by their similarity. Everyone talks and everyone only half-listens. And I join in. I pull out a bit of the newspaper I found in a dumpster that morning. It is still damp and it smells rather unpleasantly of fish oil; I smooth it out with my hand and put on my glasses.

126

I announce: "They write here that the Egyptian president has been killed. He died on the way to...."

The men stop talking, my news has taken them aback. The grave-digger looks over my shoulder.

"Huh, you Simple Simon," he says. "That was five years ago...!"

I falter. Maybe he's right; the newspaper is already yellow with age. But what difference does it make? As if time were of importance! I begin to feel sorry for the Egyptian president. Sometimes I read how many telegrams of congratulation presidents have to send; there's always some special occasion or other. I remarked on this to the postman. They must spend all their time standing in the line at the post office!

"You really are an idiot," he said. "They don't do that themselves. They have people to do it for them...."

I read on, even though the letters have already been dead for five years. But they seem alive to me. A bomb has exploded in a car and killed some people. A war is being waged in the streets of a town and the police have dispersed demonstrators with tear gas. There is a demonstration against guided missiles. Year after year the same news; I can't understand why they tell me the newspaper is five years old. The news will all be the same again tomorrow.

I imagine the demonstration: footsteps pounding the pavements. Millions of feet hitting the ground. I stride along beside them for as long as I have the strength. Then I sit down on the edge of the pavement and lean up against a tree. I can't go any further, but the footsteps go booming on, everything is shaking, windows are rattling.

A goods train goes through Little Station, the impact of the wheels sending the dust flying. You can't hear anything, just the rush of blood in your ears.

The conversation dies out. The men withdraw into themselves while the hurricane passes through the bar. The train rushes by; there is a silence which promises nothing.

I walk along the street once more, pushing the cart before me, but no longer sweeping.

Not that there is nothing to sweep: so long as people exist, litter will too. There are more cigarette butts, letters, bits of paper, patches of spittle on the pavements and roads. I push the cart as far as the Medical Faculty. Now comes the most beautiful moment of the day: they'll give me an injection.

There's a hospital in a side wing of the faculty; the corridor is shiny, it smells pleasantly of medicines, the tiles on the walls reflect the white figures of the doctors and nurses. There are flowers and little trees in pots beside the large windows. At the entrance you have to put on soft slippers. I slide along the nice clean floor like a ballet dancer.

There are always a few humble patients in front of the office. I sit down on the leatherette bench and relish the oppressiveness of the silence. Everything is clean and dignified. Some people don't like hospitals. I do. There's the kind of order here that you will never find in my streets. I feel like the Great Road Sweeper, who rules over the litter.

I wait patiently; the longer I sit, the better I feel. I let other patients go in before me, although they came later, until I'm alone there and no one disturbs me by coughing, sniffing, clearing their throats or whispering. Then the nurse looks around the door, up and down the corridor and murmurs:

"Come in...."

My excitement grows, like a snowball rolling down a slope, shivers run down my spine. The office is magical, shining chrome, little packets of medicines standing in glass-cases like an invincible army. Next to the wall is a narrow bed covered with a plastic sheet: the bed of bliss.

"All right," the nurse mutters. "Pants down and lie down!"

My fingers tremble as I undo my pants buttons, pull down my shorts and press my withered genitals to the plastic sheet; I can feel the chill in my groin. The nurse is young and chubby, she has a rough face and pig's eyes, but her fingers are gentle and sensitive. First she wipes my skin with cotton; she strokes me, feeling out my cells, evoking memories of touches long ago. She caresses me. Excites me. Makes me feel sentimental. Then she takes the hypo, presses the air out of it and jabs it into my bottom. A short, sharp pain as the needle is thrust through the tense skin and penetrates into the flesh. I let out a little hiss of delight. The hot solution flows through the needle and lights a fire in my body. Cool below, burning above. I shiver. The nurse pulls out the needle, presses the cotton to the spot and says, "That's it! Cover up that tool of yours...."

I lie there a little longer absorbing the pain and the pleasure. My body must have time to calm down and my feverish blood to cool, they inject me with insulin, because I have diabetes badly. I've taken it for years. It's a drug I can't live without. Sometimes it gives me relief, but occasionally I don't feel well after the injection; my legs go weak and mud seems to settle in my veins. That's how it is now: I have come out of the office feeling as if I am carrying a sack of grain on my back. A fan is whirring in my head, mining machines are rumbling in my stomach and crocodiles wading through my intestines.

Outside it is better; the wind eases the pain. My legs carry me to my cart, my hands grasp the handles and I-My Brain go back to the trailer in Polná Street. Walking brings me relief, but heaviness is lying in wait around the corner to hit me over the head. It may not pass until I lie down in the evening: at midnight I will dream about my son. I will suffocate with fear and break out in a cold sweat.

There are two more dumpsters on the way. There is nothing interesting in the first, but in the second there is a black plastic bag tied up like a package with string. I can always find a use for a bag like that. I can put my snacks or bread in it to stop them from going stale. I pull the bag out, clean it up a bit, wiping off the potato peelings, and I throw it into my cart. Then I move on. I have gone a few meters, when I start wondering why the bag is tied up, maybe someone has left something in it.

I pick up the package and weigh it in my hands; I can feel something soft and supple inside and I immediately imagine it contains rotten meat full of worms. I have found a piece of meat from time to time that a housewife has forgotten and then thrown away; in no time it is covered with horrible white worms, that crawl all over the dumpster. If there is meat in the package, it would be better to throw it away immediately. However, my curiosity gets the better of me. The bag is quite heavy, maybe it is old clothes or shoes. Here you never know what surprises your fellow citizens have in store for you.

I sit down on the edge of the pavement and put the package down next to me. I need to rest anyway, because my body-the stranger is protesting again and I-My Brain can't control it. I sit there, feeling the pain playing up in my bowels. I think I can hear footsteps once more, the pavement is rumbling, people must be going to demonstrate, so the newspapers will have something to write about. But no, it's a truck going down the street, belching a cloud of black fumes in my face as it passes. The footsteps die away.

The string is tied tight and my fingers are stiff and clumsy; I can't grip the knots, my nails break, my bones crack. I begin to lose patience and I would move on, but my legs don't want to. So I sit. Then I manage to undo one of the knots after all and the string gives way. I listlessly unwrap the ball; the top of the plastic bag opens and I can see something white inside. As I thought, it is meat; I wait for the worms to appear and I'm ready to recoil in loathing.

The bag is unwrapped. I recoil with a shriek. I'm stunned and struck dumb. My blood surges into my brain and pumps wildly through my heart. I break down into millions of cells and my eyes stare as if through an eight-sided prism: on the plastic bag there lies the shriveled body of a baby. Its thin hair is stuck to its head, there is dry blood on its skin, it stinks of urine and mucus. It is a boy: his tiny penis is squashed between his legs, his arms are drawn in to his body, the string has cut into his sides. Appalled, I gaze at my find, my head is empty, it hasn't the strength to give orders or even think or not think, it is just a hollow drum, in which blows resound. Suddenly, however, (to my horror!) the little body moves, the plastic bag rustles. Shocked out of my senses, I think for a moment that there are already worms in it, too (or is it just the wind that has lifted the bag?), but the hand changes its position, the leg trembles, a spasm passes through the body. It's alive! (Alive?) I poke its tummy with my finger, pull its heel; the body really is pulsating, the chest rises irregularly, the eyelids flutter. My drum of a head is suddenly full of impulses and my old legs, which at other times think for themselves, sound the alarm: all the cells in my body are on the alert.

It's only a little way to my cramped apartment, so I hurry home. The bag containing the boy is lying in my dustcart. I hurry, almost run, my bowels rattling. Although I don't have far to go, by the time I reach the old block of apartments I am wet with sweat and there's a hoarse whistling sound in my lungs. My hands are shaking when I wrap the body up in my feather quilt; I have to stand still for a while, get my breath back, let the blood in my veins calm down.

Only after a while am I capable of doing anything. First I should feed the poor creature, but with what? I remember that outside in the passageway there is a bowl of milk for the cats. I should heat the milk, perhaps boil it first, but there is no time. The little boy is not moving, he has grown weaker, maybe he's no longer alive. With my left palm I lift the back of his head a little and try to pour the milk from the bowl directly into his mouth. It's no use; the milk runs down his chin and on to his neck. I dip my little finger into the milk, open his lips and stick my finger into his mouth. That doesn't work either: his little head droops on one side or the other, his body is stiff and cold. I am about to give up.

Then all of a sudden! The boy twitches and I feel the lips tightening on my finger. He's pulling! He's sucking! I quickly dip my finger into the milk again and stick it in his mouth. And once more, he feels the finger with his lips and sucks on it. Little by little I scoop up the milk and dribble it into his body. It seems the boy has more or less enough; he suddenly stops drinking and lets out a piercing, despairing wail, making me jerk in fright. But I immediately feel relieved: he is crying, shouting, kicking and is therefore alive and is over the worst.

Suddenly everything blurs in front of my eyes; I glance back into the past. The cloth of my memory becomes taut and the first drops of recollections begin to fall on its layers. Aha, that's how they came to show me my boy when he was born. He was wrapped up in some kind of sheet and he was yelling at the top of his voice. Only his head was sticking out and there were still traces of blood on his face. I didn't know then that my wife was dead. And now it is as if he has returned; he is crying and I am equally helpless. I am at a loss to know what to do and am choked by anxiety. I was at a loss then, too, when during the war they brought him to me battered and bloody. A boy not yet an adult, almost a child, his life ebbing away through his veins. I washed his face with water, but I knew that it was the Descent from the Cross; he died in my arms.

The sound of crying returns me to the present; I decide that I will warm some water and wash the boy, then I'll take him to the chubby nurse in the hospital, let them take care of him. I put a saucepan of water on the stove, I take an old flannel shirt out of the cupboard and I tear it up. When the water has heated up a little, I dip the rag in it and carefully lift the boy in my arms. He howls. I wash his face, body, hands and legs, turn him over on his stomach and clean his back. Then I wipe him with a towel and wrap him up in the remains of the shirt, so he won't catch cold. I wrap him up in the quilt.

He stops crying and it seems to me that he has fallen asleep. My boy fell asleep, too, before he died. At that time I thought that sleep would give him strength. He had opened his eyes briefly, but he could no longer see with them; he tried to smile and his head dropped to one side.

Now to the hospital. I move the boy onto the pillow and carry him to my road-sweeper's cart. I take hold of the handles and I want to go, but the muscles in my legs and arms are as stiff as a ship's ropes. I don't have the strength. I sit down on the edge of the pavement and try to get a grip on my excited body cells. My Body-the Stranger refuses to obey, it doesn't take into consideration the urgency of the situation, it betrays Me-My Brain. Once more I hear the trample of feet, indifferent footsteps, which hurry in their hordes to save the world; they have no idea that in my cart lies the One who chaos has given birth to, the One who has stepped out of the trash and is coming to make Order. I remember that in fairytales future princes were also found abandoned in baskets, and even Old Testament Moses had quite mysterious origins.

But these considerations do not help; I can't move. I need another dose of insulin, otherwise I will just remain sitting here and worms will make their homes in my veins. Hot waves of weakness now rush into my head, filling me with a feeling of powerlessness; they progress downwards, rushing through my body like an express train and coming out through my big toes. My tongue swells up, becoming a large, rough rag in my mouth, weights of sand are tied to my wrists and my ankles. My eyes sting like puddles of vitriol. I feel something wet flowing from my nose.

I sit like this and the pressure in my head changes into a sweet sleepiness; my eyelids droop and the pain flows out of my body, tufts of candyfloss taking its place. Now I feel fine; my Body-the Stranger has ceased to put up a resistance.

I don't know if I am just dreaming it, or if it is an incident from another day; someone pokes me with the tip of their shoe and I hear a voice, "You drunken old man, you should be ashamed of yourself, boozing like that...." I roll over on my side, hit my head on a tree and cut open the skin over my temple.

The blow brings me around; I am aware of a sharp, piercing pain, I probe the wound with the tips of my fingers and feel the sticky blood. Electric needles prick my head, drilling into the very core of my brain, into the deepest hidden crannies, to the God of nerves. The pain is so intense I don't feel it: I am Pain.

My Body-the Stranger gets up to leave and I take myself off with him. Together we push the cart to the hospital. I don't know whether the boy is still alive, whether I am a mother or undertaker, bringing him into or accompanying him out of this world. At times I forget what I am doing and where I am going, what I am carrying apart from the casing of my skin; but it isn't important. I am moving and that is all that matters. I have the feeling I have been walking along like this all my life, dragging my burden, my cart, and carrying in it an important message: trash.

I park the cart in front of the hospital and feel for the boy wrapped in the pillow. I can't see anything, just a long, narrow tunnel with a bright light at the end. I walk on blindly, I know the way by heart. I pass by the porter's office, along the slippery floor reflecting my own picture over and over again in its flat tiles. There is no one sitting in the waiting room, the imprint of bottoms can be seen as dark patches on the leatherette benches. I stand in front of the office door (my hands are full) and I kick the door. I almost fall over. I know I can't last long; I kick once more, but the door doesn't open.

My hands begin to drop and the joints in my knees give way like loose screws. Drums are beating in my head again and the light at the end of the tunnel is flickering transparently; someone is walking towards me. I kick the door again and it suddenly opens.

"You crazy old man!" yells the nurse. "Are you out of your mind?"

I thrust the boy and the pillow at her and I sense rather than see her astonishment, horror and alarm. I don't know whether she has taken the child, because the weight remains in my arms. I stumble out. I lean up against a tree, slide down to the ground and the burden of my arms drags me down to the roots. I'm bent over and I grow into the ground. My toes sprout. I'm heavily light. Feet trample past me, stepping over me, more and more coming all the time. They are all hurrying to the demonstration, to prevent Evil from happening.

The feet speak harshly to me: "Drunken old man! Getting yourself pissed like that...."

Well, one day I will get angry...! One day when I get angry, I will take a big broom and I will sweep them all into one enormous pile. All that dirt, puss, all that disgusting garbage. Only...I won't get angry any more. I don't have the strength. I am walking toward the Great Heavenly Broom.

The feet speak harshly to me: "Drunken old man! You should be ashamed of yourself...."

The tunnel suddenly widens and the light is soft. I walk along with ease, I just have to half-close my eyes. It takes some time to get used to it. I am walking towards myself and in the middle of the tunnel I meet myself. We shake hands and together we go on, to the place from where we came.

I think we will have something to talk about.

JÁN LENČO
- prose writer, journalist;
born in Žilina (1933)

Ján Lenčo worked as an editor, teacher, administrative officer, as well as a cinema manager.

His debut was a collection of short prose works, **Cesta na morské dno** (*Journey to the Bottom of the Sea*, 1966), where, in minimal space he raises weighty questions of human existence. The short novel **Didaktická kronika rodu Hohenzollerovcov** (*The Educational Chronicle of the Hohenzollerns*, 1968) is a historical metaphor on the misuse of power. He deals with questions of the lack of freedom in the works **Nepokoj v minútach** (*Turmoil in Minutes*, 1968), **Ďaleká a blízka** (*Far and Near*, 1968) as well as in the book of short stories **Pomsta zo záhrobia** (*Revenge from Beyond the Grave*, 1971); this includes the story "Na ceste do P." ("On the Way to P."). The role of the ordinary man in history is also the subject of his novel **Egypťanka Nitokris** (*The Egyptian Woman Nitokris*, 1972) and the book of short stories **Hviezdne okamihy** (*Stellar Flashes*, 1974). In the novel **Rozpamätávanie** (*Recollecting*, 1978) he reveals in an unconventional way the difficulties that arise in the relationships between members of a teaching staff. The novels **Čarodejník z Atén** (*The Wizard from Athens*, 1978) and **Zlaté rúno** (*The Golden Fleece*, 1979) are intended for young readers. Other works of his also use history as an allegory – the novels **Odyseus, bronz a krv** (*Odysseus, Bronze and Blood*, 1982) and **Žena medzi kráľmi** (*A Woman among Kings*, 1985). The novel **Roky v kine Úsmev** (*Years in the Cinema Smile*, 1987) is a satirical probe into conditions nowadays in a small town. His leaning towards short texts and science fiction is evident in the book **Socha z Venuše** (*The Statue from Venus*, 1988). In the satirical short pieces **Pravidlá a výnimky** (*Rules and Exceptions*, 1990) he considers man in the process of social transformation.

In his own words:

If I am interested in people as such, I can't be indifferent to their past, present and future. It wouldn't be a good thing if all my books did not have a lot in common, and even worse, if their common denominator were not the most important thing: people in a "model" situation, moment or sequence of situations, in which they struggle with all kinds of forces, and try to shape their existence according to their own ideas. From this point of view I wish to make a point of depicting history as the present and the present as history. The same also applies to the future, that is, to the genre of science fiction. So far as the question of form is concerned, I am a traditionalist and I am not ashamed of it. My greatest ambition is to achieve what is often scorned in modern literature as old-fashioned: simplicity, transparency, clarity.

(1988)

Humor and satire in life and in literature have always seemed to me like twins. If I consider their grammatical gender [in Slovak], humor is a good-natured and kind-hearted husband and satire a malicious and nagging wife....

The process of writing – don't wish to make a mystery or myth of it – is a secret, a great non-self-discovery. I guess it would be best if in the process of maturing, the original idea was purified, while enriching everything that one experiences or comes to know, or that troubles and torments one....

In literature the posing of questions, I stress, the **right** questions, is incomparably more important than the formulation of answers. Answers a priori provoke distrust and are potentially misleading, while questions are more human, more stimulating and more creative.

(1993)

ON THE WAY TO P.

Outside the window the country flashed by. It was as monotonous as the bumpity-bump of the wheels.

The man who was sitting opposite me had been sizing me up for some time. It was clear he was gauging the possibilities of speaking to me. He was an old, grey-haired man with a good-natured appearance. Since I don't much like starting conversations with people I don't know, and like listening to them even less, I pretended I was dozing. From time to time I surreptitiously lifted an eyelid, to see whether my fellow-traveler had given up his intention. A silent, but frenzied duel arose between us, a duel between our astuteness, cunning and endurance. Who would win? On this tiring journey through monotonous countryside nothing seemed more important than this contest of wills. At least it was a welcome distraction, relieving the boredom. In the end, I lost, no doubt because I let myself be carried away by the enjoyment and pleasure of the game. I forgot to be on my guard.

The old man let out a triumphant chuckle. He chuckled for a long, long time, clearly enjoying himself.

His chuckling wasn't at all monotonous. It was as varied and changing as the countryside in spring.

"I'll tell you, sir, the story of my life. How could I not tell you? When I come to think about it, talking is now my only pleasure. The only pleasure of my grey days. The only pleasure on this journey. You could say it is what I'm here for. After all, everyone who wants to live more or less reasonably must give his existence some kind of purpose. He-he-he! Think about that. Some purpose, some little purpose, however small. How, otherwise, would you get over your disappointments, how would you improve yourself, how would you excuse yourself, how would you comfort yourself, deceive yourself? It's all a question of purpose. It's a well of pleasure. Since I am already drinking from this well, I can't resist offering you this pure, healthy, spring water, too, sir. Spring water, even though it is drawn from a well. How would it be if I didn't share it with you. After all, we are humanists. We carry two thousand years of Christian humanism within us, one century of that, hm, that new, scientific humanism. I can't help sharing with you, sir."

I wanted to cut in, to interrupt him with a comment to the effect that what is a pleasure for one person needn't be a pleasure for another, that it is very often an expression of greater consideration for others not to try to please someone who does not want to be pleased.... Why try to please someone against their will, when they just don't want it? Why?

But instead, feeling rather guilty, I merely asked him the banal question: "Where are you going?"

"To P..., sir. To P.... A nice little town, a nice little world. Our little town, our little world."

I was traveling to the station after P.... Shivers ran down my spine. I'd have to listen to a lot more from him.

"To P..., sir. That's my destination. But not the final one. Oh, no! He-he-he! From there I have to go further and higher." He began chuckling to himself again. It was as if he had grown, as if he had drawn from his own words and laughter a strange kind of strength. It was impossible not to listen to him. He was a master of words. I had never yet met anyone who had such a command over words. They were his obedient, hard-working slaves, and he generously rewarded them with laughter.

"I'll tell you, I'll tell you everything, how could I not tell you, why should I not? Before I begin, I'll tell you one thing, sir. Maybe you will agree with it, maybe you won't, but that doesn't matter. He-he-he. Sir," here he lowered his voice secretively, as if he were about to disclose some important news, "listen to me carefully, mind my words."

Once more he began laughing. He laughed till he was shaking all over, till he almost choked. Tears of laughter ran down his face.

Involuntarily, not wanting to, quite against my will, I began to laugh with him, too. We laughed together. The ticket inspector arrived and he also began to laugh. My fellow traveler suddenly stopped unexpectedly, gave him a stern look and handed him his ticket. The ticket inspector frowned guiltily, punched our tickets and left. We heard him cough in a puzzled fashion in the corridor.

"I'll tell you something, sir, but don't divulge it to anyone. Promise me you won't divulge it to anyone, that never in a weak moment or second will you let it out. A secret to be kept more secret than all other secrets! If anyone should find out that I had told you, I would be in hot water. And you, as I already guessed, even when you were pretending to doze, he-he-he, are a good man, sympathetic to your fellow men, you wouldn't want to get anyone into trouble. You, yourself, could be in trouble, sir, as well...." He lowered his voice even more. I could hardly catch his words. I listened hard. "Alongside this reality of ours in which we live, there exists another, a different one. Completely different. Very few people know about it. It has quite different rules, other laws, a different history. And that hidden reality, sir, is far more important than that which we know. That hidden reality influences – but *influences* is a feeble word for it, it *motivates* the reality in which we live. We live in the tops of the trees, sir. Just like our ancestors. The tops of the trees, that is our reality. And the reality I'm telling you about, that is the roots that give the leaves their greenness, the branches their moisture and life to the whole tree. That's how it is indeed, sir.

"Don't you like what I'm saying, my good, gullible fellow-traveler? Don't you like it? Badly educated by literature, I thought so at once. Your fault, not mine. Of course, they taught you, and you got used to it, that the moral should never come at the beginning. It should arise inconspicuously, quietly and tactfully from the story. Or at least be at the end. First the story, an interesting story, then we get to the point. And the point includes a little moral.

"Sir...," he once more burst into laughter, but a different kind of laughter now, somehow more good-hearted, indulgent. "I have first told you the point and only now am I going to come out with the story. I divulged the point, I couldn't stop myself. And why, sir? Not because I disagree with the laws of narration and am against the spirit of them. That wouldn't be true. No, it certainly wouldn't."

He pushed out his lips self-importantly. "I have a different moral, a different point at the end. You will be surprised, dear sir. I'm preparing a great, unexpected surprise for you. What I have already told you will seem nothing in comparison to that. Indeed, sir, if you will be so kind as to have a little patience, you'll experience something you've never heard before. You will, whether you want to or not.

"Around our reality is another kind of reality. And who organizes this hidden reality, who secretly creates this visible reality? Who, sir? He-he-he. What do you think? Who do you suppose? Go on, you'll never guess!

"I'm traveling to P...today, I traveled to P...forty years ago. By this same train, sir, and I didn't have such agreeable company as I do today. There was not a soul to listen to me. Yes, it's forty years since I began work in P...as a very young teacher of Slovak and History. I was to teach at the grammar school there. It was my first job.

"It wasn't a big town, the grammar school wasn't a big one either, there were only about fifteen of us on the staff, but I've no need to tell you, you know what it's like, sir, even a small group is a group and a little hell is still hell. It's a question of quality, not quantity. I quickly found my place among the staff. I began to teach. I taught my subjects, Slovak and History, my mother tongue and the mother of wisdom. I taught, sir, as my superiors and the syllabi required, yes, indeed. I became part of the everyday routine of the school, I spared no effort and was very conscientious, just for the miserable salary teachers were paid. I taught, I looked forward to the holidays and to promotion, that's the kind of humble and withdrawn person I was."

It was really at this moment that I noticed something teacher-like about him. As if he were explaining. While he talked, I took a closer look at him. He seemed to have gotten younger. As if he now had fewer grey hairs.

I listened.

"There was nothing strange about the running of that school. It was quite an ordinary, average, typical school of those times, the centuries' old traditions of our educational system were its driving force, they kept it going. Everyone knew what he should do, everything was laid down, planned in advance. You could only develop your own initiative within the limits of what was required. If you had asked yourself what you would be doing in, say, seventeen years, on a particular day, you would have known exactly. Such a small, stable world, an island of security. Ceremonies, conferences, final exams and so on. In a word, a school. I can't say I felt happy there. I'm not of a calm and equable temperament, I find security and uniformity very difficult to bear."

I was surprised to note that now, when he had gotten around to something more concrete, his language was more matter-of-fact, less clownish. It was as if this man had never laughed. As if he was not capable of laughing. I looked at him. He was serious, lost in thought.

"But I won't bother you any more with the introduction. Who likes introductions, however short?"

I smiled guiltily and said apologetically, "Oh no, why?"

"I'll get on with it now. I'll just stick to the story from now on. I've talked around and around the subject quite enough. Just listen, please, just listen to me.

"There was just one thing I enjoyed at that school. When I had a break between lessons, I used to walk through the corridors. The school didn't have a cloakroom, so the children used to leave their coats in the corridors. I would walk past them and, forgive me the expression, each time I would snitch something. Just imagine, sir, a teacher who stole things from his pupils! Once it was a cap, another time a scarf, sometimes even a purse. Everything I had taken so easily, I hid very carefully. I knew, sir, I knew what I would need it for."

A delusion of the senses. Again it seemed to me that he had grown younger, much younger.

"The deputy headmaster, Matej Grópius, taught Latin and Greek. He was a good, honest man, worthy of respect, at least according to what was generally expected of people then. He was a real expert in his field and an excellent teacher. He was held in respect by both the children and his colleagues. No one would think of questioning anything he said. When the school was getting all excited about my thefts, when no culprit could be found, I remember I suggested that a search should be made not just among the schoolchildren, but also among us teachers. On that occasion Grópius hotly rejected my suggestion: How could such a thing even occur to you, sir! They pay us very poorly, it's true, but we would never lower ourselves to theft! Grópius had a good family, a wife and two children. He divided his free time between them and the school. He was particularly fussy about school administration, it was his hobby. He would sit in his office late into the night dealing with such matters. He was still a young man and it was generally expected that when our headmaster retired, he would take over his post. He really did have all the necessary skills, qualifications and prospects.

"I had been at the school only for a short while, when I noticed, you know what? I get great amusement, delight, pleasure out of noticing everything. I noticed that Grópius had a gold watch. I admired it one day when I was speaking to him and he happened to pull it out of his pocket. He was pleased. It's from the eighteenth century, he confided, given to his great-grandfather by the palatine himself. Then some time passed, maybe two school years, but what is that in comparison with eternity, what is it in comparison with me? He once asked me the time. I said, Where's your beautiful watch? He told me it wasn't working and he was having it repaired. Which watchmaker did you give it to? Not Čavard by any chance? No, Maňák. You did the right thing, I reassured him. Čavard's no good. Last year he almost ruined my watch. A good thing you chose Maňák. He'll repair it, it'll look like new.

"So his watch was in Maňák's workshop. Excellent. And when will it be ready?

"You know how it is, he said regretfully. Too much work and too little time. I don't have the time to pick it up during the day, and I can't send a pupil for it during school hours. So I agreed with Maňák that I would pick it up at his apartment tomorrow at seven.

"Good. Excellent! Nothing could be better. I had it all worked out.

"Maňák the goldsmith lived on the outskirts of the town, in a dark, deserted little street. His workshop was on the ground floor and his apartment above it. Like most of the small tradesmen.

"I knew that Grópius used to go into his office regularly at three. I spent the whole afternoon and evening marking written tests in the staff-room, which was next to his office. At exactly three o'clock Grópius went into his office and at exactly a quarter to seven he left it. I knew where he was going.

"I opened the deputy headmaster's office with a skeleton key, slipped inside and turned the hands on the wall clock ahead an hour. I left the light on, then I went out and locked the door. I went to find the janitor. The Deputy Head has already left and he must have forgotten to turn out the light. Would you be so kind as to open it, so I can turn the light off? The janitor went with me and when we entered the room, I pointed to the clock and sighed out loud, It's late. It's already eight o'clock! The janitor glanced at the clock and automatically repeated, Already eight. Then he turned off the light and when we had gone out, he locked the room.

"I'm staying a bit longer, I said, these awful written tests. Another hour, until nine o'clock.

"When his footsteps had faded into the distance, I slipped into the Deputy Head's office and set the clock to the right time.

"Grópius returned at a quarter past seven. He worked for another hour. At a quarter past eight he looked around the door of the staff-room. Aren't you going home yet?

"Not yet. This will take me until about nine.

"I quietly crept out of the school. No one saw me, no one heard me. I had bought a new pair of shoes with rubber soles just for this purpose. Keeping a careful look-out, I arrived at the outskirts of the town. It was no problem to break into Maňák's shop. I took all the more valuable items, watches, earrings, necklaces and diamonds, wrapped them up as a little package and sweated. I set one of the watches at eight o'clock and then smashed it to stop it at that time and I threw it on the floor. It looked as if the thief had dropped it by mistake. Apart from that, I cleverly caught a woolen thread on a splinter on Maňák's work bench. It was one I had pulled from Grópius' winter coat some time before. Then I returned to the school. Luck was on my side. No one saw or heard me.

"I stuffed all the loot from Maňák's shop into the drawer of Grópius' desk. I added the scarves, caps and purses that I had stolen from the children a lot earlier.

"The news about the break-in at Maňák's shop flew around the town early in the morning.

"Two policemen arrived at the school. The usual formalities. Maňák had reported that Grópius had been at his flat at seven in the evening. The police wanted to know whether by any chance he had noticed anything.

"They said the shop had been burglarized at eight. Grópius claimed that by then he had been at the school for three quarters of an hour.

"I was called into the headmaster's office. It's just a formality, said one of the policemen. After all, we all know the Deputy Head. He taught my son, too. The Deputy Head says that at a quarter to eight he was already in his office. I looked surprised. That can't be right. Just before eight I went to the toilet and I noticed that the light was on in his office. I knocked, but there was no answer. I realized immediately that the Deputy Head had forgotten to turn the light off. I went to get the janitor, so he could open the door and turn the light off. I happened to notice that it was eight o'clock.

"But the Deputy Head says he was here at a quarter to eight, the policeman said, taken aback.

"I suppose he must have made a mistake, I objected meekly. It's hardly surprising, he works too hard.

They sent for the janitor. He confirmed my statement. Grópius hadn't been in his office at eight o'clock.

"Then I said that Grópius had returned to the school at half past eight, that he had been very excited and he had had a little package of some kind with him. He had shown it to me and said that from now on life would be easier for him.

"The policemen and the headmaster looked surprised. The headmaster, who was most concerned about the good name of the school, said, Well, colleague Grópius, so there won't be any unjustified suspicions, please open your desk drawers. Suspecting nothing, Grópius pulled open the first drawer. He stared in horror at the watches and jewels....

"The police searched all the other drawers. They found the rest of the loot in them. As well as caps, scarves.... They arrested Grópius immediately. The headmaster lamented, Who is going to clear the name of the school after this scandal?

"The goldsmith Maňák declared that Grópius had seemed suspicious to him from the start. He had been behaving rather strangely.

"They sentenced him and, of course, dismissed him from the school. Together with the janitor, I was a star witness for the prosecution. The thread of wool also helped.... An inspector came to investigate the whole affair from the point of view of the school.

"I brought to his attention the fact that I had on several occasions demanded a strict investigation into the thefts in the corridor. I mentioned that Grópius had rejected the idea. The inspector criticized the staff as a whole, including the headmaster, and praised me for being the only one to stick to his principles and be vigilant.

"The post of deputy head was temporarily entrusted to our oldest colleague, Mamatej. At a meeting with the inspector, I warned the latter of his shortcomings, which could have a far-reaching malign influence. The inspector looked at me appreciatively. He rewarded me.

"A week later I received a letter of appointment, I became deputy head.

"I hope so, too, I said, when the headmaster expressed the hope that we would get on well together.

We didn't get on badly; in fact, I can even say that he became quite fond of me.

At the meeting when I took up my new post, I declared that I would do everything to clear the good name of the school. No trace of that thief and hypocrite must remain."

As he talked, my fellow-traveler grew visibly younger. He straightened his hunched back, his hair turned black and became thicker.

"That's how I helped myself, sir. I cleared the school, I renewed its former respected reputation. But I didn't want to remain idle. Idleness is not for me. No, indeed, sir. I looked around for further work and I lulled the headmaster Vachtan into a false sense of security. He was a man who had something in common with the revivalists of the last century. He was strict, moral and morose. Ever since his wife had died, he lived only for the school. There was nothing vulnerable about him.

"But I told myself, sir, that I would find something vulnerable about him, no matter how. Who hasn't got a weak spot? After all, we are all human.

"Physical education was taught by my colleague Matara. He was young, healthy and still full of life. I soon observed there was something in him that I could take advantage of. Sex.... I noticed that when something like that came up in the conversation, his eyes immediately lit up, they shone. He tried very hard to resist temptation. And don't forget, he had the key to the gym teacher's room.... He courted my favor, showed his admiration and respect for me. I told myself, why not take advantage of it?

"There were two girl cousins in the seventh grade. They didn't have a very good reputation. People used to say of them that they had had their first experience of...well, you know what, a long time before. And they also used to say that what one didn't know, the other was sure to.... They were pretty girls, nicely-developed, well, I don't have to explain.

"One day I walked to school with my colleague Matara. What if..., I said to him.

"When he understood what I had in mind, he suddenly got excited. We talked at length about group sex. He tried to tame his fantasies and words, he had too much respect for my position. It needn't be so despicable. It must just be done sincerely, unselfishly, I told him. And reliably. So that everyone involved agrees with it. Let's take just those two from the seventh grade, the Marejková cousins, or whatever their names are. They have nothing to lose and they can give pleasure to others. What if..., I stoked up the fire of Matara's imagination.

"It burst into flames. It would be possible, he said hoarsely.

I licked my lips encouragingly. The girls would be glad to get nearer to the teachers and, well, we....

"When I assured Matara that I was seriously interested, he offered to organize everything. He had to swear to me that he would say nothing to anyone for the moment, and that all the staff who took part in our activities would wear masks on their faces.

"A few days later we met in the gym teacher's room. The Marejková cousins and we two. We in masks.

"Before I went there, I used brown ink to paint a large birth mark below my navel.

"We pulled down the blinds, lit candles, opened some bottles, played quiet music on the gramophone.

"The girls were the first to undress. They knew what we wanted of them. And they knew how to undress, yes, sir, the strippers nowadays could learn something from them. Nice and slowly, with every little bit of clothing; you thought you couldn't stand any more. When they were quite naked, we undressed, too. Completely, apart from our masks. It was obvious that it was not the first time the girls were in this situation. They knew what to do. They knew, sir, oh, oh, oh" – he gazed sideways with a rapturous expression on his face and smacked his lips with pleasure. "They knew, they certainly did! One of them was a bit reluctant at first, saying that we should put out the candles and so on. And that there was only one couch there, so not both at once. But Matara insisted. He said everything I wanted him to. I kept quiet, I didn't even open my mouth. That's the way I do it, sir, let others do the talking for me."

I listened to him. He really was getting younger all the time. He had lost at least ten years.

"Sex, sir, is a cunning little devil. Each one of us carries it within us. We have to feed it, if it is to keep out of unnecessary mischief. I hinted to Matara that he could involve others. He would look around for more men and women colleagues and the Marejkovás would get hold of some girls. Matara didn't disappoint me. There were gradually more and more of us. Some without masks, but some with them. We couldn't manage any longer with just the one couch and the gym teacher's room. We needed more space. We moved into the gymnasium and spread out the horsehair mattresses. We were quite pleased with the effect. Yes, we were. We met once a week, later twice. We got bolder, we became used to each other. How many girls I – forgive the expression – worked on! You just can't imagine how strange it felt when I tested them in a lesson, while remembering what we had been up to together! You just can't imagine!

"I got a real kick out of the third graders. Such modest little maidens.

"As I have already told you, we had to make do with mattresses. We enjoyed each other and ourselves. We thought up all kinds of competitions, too. To make things more interesting and more fun. It was really nice! Really nice."

He smacked his lips dreamily several times.

"We let some of the schoolboys join us later. But we were cautious. Only those who hadn't been in trouble before, those we could trust.

"How many girls were deflowered! Well, so what, we had a good time, we came into our own.

"Of course Vachtan, the headmaster, had no idea of what was going on. On occasion I vaguely hinted that something unheard of, some disorderly conduct, was going on in the school. But Vachtan was so moral and naive that it never even occurred to him what it could be. He didn't take any notice of my hints, he ignored them.

"From time to time at staff meetings I expressed mysterious surmises about a gradual moral degeneration. Each time a bit more insistently. I demanded that firm measures should be taken. But no one guessed what I was getting at.

"One day I realized it was high time to act.

"I told Matara I would be coming late that evening and we agreed on a password. Then I called on the policeman who had led the inquiry into Grópius. Forgive me for coming to you like this, I feel ashamed myself that something like this is at all possible, but.... I told him all about the orgies which were taking place regularly in the gymnasium. I begged him to organize a raid at exactly eleven in the evening. He was amazed, he just couldn't believe it, he wrung his hands, clearly appalled, and kept asking me more and more questions. In the end he promised to look into the matter. At ten in the evening I rang the bell at Vachtan's flat. Sir, as deputy headmaster, I'm not willing to put up with it any more! I gave him an account of what was going on in the school. I demanded that he intervene immediately. I'm going at once, he muttered in consternation, just as soon as I can get dressed! He was in his pajamas and while he went to change, he left me alone in the hall. I quickly hid my mask in his pocket. On the way to school I told him the password to use so they would let him into the gymnasium. Vachtan was in a hurry, he didn't take much notice of me, the thought of what was going on had completely shocked and horrified him. I stopped and waited at the corner of the street. A few minutes after he had entered the school building, a police car came tearing up. I accompanied the police and led them into the gymnasium.

"Dozens of young bodies were lying on the mattresses. Those who weren't wearing masks covered their faces in horror. The atmosphere was charged with erotic tension.

"Headmaster Vachtan was staring in front of him, he looked as if he had turned to stone.

"Blue uniforms mixed among the naked bodies. I pointed to Vachtan. My finger didn't shake at all. I burst out angrily, This has been going on for a long time. I warned the headmaster over and over again, but he refused to intervene. Since I had no other choice, I went to the police. Now it's clear. The headmaster Vachtan and our colleague Matara have been organizing orgies and dragging young people into the mire of sin. I couldn't look on any longer and just do nothing! I cried indignantly.

"They took us all away for interrogation at the district police headquarters.

"A long investigation followed. They expelled dozens of children from the school. A number of things confirmed Vachtan's guilt. For one thing, he had a mask with him, for another, he knew the password needed for Matara to let him in, and in addition to this there was the birthmark under his naval, which enabled several of the girls to identify him. The birthmark I had noticed once when we had visited a sauna....

"Another thing that spoke against him was that, owing to his advanced age, he had on more than one occasion failed when it came to the sexual act....

"That, yes indeed, sir, that is how it all happened and that is how it ended.

"I was happy, too, I had done well and had stopped that moral decline. Yes, indeed."

He was getting younger and younger. By then I wouldn't have recognized him. He paused for a while, lost in thought.

"They appointed me headmaster and publicly acknowledged my deserts. The minister thanked me in person. He begged me to be equally principled in my new post.

"I'll do everything in my power, sir, I promised him.

"As headmaster I conscientiously worked for the good of the school. I was particularly strict when it came to thefts and moral delinquency. At headmasters conferences I became one of the minister's favorites. He showed his trust in me by often appointing me a member of inspection committees. I got to know the conditions at all the grammar schools in the country.

"At my own school I tightened up considerably on education in the official spirit. I would hold forth on this subject at every meet-

ing of headmasters. In private conversations with the minister
I often expressed my concern that some schools were not keeping
to this spirit.

"When talking to my colleagues, the other headmasters, I was
more liberal and more benevolent.

"I gently hinted that there was no need to take everything literally. On each occasion I would wink meaningfully. After all, the
minister himself.... They believed me, because my good relationship with the minister was general knowledge.... After all, the
minister himself.... I gradually allayed their fears. The reserve and
official manner which prevail during school inspections disappeared. I became more and more popular.

"A wink and the little phrase After all, the minister himself...
opened the way for me to my colleague's hearts.

"As their defenses fell, so I advanced; further and further and
higher.

"I started with the grammar school in T. It seemed the most
suitable soil for the crop I wished to sow. The religious order of
Piarists had been working there for many years.

"The headmaster at the grammar school in T. was a majestic,
grey-haired gentleman of the name of Franko. He was known not
to be too happy about the present situation, sympathizing more
with what had been than with what would one day be. They only
tolerated him because they couldn't prove anything against him.
After several visits, I unobtrusively hinted that I didn't go along
with the opinions of the other inspectors and I showed him my
sympathy. He immediately confided in me. People who are dis-
satisfied with the way things are automatically assume that others feel the same way. All you need to do is give a slight hint,
reach out to them and they immediately confide in you. And they
are terribly flattered if they feel that someone higher up the ladder thinks like they do. They begin to respect you.

"When I found myself alone with Franko in his office, I whispered suspiciously, Are you sure there's nothing, hm...installed
here?

"He turned very pale. No...! Then he corrected himself uncertainly, I don't know....

"You know, even the minister..., I chirped. He looked at me in
surprise. I had gone beyond all his expectations. I can assure you
that everything will be all right, I'll iron out any objections on the
part of my colleagues. But you know, we must pay strict attention
to the official spirit at the moment.

"I know..., he breathed a sigh of relief, wriggling disconcerted-
ly, poor man. He was afraid he might have misjudged me.

"Don't worry, I reassured him. You needn't be afraid of me,

but.... Have you ever tried out the magical effect of the word *but* and a short silence after it? There's no need to be afraid. The spirit which is considered troublesome at the moment may become the official one tomorrow. We know how these things go. And then those who supported it when it was out of favor will be in the best position. They will be brought into the limelight, rewarded, set up as an example. It will be taken into account when it comes to pensions, too, how else, they deserve it; after all, they were true to themselves even in the most difficult times. It can happen. I put all my art into that word *can*. Franko looked anxiously about him and assured me that his school was governed by someone who, though he assumed the mask of the official spirit, was not favored by the present time. He chose his words carefully, he spoke quietly, cautiously. That's not enough, I objected, That's not enough by a long shot. Such an attitude could one day look like buck-passing. You must be active. We'll put up with it for a bit longer somehow or other. After all, even the minister....

"Eagerly, impatiently, he asked me, And what should I do?

"I can't advise you about anything officially, but..., a deadly silence reigned. I stared hard at the picture of the head of state and I began to think aloud, as if to myself. There are schools where although the children have new textbooks, as a matter of principle the teachers teach according to the old ones, they use every opportunity to pick holes in the logic of the official spirit, they issue all kinds of pamphlets and so on. He understood. He trembled with joyful excitement. He caught my hand.

"OK, OK, I get it now, he enthused. I have only one little question. When he had plucked up his courage, he asked me, Will it last long now?

"I hope not, I replied and we parted cordially.

"Franko lost no time in mobilizing all his friends among the headmasters. They knew him, trusted him and confided in him. It wasn't long before I discovered this for myself.

"Among the headmasters the news spread like wildfire what I was really like. Those who obstinately held to the official spirit, didn't believe it. Those who had sold themselves in spirit to the enemy became suddenly more cordial to me. This enabled me to pick them out reliably.

"When I declared the virtues of the official spirit at the headmasters' meetings held at the ministry, I always followed my words with a meaningful cough. This only strengthened the resolve of the dissenters. They assigned to my coughing a hidden meaning, they saw in it what they longed for.

"I was most successful at the ancient grammar schools in K., in O. and in S.

"The headmasters of these schools became, you might say, activists of the non-official spirit.

"But there were other schools that were caught quickly and easily. In L., in H. and in G.

"When I discovered shortcomings in teaching according to the official spirit at one of these grammar schools, I publicly praised the headmaster for his excellent work from the professional point of view and I proposed he should receive some kind of recognition. In a private conversation between the two of us, I told him: Be careful, sir. You can never be too careful. After all, even the minister.... We must put up with it for some time yet. Clench our teeth and fists, not be in too much of a hurry, hold out. I hope it won't last much longer. It can't!"

Once more he paused for a while. He looked fresh, rested. By now he was very young.

"You wouldn't believe, sir, how quickly this hostile spirit grew and spread throughout our schools. You'd never believe it. When my respected colleagues realized that there was no danger threatening them, that we secretly approved of everything they did, that they would not be punished, they became bolder and bolder. One by one they showed their true colors. They competed with each other to prove they couldn't stomach the official spirit.

"I warned the minister more than once of the danger, I tried to persuade him that it was growing all the time. I spoke about it at our headmasters' meetings, too. But I never forgot to cough. At one meeting, where I had aggressively attacked signs of the old spirit in the teaching process, one of the headmasters patted me on the back in a friendly manner. We know you have to do it!

"At my own school I laid more and more stress on the official spirit. I insisted my subordinates make it an integral part of every subject. Maybe you remember those times, sir. For my headmaster's pay I forced others to believe in a prosperous future.

"One thing happened to me. A student in his final year couldn't resist the temptation and wrote a provocative and subversive notice. It was at a time when thanks to the enemy, there was not enough pork.

"The student wrote: There is not enough pork because we are being chased so fast into a happy and wonderful future that the swine can't keep up with us.

"I immediately started an investigation. The grade master was fired on the spot and the boy expelled.

"He was excluded from all the schools. I told his father I would try to get the ministry to reduce his punishment. I begged the minister: the boy was misled by the temporary shortage; after all, we know that young people don't have enough experience, that

149

they tend to consider temporary states as permanent. I'm all for a severe punishment, he should be expelled, but only from our school. Let's give the boy a chance to come to his senses and make up for his offense.

"For that his father brought me five kilograms of pork, which at first I didn't want to accept.

"A lot was written about that case, sir, both in teaching journals and in the general press. Everywhere they praised me. Some people appreciated my principled and uncompromising attitude, others my magnanimity.

"Meanwhile other schools went on being undermined and subverted by the spirit of hostility.

"In K., for example, they provocatively took down all the portraits that should officially have been on the walls and decorated all the classrooms with the old ones instead. They changed them for the official ones only during school inspections.

"The grammar school in S. was no better. The headmaster forbade all the teachers to teach according to the official textbooks. Every teacher had to reassess their subject from the point of view of the hostile spirit and write their own duplicated texts. The headmaster checked them himself and crossed out everything that was not correct with his own hand.

"And in O.? There the school radio regularly broadcast reports that put doubts in the students' minds about the infallibility and the absolute superiority of the official spirit and which propagated the pernicious ideals of the enemy. That's how low the grammar school in O. had sunk. Yes, indeed! Gradually more and more schools were caught in the net of foreign ideology.

"The students' magazine that was published at the grammar school in L. organized a competition (not anonymous) for the best topical joke at the expense of the official spirit. At the grammar school in H. they were even more daring. They built up a store of slingshots in the school cellars, just in case they would be needed. And in G.? You just wouldn't believe me, sir! They founded a special organization, which had its own radio transmitter. They broadcast to foreign countries things that everyone knew in this country and abroad. Tell me, sir, what could be a greater crime?

"From the tiny little seed I had once sown, there grew a really enormous tree.

"Now's the time to cut it down and saw it up into logs to warm myself by, I finally decided.

"At the very next headmasters' meeting at the ministry I held forth once more. I was extremely careful not to wink or to cough by mistake. That would have been a disaster.

"The enemy spirit has flared up in our schools, it has spread like the plague, multiplied like locusts. The state of affairs which now reigns can no longer be endured or tolerated. Instead of our kind of education, a foreign kind is being legally allowed to develop without anyone trying to stop it!

"The minister gave me a troubled glance. The hall listened to me with stunned interest.

"I can give concrete examples and cases. How is it possible that today, today...! I began with the grammar school in T., with its headmaster, Franko. Then I passed on to other schools. I mentioned everything I knew. How can something like that possibly happen! I stormed. Our school system must be cleaned up at last, that smithy where our bright and beautiful future is hammered out, we must pull up the weeds of the enemy spirit. I propose we set up a commission without delay that will closely scrutinize the situation in all the schools, and on the basis of this survey, I ask the minister to take uncompromising measures!

"The commission discovered terrible, unheard of facts. They confirmed my words. All the headmasters were fired. Several of them found their way to prison. It was shown that the enemy spirit had far deeper roots than had been generally supposed. The struggle began to uproot it. Informing, uncertainty, fear.

"Nothing was found at my school. On the contrary, everywhere it was quoted as a shining example.

"They also counted in my favor the fact that I had repeatedly warned against the danger which threatened.

"Before I knew what was happening, the postman brought me a letter appointing me as deputy minister.

"My main task, which I fulfilled conscientiously, was to guard the purity of the official spirit.

"And the fact that today we have the kind of school system that we have is partly to my lasting credit."

He was now very young. His wrinkles had been smoothed out, his skin had a shine to it, a freshness, he had thick, black hair. He was bubbling with untamed strength and energy.

"And what then?" I asked him timidly. I was very curious. "What happened then?"

"Then I became a minister. And not long ago, when I was again speaking at a large official meeting, there was a sudden flash, a deafening blast...."

"P...!" blared the station loudspeakers and the train ground to a halt. "We are in P...."

"I'm getting out here," he said and stood up. He shook my hand cordially as we parted.

I leaned out of the window. When he passed by, I posed a question to him: "And why have you come here?"

He stopped, looked at me as if we had never seen each other before. Once more he chuckled to himself. It took him a long time to control himself before he replied.

"In order to do everything I told you about on the way here."

I gazed after him. A moment later he disappeared in the crowd. The train began to move.

DUŠAN MIKOLAJ
- *prose writer, journalist, playwright;*
born in Lodno (1948)

Dušan Mikolaj has worked as a reporter and publisher, for a long time as editor of the magazine *Slovensko* (Slovakia), then of a literary magazine for young authors *Dotyky* (*Touches*); he was editor-in-chief of the monthly magazine *Národná osveta* (*National Culture*), and he was responsible for activities in the field of cultural education at the Ministry of Culture.

His first short stories were published in an anthology (1973). His solo debut was a short novel entitled **Také korene** (*Such Roots*, 1979) about the lives of two brothers in their native village and about their hard struggle to make a living. In the lyrical stories in his book **Kone** (*Horses*, 1981), it is possible to see his love for these animals, as well as his detailed knowledge of this environment. A greater leaning towards essayistic elements is clear in the prose works **Po čom túžim** (*What I Long For*, 1985) and **Holúbok mieru** (*Dove of Peace*, 1986). He also wrote a biographical essay about the partisan poet Ján Brock, **Stanem sa básnikom** (*I Shall Become a Poet*, 1990), and a novel about the life of the Slovak painter Miloš Alexander Bazovský, **Tlejúce slnko** (*Smoldering Sun*, 1994). In the collection of stories **Smrteľné nebezpečenstvo** (*Mortal Danger*, 1994) he depicts unusual events in the lives of ordinary people in the setting of his native region of Kysuce and the High Tatras; the story "Muž s infarktovým srdcom" ("The Man with the Weak Heart") is from this book.

He is the author of a radio play, **Posledný žrebec** (*The Last Stallion*, 1983). He devotes much of his time to journalism.

In his own words:

I have been asked on more than one occasion what must capture a writer's interest for him to write something worthwhile. If I was sure about this, the list of my books would take up more than just two lines, although I think that from time to time my interest is also caught by something quite ordinarily, unexceptionally beautiful. Nature, for example, in spite of the fact that it thrives better in my heart and inner eye than in the neighborhood of greedy mankind or within contemporary prose. Ordinary friendship, although nowadays few people can rely on it with any certainty. The depth of words, which cause me no small trouble when writing, but which when read in the right context can catch my attention like a spot of color on a painter's canvas. A story with an ordinary message, which I am at last beginning to respect, or at least I am beginning to realize the value of an apparently negligible human life, which as the basic element of spiritual life on our Earth, was present at the beginning of creativeness and cultural history and without whose permanent presence art will either vegetate or will cease to be communicative. In stories about people, their ability to communicate in an interesting way is a vital element not only in prose or other kinds of art, but also, let's say, as a moral imperative in human relations.

And when it comes to communicating in an interesting way, it is above all pure, genuine, spontaneous and humanizing humor. We have begun to neglect it shamefully, partly because we take ourselves in particular far too seriously....

(1997)

THE MAN WITH THE WEAK HEART

Roman Zelina got off the bus at Podbanské. Mist was hanging in the valley and vague outlines were all that could be seen of the hotels, chalets and huts. The peaks of the Liptov hills were already lit up by the rays of the rising sun. Roman had a light canvas rucksack on his back and he was carrying a pair of cross-country skis attached to the sticks by a plastic clip. It was his first time here. When he had found his bearings, he crossed the wooden bridge over a mountain stream shouldering its way down between the granite rocks. The asphalt path was dry at first; higher up little islands of ice became more and more frequent. As soon as the path was covered with an unbroken layer of snow, Roman impatiently fastened on his skis and pushed off, thrusting his sticks into the hard snow compressed by the wheels of forestry vehicles. He took long sliding steps forward, imitating the skating style of cross-country skiers, which had recently become a new competitive discipline. He could feel his body, stiff from sitting too long in an unheated bus, begin to warm up, the blood flowing into his muscles, well-trained with regular body-building exercises. He breathed deeply, feeling satisfied that he had managed to choose the right wax for the running surface of his new skis.

He had been given these skis only the day before. He had chosen them as his present for his eighteenth birthday. They carried him ahead easily and he felt as if he was on a precisely adjusted machine. I must use this day to the full, he said to himself. To remember forever the first moments of that magic threshold to adulthood. He had wanted to celebrate his birthday with his friends from school, but he hadn't managed to persuade even one of them to go with him. He took it as a sign that in the future he would have to make his own decisions more often.

The divine simplicity of the eighteen-year-old!

When the road leading into the forest forked into the Tichá and Kôprová valleys, he chose the latter. Kôprová looked more open. At the very beginning, behind a wooden fence, there was a log cottage bearing the official plaque of the Mountain Rescue Service. In the yard a young woman in a short, sleeveless fur jacket, which she wore unbuttoned, was hanging wash out on the line, while a young German shepherd romped around her. Roman liked her short, fair hair, her slim figure and shapely breasts and also the way she reached up to the line of fine underwear. He remained standing where he was and couldn't tear his eyes away from her. He was attracted by her movements and by her body. When the woman caught sight of him, he set off at once in his most elegant cross-country style. He continued in this fashion even when the house had disappeared behind the trees.

That, too, was natural for someone of Roman's age. He was happy with the way he was skiing and also that he had at last set out on a real mountain trip. Although he was more familiar with the Kysuce hills and he understood them better, since he went there from time to time with members of the local rambling club, he had to tear himself away from them one day and get to know the higher ranges. It was not yet a need arising from being overweight. It was rather respect for the majesty of the mountain landscape, as he had come to know it from nature films and books on mountaineering. The period of adventure stories colored by the imaginations of their authors had been replaced once and for all by books based on the first-hand experiences of well-known explorers.

His plans were rather vague. As he got further from Podbanské, his elation began to fade and his pleasure was mixed with a feeling of loneliness. He didn't meet a single tourist in the valley. The stretch the snow plough had cleared came to an end, to be followed by an untouched area sprinkled with a dusting of fresh snow. This revealed that someone had in fact already passed that way.

Coming across the tracks of wider skis, flanked by the regular prints of steel rings interwoven with leather straps, Roman Zelina decided to follow them. They led him as far as Temné smrečiny. There he caught sight of a man. He had old-fashioned skis of hickory wood with balls on the tips and bamboo poles stuck in the snow beside him. He was standing motionless, gazing in the direction of the waterfall trickling down from the Temné smrečiny tarns. The water could only be heard, it was covered with icicles nailed by sharp sunrays to the stone face of the mountain.

The man was silently watching the cold ice shimmering like crystal in the rays of the sun. When he heard the swish of skis, he started. Roman Zelina greeted him, but the man only nodded his head. It was impossible to say whether he was returning his greeting. A moment later he moved off, going in the direction of the forest. Once among the trees, he began to climb uphill.

The ascent was strenuous. The man had to bend forward at every step. As if he were leaning into the wind. In the thick young undergrowth heavy with snow fallen from higher branches, his long skis caught on the tree trunks and his poles sank right up to the hand grips.

Roman Zelina couldn't understand where the man was heading. At home he had studied the tourist guide. Following its advice, he had planned to go to the end of one of the two valleys, have a rest and come back the same way. He had covered the route quicker than he had expected. It wasn't even noon. He decided to follow the man a little way. No doubt he knew of a short cut that would take him down to the valley.

The distance between them grew gradually shorter. It was easier for Roman to make progress on his narrow skis. He avoided the treacherous places where the man had really had to struggle. He was now close behind him and the man hadn't looked around even once, although he must have known that someone was following him. He was obstinately wading through the snow, which was getting into his sleeves and up his ski pants, the sweat was trickling from his neck down to the small of his back. The damp patch on his waterproof jacket was growing larger and larger.

When he had struggled out of the forest, he leaned up against a tree. He breathed out, "Phew, that was a hard job," he said, as if to himself.

"It'll be easier on the way down," Roman remarked.

"After you."

"Which way are you going?"

"Me? To Závory."

"That far?"

"Now that I've fought my way through that thicket...."

"Right up to the ridge?"

"Yes. I'll have a look at the view."

"And then?"

"Down Tichá valley."

"But that takes all day. In summer, providing the weather's good," Roman Zelina quoted from the tourist guide.

"Tomorrow's the first day of spring," said the man.

"But there must be more snow up there than here."

"No doubt there is. That's what Eskimos made skis for."

"But even so, it isn't exactly safe. What if somebody should break a ski?"

"I'd like to have your worries."

The man moved away. He was on a slope lit up by the sun. His shadow on the snow looked as if it was made up of scattered poppyseeds. Roman Zelina remained standing, not able to make up his mind. He very much wanted to return home as quickly as possible, turn the heat on in his attic bedroom in his parents house, furnished in typically student style, and read long into the night.

Roman saw the man start off towards his goal, with no thought for him. He didn't feel like going back through the woods. He did not even know whether there was a negotiable way down. For a moment he forgot to exercise caution. He even began to tell himself that it was vital to go on. What if the man should need help. There was no one else to be seen far and wide.

When he looked towards the shoulder of Kriváň peak from Kôprová valley, it kept appearing and disappearing behind a tattered curtain of firs and spruces with clusters of overripe cones. As when a card-player cautiously uncovers the corner of an ace of spades behind a black ten. Now Kriváň could be seen in all its majesty. It spread itself wide, its sloping head pushing into the background all the other peaks and crags lined up in several rows. Roman Zelina knew nothing about these stone corpses. However, against the bright blue sky they had a strongly calming effect. As if they belonged to him, too.

A warm dry breeze was blowing on the open hillside. In that blue calm the sun's rays seemed to slow down the man's movements, forcing him to rest at frequent intervals. The man would stop, bend back his head and gaze for a long time into the sky with its orange sun. Then he turned his attention to a broken arolla pine. To a boulder encrusted with lichen. Then to a nest formed by dwarf pines with their tips sticking out through the snow. To Roman it seemed as if the man was becoming part of the mountain scenery, carried along on the waves of the breeze announcing the slow arrival of spring; he was going back to the times when the mountains were still being formed from the red-hot planet.

The man's impossibly slow tempo was beginning to get on Roman Zelina's nerves. No matter how slow he tried to go, he was soon on his heels.

"You've set yourself the right pace for a tour," the man praised him. "At your age I didn't have the patience to drag along either. Light feet, regular breathing, a strong heart."

Roman was pleased to see the man was at last paying him more serious attention. He took it as acknowledgement of his performance. Like a pat on the straining neck of a racing horse.

It made him bolder. He hurried toward the horizon over a plain surrounded by an unbroken rim of rocks. It could serve as a large cauldron. A clean white cloth spread on a table. A bed made up for a giant. Both a no-man's-land and a land offering itself to anyone who made it his destination. A tiny closed and complete part of the vast globe.

A pair of chamois were making their way across it. Unhurried, free, fearless. They looked confident, but vulnerable at the same time, calm and yet eager, hot blood pulsing under cool skin. They were leaving two rows of prints in the virgin snow. White writing on an equally white surface. Like Kysuce embroidery. Legible and comprehensible in its inconspicuousness.

The chamois paused for a moment. They gazed at Roman, then quickened their pace.

Roman Zelina took it as a challenge. At last he could see how fit he was. He made after the chamois. The distance between them grew and soon they were lost from sight, as if they had fallen into a rocky ravine. Roman did not slow down. He was overcome by a desire to reach the ridge as soon as possible. A particular point, which he could remember as the highest he had ever been. A successful climax to the day. His own present to himself on his eighteenth birthday.

He reached the saddle out of breath and perspiring profusely. His muscles were tense. And his senses numb. Earlier feelings of wonder quickly evaporated. They now seemed ordinary and monotonous. Nothing but snow and mountain peaks. Time seemed to have frozen in the chill of the numbed panorama.

He took out of his rucksack two slices of bread with a thick layer of cold scrambled egg mixed with bacon fat and onion in the middle. He ate them with a couple of apples. Their skins had begun to wrinkle, but they were still juicy. He munched them to the core, chewing even the seeds. These he enjoyed the most. He remembered his father and his fruit-laden orchard behind the house.

He waited for the man. It seemed an age before he caught up. His face was flushed red, he was breathing like a bellows with a hole in its leather bag. An old man's expression on his face, although down in the valley Roman had guessed he was no older than his own father.

"Shall we go?" Roman asked him.

"I'm going to have a rest."

"Did the climb wear you out that much?"

"What's strange about that?"

"My shoulders ache a bit from the sticks," Roman said apologetically.

"This was my favorite spot."

"Did you come here alone?"

"With friends, and sometimes alone. Before the age of chair lifts and tows. We plodded on, over range after range, on our own two feet. Without grumbling. Skiing downhill over the untouched snow was our reward."

"So you know the easiest way down," said Roman.

"The wonderful thing about it was that we didn't keep to the marked routes. So far as possible, we chose a different route every time."

"Which was the safest one from here?"

"I can't remember," said the man. "It's a good few years since I was here. Before I'd had time to get married. Which was a mistake, anyway."

"You don't know your way around here?" Roman stared in disbelief at the well-nourished, but strained face of the man.

"I expect I'll find my bearings. Although the forest can change out of all recognition over the years. It grows in all directions, while you waste away. You waste your life on stupidities. You believe that the most important thing is to earn and win money. The more the better. So you can spend it. Your children and your wife are the same. If you're lucky, you may come into a good pile. It's only in the mountains that neither time nor money count. And a stone lasts longer than the heaviest gold ducat."

"We're living beings," objected Roman Zelina. The man seemed to see life in a completely different way. It annoyed him.

"Wisely said," the man remarked. "You have to give the body what it needs. After a tour like this it deserves it." He took a thermos bottle out of his knapsack. He drank in gulps, putting it down only when it was empty.

"Shall we go?" asked Roman Zelina.

"If you need to, then go."

"It must be about three o' clock."

"I'm in no hurry."

"But I may miss my bus."

"Then why are you hanging around?"

"Don't you need to get anywhere?"

"I've traveled enough."

Roman Zelina said goodbye. He hoped that if he made a move, the man would get up too. Surely he wouldn't stay there alone.

He didn't hurry. He didn't know the way. He tentatively pushed off, traversing the hillside. His light, narrow cross-country skis were not easy to control on the steep slope. The sun's rays sparkled on the grains of snow, blinding him. Roman had no experience of skiing in conditions like this. He seemed to be descending a gently-sloping plain, but it was sending him flying in the direction of the rocks. His attempts to turn failing, he threw himself on his bottom, but still went on sliding forward. He came to a halt only when he got caught in some dwarf pines. A few meters from a sudden drop. Alarmed, he hurried back along the trail his skis had left in the snow.

Against his will, he returned to the man. So he could at least point in which direction he could get safely down to the valley.

As he approached the saddle, he caught a brief glimpse of the man against the background of the clear sky. He was disappearing from sight. Roman tried to catch up with him. Ahead lay a large slab of heavy snow. It creaked quietly under his skis and narrow cracks appeared. Roman imagined the fissures growing wider and deeper, the broken slab beginning to move, large bits of snow sliding downward. Soundlessly and almost unnoticeably at first, then gradually speeding up, until he found himself in the middle of a perilous island. He froze, afraid even to breathe. In his imagination, the occasional, almost inaudible cracking sounded like the roar of an avalanche. He caught sight of the man. He was quite close, but he was afraid to call out to him, in case his voice, now squeezed tight in the middle of his throat, should really set the uneasy mass of snow in motion.

The man looked wonderfully content. He was leaning on his ski poles, his face upturned towards the sun. He was resting again, as if nothing had happened.

"Are you sure we're going the right way?" asked Roman, when he had reached a safer stretch of snow.

"You still here? I thought you were already on the bus," said the man, not even looking around at Roman.

"'Fraid not. Somehow I couldn't find the trail markers," Roman said, making excuses. "You can't find a single one here. Somebody's not doing his job!"

"If there was no snow, you'd find them on the rocks. In the forest they usually paint them on the trees."

"But in which part of the forest?!"

"You have to find that out."

"Well, I'll go on ahead," said Roman.

He pushed off in the direction of the forest. The man, who had fixed cable binding for the downhill run, skied alongside and even overtook him. He was descending adventurously. He was a good skier, even though his style with Christies in the Telemark was very old-fashioned. All of a sudden he braked. He came to a halt and bent over at the waist. His hands shaking, he fumbled in his knapsack. Bits of ski wax, a rubber ski clasp, a plastic bag containing some bread and an orange fell out of it in turn. Then a little box. Just as he was reaching out for it, his lower ski slipped. He fell face down. When he managed to get up, he scrabbled in the snow with quick movements like a dog.

He found the tube of pills, tipped one out on to his palm and quickly put it in his mouth. His eyes closed, a blissful expression came over his face. But his pointed Adam's apple was jumping up and down in his neck. He was breathing like a child that has just stopped crying.

"Are you all right?" Roman asked.

"It'll pass," the man said in a hoarse voice.

"What kind of medicine is that?"

"Just nitroglycerin. For the heart."

"You take it? Regularly?"

"I don't make a point of it. I'm not great at self-discipline. I only bother if my heart demands it. Ever since I left the saddle it's been saying it would love a pill. I've been trying my best to dissuade it. I offered it vitamin C dissolved in tea with a drop of cognac, but as you can see, it's not going to let itself be fooled."

"You've got heart trouble?" Roman asked, not wanting to believe his ears.

"That's what the doctors say. They don't recommend that I drink spirits, with the exception of a small glass of cognac, and they've forbidden smoking. If I took their advice, I shouldn't even show a sudden interest in women. Instead of manly pleasures, they've prescribed all kinds of dreary things. Just because without wanting to I've scared them a couple of times. All you have to do is have one or two little heart attacks and you get the hospital's whole department of internal medicine running around you."

"You're exaggerating."

"I'm only repeating what the doctors say. The ones who specialize in these things."

"If you really have had a heart attack...."

161

"And not just one, I'm told."

"Why didn't you say so when we were still down there?"

"You don't object to my getting this far, do you?"

Roman didn't answer. He needed someone with him who he could rely on. It was becoming clear that this man certainly didn't fit the bill.

"Has the medicine taken effect? Are you feeling better?" he asked him.

"As better as you can feel with a heart like mine. If the specialists were here, they'd no doubt like to listen to it. But I've given them the slip at last. They can't reach me here."

"Don't you think you're risking your health?"

"It's my heart. No one else's. I'd never have gotten here with anyone else's heart."

"Do you have the strength to go on?"

"Don't worry about me. I'm just tired. I'm not used to going this far anymore. Nor to this fresh air. It's made me feel quite giddy. As if I'd been smoking marijuana."

"Then stay here and have a rest for a while. While I'm waiting I'll go and look for a trail marker. To save us time later."

Roman Zelina cautiously pushed off downhill.

"You really don't have to bother about me."

"When I find the trail, I'll let you know," he called from below.

The flashes of anger that seized Roman from time to time were suppressed by a feeling of responsibility for the sick man. He wandered here and there through the forest, which was as thick as that in the Kôprová valley. He didn't want to go too far from the spot where he had left him. He wasn't even reassured when he heard the man set off. Every few minutes he stopped and pricked up his ears, in order to catch the irregular swishing sound of his skis. His attention was alerted when the sounds faded and were swallowed up in the silence of the darkening wood. Whenever he didn't hear the skis for some time, he would call out. If there was no response from the man even after several shouts, he returned to him, to see whether he was all right. Each time he spoke to him, but the man seemed to be losing an awareness of his surroundings and his movements had become more or less automatic.

It seemed to Roman that he was being very noble to take care of him like this. He imagined himself in the situation of an experienced mountaineer rescuing a comrade in peril of his life.

Reality was more prosaic. He needed to find a tree which had, though overgrown by grey moss, a red strip between two white ones painted on its bark. An ordinary trail marker, which would direct them out of the forest.

162

At last he caught sight of one. From the first tree, he could see another with the same mark. He sped towards it, then to the next. He realized what he was doing only when he had gone quite a long way.

"Hey," he shouted. "I've found the trail."

There was no response from the man. "I'm fed up with this," Roman Zelina suddenly said. "I'm not going to go back a hundred times. Forget him. After all, I'm not responsible for a madman who drags himself off on such a trip after two or who knows how many heart attacks. The doctors take all that trouble to get him back on his feet and he can't resist coming here to have at least one more look! And I'm expected to play the good Samaritan."

"He-ey! The marked trail's this way. Can you hear me?!" he shouted so loudly that his throat hurt. Straining his ears, he listened for an answer.

Nothing. No response.

Roman Zelina moved on to the next trail marker. In front of him lay the longed-for path that, like in the fairytale about the ginger-bread cottage, led out of the dark forest. The children had fled along it as if a fire were burning at their heels, wild strawberries spilling out of their basket. Roman fled after them. He was almost out of the forest. He halted for a moment. Once more he called out. Then listened. No answer. He made a move. Reluctantly, in the direction of the spot where he had left the man.

The marks of the man's hickory wood skis led in a completely different direction. Down a steep slope to a stream. The man was filling his thermos with water.

"Come on, I found the trail," said Roman.

"Fine," said the man. He was drinking water from the stream. It must have been terribly cold. Roman tactfully warned him.

"I guess it's my business what water I drink," the man frowned.

"I just wanted to say that we should get a move on at last."

"You found the path? Then what are you waiting for? You don't have to hang around because of me."

"You come on too. It's getting dark."

"I'm fine where I am."

The man sat down in the snow and again drank the freezing water. He was gulping it down and Roman's teeth felt cold just to look at him. He made him think of an animal, wounded or worn out with old age. It had withdrawn to a deserted spot and wished to rest undisturbed, to lick its wounds. Or even, who knows, to end its life in dignity, with no witnesses.

To eighteen-year-old Roman Zelina such an end seemed inconceivably cruel.

"Come on, please," he said, as quietly as he could.

The man took no notice of his rescuer. He closed his eyes and huddled up in a ball. He was shivering with cold. Roman Zelina could not let him stay there alone. He decided he would do what the situation demanded of him. He seized the man under his armpits and tried to pull him to his feet. His skis got in the way, but without them he would have sunk deep into the snow. The man was terribly heavy. Like a sack of potatoes. He didn't try to help him in the least. Roman jerked and shook him angrily. He was soon worn out. The man was also losing patience.

"Leave me in peace."

"Come on."

"By God, I'll sock you one."

"You'll catch cold."

"What business of yours is that? Why do you keep interfering? The doctors and nurses order me around. When I've at last slipped out of their hands for a while, this damn boy has to get in the way! You've been trailing me ever since we got to the waterfalls. Like a bloodhound. Who asked you to? Are you really so dependent that you need me to babysit you? If you can't make your own decisions, stay at home tied to your mother's apron strings."

"I thought...."

"That's exactly what you should be doing. If you don't understand the mountains, and by God you don't, then keep away from them. That's good advice."

Roman Zelina felt the man was being unfair to him. He didn't appreciate his sincere concern at all. It was untactful of him to reproach him for his lack of experience. He felt cruelly and deeply wounded by his bad temper. The man had touched a sensitive spot in Roman's hard-won self-confidence. He felt on the edge of tears. He hesitated uncertainly. If he didn't know how to win the man's trust, he should leave.

He would freeze to death! Simply freeze to death. But he probably doesn't care, Roman Zelina told himself. He just doesn't want me to help him. So why should I care?

He firmly resolved to descend. The forest was getting dark. When he got out of it, there would be a bit more light, even though the sun had already set. He was soon back on the path where the foresters' trucks had left hard tracks in the icy snow. The running surface of his skis rattled over the bumpy surface. However, Roman was concentrating so hard that even at the greatest speed he could make his tired body go, he managed not to fall.

This improved his mood and self-confidence. Although it had seemed to him not long before that he had no strength left, he was increasing his speed. He propelled himself forward with his legs astride, left ski, right ski, pushing off with both sticks at the same time. As he got farther and farther from the spot where he had left the man, the tension disappeared. He was concentrating on giving his best cross-country performance. He was proud of the way he had gotten the hang of the skating style.

He was approaching Podbanské. In order to relieve himself of his last worry, when he came to the crossroads, he would stop at the Mountain Rescue Service. He would report what had happened and then catch his bus in plenty of time.

From the hall Roman Zelina was greeted with the smell of smoked sausage boiled in cabbage soup. He paused in confusion on the threshold of the heated room. Like a carol singer with stage fright. The woman he had seen over the fence that morning was lightly dressed for indoors.

"You forgot to knock, young man," said a man with a thick, curly beard. He had the logo of the Mountain Rescue Service sewn on his red pullover.

"I'm sorry," stammered Roman.

"Has anything happened?" the woman asked calmly. She had honey-colored hair hanging over her shoulders. She looked only a little older than the girls in his class, but she had the mature air of an adult.

"Yes. Something may happen. Up there."

"Where?"

"In the forest. At the top of the valley."

"Which valley?"

"Kôprová, no.... That's the one we went up. We decided to return by the other one."

"Over Závory," concluded the young woman.

"I still have no idea what this young man is talking about," said the Mountain Rescue officer.

"Does someone need help?" the young woman prompted Roman.

"Yes, he's sure to," Roman reacted almost enthusiastically, as if he had at last remembered the real reason why he had stopped there. "An elderly man. Up there in Tichá valley. Beside the stream," he tried to describe as exactly as possible the place where he had left the man with the weak heart.

"So that's it," said the Mountain Rescue officer. "Now I'm beginning to understand you. Of course, I'd rather stay at home where it's warm, but I'll be dressed in a moment and I'll hurry up there."

"Is he a relative of yours?" asked the young woman.

Roman Zelina shook his head.

"Then you don't much feel like going back with me," said the officer.

"Should I?" Roman asked indecisively.

"It's up to you. But I don't want to have to rescue two people instead of one."

"Let him have a rest," said the young woman. "Look, he's ready to drop."

The Mountain Rescue officer slipped on his quilted red anorak. He was soon starting up his jeep outside in the yard. After several attempts, the engine sprang to life and rattled away noisily.

"Sit down. You must be hungry," the young woman said to Roman Zelina.

"No thank you, I'm not at all hungry," Roman replied and tried to explain that he had had enough food with him.

"Then I'll pour you some tea. I don't suppose you'll refuse that," the woman said, looking at Roman calmly and optimistically. When she gazed at him with those light-brown eyes, he had to look down. He could feel himself blushing.

"I won't disturb you," he said.

"You're not disturbing. Nor keeping me from my work. Not many people stop by here. I'm glad when I can talk to someone."

Roman glanced at his watch.

"My last bus from Podbanské will be going in a minute."

"Won't you wait? Aren't you curious to know what's happens to that man?"

"He'll be all right," Roman stuttered. "He said he was an experienced hiker."

"You're probably right," said the fair-haired young woman. She stepped towards Roman Zelina, as if she wanted to help him take off his rucksack. He just mumbled something, said goodbye and hurried out of the house. The Mountain Rescue officer was leaving in his jeep, driving up the valley.

Roman Zelina ran up to the bus stop just in time. He got on the half-empty bus, sat down and closed his eyes. A feeling of profound melancholy washed over him. He was convinced that having fled this place in such a cowardly fashion, he would never dare show his face there again.

RÓBERT MÜLLER
- prose writer, poet, journalist;
born in Bratislava (1961)

Róbert Müller has worked as a geologist, he was director of the Záhorie Museum in Skalica, and at present he is an authorized expert on precious stones, minerals and the extraction of minerals.

His first book was a collection of short stories, **Naša láska bola modrá** (*Our Love Was Blue*, 1992). This extraordinary assemblage of human relations, depicted in a rather Kafkaesque way, with elements of mystery and absurdity, presents society's degrading influence on people. The book **Oko ako ty** (*An Eye Like You*, 1993) contains a selection of his poetry. In his short novel **Béla, priateľ Fénixa** (*Phoenix's Friend*, 1995) he ponders the position of man in the modern world. In his prose work **Stratené veci Ríma** (*Rome's Lost Causes*, 1998) he speaks in an untraditional way of the lack of mutual human understanding. The book of short stories **Strážni anjeli** (*Guardian Angels*, 1999) shows his own reaction to the dilemmas of Slovak history and of our modern times. The short story "Otázka" ("The Question") is taken from this work.

Róbert Müller also devotes time to journalism. He made good use of his expert knowledge in the work **Fantastická mineralógia** (*Fantastic Minerology*), in which, apart from other things, he sums up opinions about precious stones since ancient Greek and Roman times.

In his own words:
Stone grows in the course of time like a tree: it has its birth, length of life, it has its year-rings. Stone was here before human beings, but it was humans who first noticed its beauty and durability. Stone was the first natural material that ancient people learned to shape and use, both as a tool and as their first weapon. The path of progress from hand axes to nuclear weapons was not a simple one. People gradually learned to understand the microstructures of crystalline substances and discovered how to release enormous

amounts of energy from natural radioactive materials. The human race has already had a taste of what it means when stone "weeps," but I am not sure if it has learned a lesson from it....

But stone is also silence. Mystical silence. The need for silence has existed, so it appears, from time immemorial. In silence we have a clearer awareness of ourselves, we seem to get nearer the truth, nearer to the core of things. Healing silence, quieting and calming the human senses exposed to so many enticements. There is a plant called the Japanese Bay [laurus japonica] which cannot bear shouting, loud voices, noisy laughter, wailing and general uproar. The leaves of this plant turn away from the noise. On the Solomon Islands, as Robert Fulghum wrote, the local people use a special method for felling trees: they don't use axes or other tools, but shouting – they all begin to shout at the tree and the tree succumbs and falls. Man seems to have encoded within him the need for silence to counterbalance chaos and noise, to maintain a state of equilibrium in our busy, chaotic, disordered lives. When you look closely at a stone, its perfect existence helps you to quietly shed tears.

(1997)

THE QUESTION

We sent Julinka a little duck on a piece of elastic. You hang it from the ceiling and when you pull it down and let it go, it flies upward and flaps its wings. She played with it for weeks on end. She would pull on the elastic, clapping her little hands and gurgling with laughter when the plastic duck flew upwards.

His wife is a bit hysterical. I'm not surprised. Until they decided to adopt a child, their lives were unbearably empty. They chose a little girl from the orphanage. Julka. A year later, the girl got meningitis. Since then his wife has been quite impossible. From time to time she has a fit. Then she'll grab an umbrella and begin to beat her husband with it, yelling that it is all his fault that she has never had a child.

She has a husband like bread and honey. Infinitely good, and what is even rarer, truthful. In all the time we have known this man, and that's a good many years now, we have never heard him complain or lament his fate; in all the years we have known him, we have never heard him ask one question that concerned himself, his wife or Julka.

It happened one evening. He came to visit us, because he wanted to know if we were satisfied with the working of a fountain with a large plastic plate, which he had once given us when we complained that the air in our apartment was unbearably dry. When he sat down in the living-room, he pulled something out of his shopping bag – a hedgehog. He had found it at the edge of the road and couldn't resist it. He clearly wanted to share with us the childlike pleasure we could see in his face when he put the hedgehog down next to a crystal cigarette box, a vase of more or less the same cut and a fairly massive ashtray.

My wife let out a little squeal of admiration. All three of us were aware of something infinitely tender and good, something that was reflected in his face as he gazed in wonder and delight at the hedgehog. He then put his finger to his lips like a child that has betrayed an important secret and immediately realized he should not have given it away so easily, so he put his finger to his lips, as if making a promise.

At that moment my wife and I realized something was missing in our lives. The three of us waited for the hedgehog to summon up its courage and prepare to defend itself. We waited for the ball of prickles to stir, staring hard at it to see whether it would move at least a few steps across the table. We waited for it to stick its brownish black nose out of its stronghold of prickles. After we had waited in silence for some time, the prickly ball stirred and the hedgehog took a few tiny steps across the table as if it were going for a walk, until it got to the edge, where it hesitated and came to a halt.

At that moment we noticed the expression of extraordinary pleasure on our friend's face, something truly childlike and good. This is what we had been waiting for almost all evening. In the end we agreed we would let it go in our garden. It's right next to our house, a reasonable size, with plenty of places to hide, and here and there tall weeds along the fence and holes in the ground, where it could find shelter. The hedgehog scuttled off across the uncut lawn beyond the tongues of light reaching out from two rooms. Finally it was swallowed up by the darkness.

My wife and I lay side by side on the edge of sleep, each of us wondering to ourselves what it was that was missing in our lives. We are fond of each other, but even so, there is something in our relationship that we feel a need to change, that both of us perceive as a deviation or a blow below the belt. When he put the hedgehog on the table, we felt it was an urgent question, which cried out to be asked and demanded a serious answer, which would reassure us, give us peace of mind and would fill our relationship once more with something strong and secure.

We were torn from our half-sleep by the ringing of the doorbell. We turned over, not knowing at first whether we were dreaming, but when the ringing showed no signs of stopping, I roused myself and went to open the door. It was late evening and he was standing at the gate. The childlike delight had disappeared from his face. He was gasping for breath, as if he had run all the way, but as soon as he calmed down a little, he blurted out, "I must bring it! No matter what, or there'll be hell to pay at home. She's been beating me with the umbrella again." In the dark I didn't see the bruise marks on his face.

"I must find it," he repeated. "Please, help me. I want it for Julinka, so she can play with it, too."

At that late hour we started looking for the hedgehog and we looked for it until the early hours of the morning. We aimed flashlights under every tomato plant, blinding each other, and from opposite ends of the garden we kept repeating in desperation throughout the night, "Where on earth can it be? It's not here, either!"

Dawn was already breaking when we finally gave up. We sat down in the living room and only then did I notice his sleepless and weary face. It told of anxiety and fear of the umbrella, or perhaps of something worse. My wife brought in three strong coffees, but he had fallen asleep on the table in the meantime, his head among the crystal we had received as a wedding present. I gazed at him, his head resting on his arm like a child and I was tempted to ask my wife whether she had realized what it was we were missing.

GABRIELA ROTHMAYEROVÁ

- prose writer, journalist;
born in Gelnica (1951)

Gabriela Rothmayerová worked as an editor, from 1991-94 she was a member of the National Council of the Slovak Republic and at present she is editor-in-chief of Slovak Radio's station Rádio Devín.

Her first book was a collection of prose works, ***Lastovičie hniezdo*** (*The Swallows' Nest*, 1982), which are set in a mining community and have a common protagonist – a little girl looking for her place in life. It is a book about a longing for harmony and understanding. "V nebezpečnom pásme" ("In a Danger Zone") is a more recent version of a story taken from that book. The collection of stories ***Po prvej skúške*** (*After the First Test*, 1984) presents episodes from the lives of emancipated women. In an equally feministic novella ***Šťastie je drina*** (*Happiness is Hard Work*, 1989) she considers the complicated position of women with duties at work and at home through the portrayal of a woman in an unhappy marriage who longs to have a child.

In 1994 she published a book of autobiographical essays, ***Zo zápisníka poslankyne*** (*From a Representative's Notebook*), about her experiences as a member of parliament. The book **Dusno** (*Stifling*, 1998) also contains articles on political and social themes. Here she brought together a variety of texts that had been published in the press and on the radio about the complicated process of transformation after 1989; apart from her own texts, she included interviews with political figures from both camps – representatives of the totalitarian regime and of the "velvet revolution."

In her own words:
If a writer or intellectual takes up a political career, they give up their talent – that is what I have learned. Politics really is no minuet, in which you circle round the floor in a genteel fashion following the steps of the dance; it is not for the tender-hearted and certain-

ly not for the just. If you want to be successful, you must win points. And points are won for the fight. And although the rules should be clear, where can you find a referee who notices every forbidden hold? Only the Lord above knows....

It disturbs me to see how easily we have come to believe in our insignificance. About a year ago my son took part in a competition organized here in this country by Atlantic College. This school was founded in the sixties by NATO officers with the idea that talented children from various countries should get to know each other when they are young, because people who know each other and are friends will not wage war against each other. At the competition, apart from tests in certain subjects, the participants were asked about all kinds of things. For example, what is the difference between us Slovaks and, for example, Americans. My son answered, none at all, we just have to know more.

I think here lies hope for our culture, if our children have no complexes about coming from a small country. If they measure up or even excel. If they don't succumb to the garish bad taste of commercialism, which would like to pretend it is culture, but its roots are only in the purse, or to put it in a nicer way, in bank accounts.

My Michal doesn't feel any handicap among three hundred and fifty students from eighteen countries of the world. And when he was talking with his roommate, Mussa, a boy from Africa, the latter apparently said admiringly, Mišo, you are from the greatest country I know! You see, everything is just a question of interpretation, as well as of culture and cultivated behavior.

(1994)

IN A DANGER ZONE

The beginning looked more than promising. They found their first prize at the very edge of the forest, beneath a cluster of small young pines. In the damp, flowering moss with its hair-like, slender, upright stalks bearing tiny reddish sparks of flowers stood a whole family of mushrooms with velvety dark-brown caps, their feet sunk deep in the sandy soil.

Ada twisted them out of the moss, blew on them and held them to her nose. Rudo cut around the portly stems and flicked the pine needles off their caps.

They pushed their way through the dense, shiny-green bristles, lifting stiff pine branches and eagerly ducking under their starched skirts. Lizards rustled through the long grass. A startled rabbit leaped up and away, leaving only a shuddering trail through the pine wood.

Spiders swayed in finely woven cobwebs shining like silk in the autumn sun, while a little deeper in the forest squirrels leaped among the magnificent branches fanning out from the tall trunks of stately pines. All around there was a majestic silence.

Suddenly the forest bent over, a deafening rumbling rent the sky, followed by a dull thudding, as when heavy, hard oak logs come tumbling down on a dry wooden floor. That the forest was a military training ground was made clear by the notices warning intruders, but this was also obvious from the blackened cartridge cases lying around in the grass, glittering now and then in a ray of sun that slipped through the thick branches.

Far from worrying them, the cartridge cases struck them as exciting, something out of the ordinary, forbidden. They had never been mushrooming before in the forbidden zone; sooner or later, they just had to try it. The soldiers came there to train at precisely scheduled times, at least that was what they had been told by those who boasted of their success in these woods. Mushrooms grew there as if someone had planted them, that's what they said.

"Isn't it dangerous?" Ada had asked the day before, the moment she had put down her suitcase, and her eyes lit up with the pleasure of excited anticipation. She was immediately determined to try it, in spite of the danger. Her friend made a brief attempt to dissuade her, claiming that the training ground was in fact a shooting range, and athough they only used blanks, even they could be dangerous in the case of a direct hit. However, her friend's husband, Rudo, allowed himself to be persuaded. He liked Ada's courage and the excitement of the forbidden gripped him, too.

The rumbling spread out, fading into a good-natured mumble, until it finally fell silent altogether. For a while the squirrels still sat warily in the trees, but they were soon bouncing through the branches and scrambling up the trunks until they were lost from sight.

"Do you think they'll start early?"

The shooting in the training ground was not due to start until the evening. Rudo didn't reply. He was already crouching at the feet of a couple of beautiful mushrooms. A fly, caught in a cobweb, was stuck to his nose, but Rudo hadn't noticed it. He was in high spirits, pleasantly thrilled by the unusual experience.

Their hands met as they picked the mushrooms from their nest. Rudo felt the fragrance of wind-blown hair and cool skin covered with fine down like a ripe peach. The thick taste of saliva in his mouth kept him swallowing as she bent over in front of him, the firm cloth stretching over her round buttocks. When she reached out for the basket, he felt her supple breasts under her thin T-shirt on the back of his hand. He dropped the open knife into the half-filled basket and stroked the bare back of her neck with fingers stained black by the mushrooms. They left a smudge, which ran down from her neck to the pale blue shirt and drew a map of his further discoveries. However, many areas of her shirt were left unexplored, as he completed his map on her naked body. He felt a loud throbbing in his head, a yielding body in his hands.

"We've really gone and done it now," Ada sighed, picking spiders and pine needles out of her tangled hair. She noticed salty drops of sweat sliding down Rudo's temples.

The sky roared again and the forest ducked in anticipation. This time they heard a whistling, which was almost drowned by the roar of an engine, followed by the sound of an explosion. In a flash they were fleeing from the danger zone, like the frightened rabbit a while before. At the edge of the forest, in front of the warning sign, they stopped to get back their breath. Ada untied her shoe laces and, holding on to Rudo with one hand, she balanced on one foot like a fully-grown brown-haired pore mushroom and shook the pine needles from her trainers.

The evening was filled with the aroma of mushroom stew, mushroom soup and the rain which signaled the end of the Indian summer. It splashed on the tiles of the terrace steps where Rudo was sitting with Ada and his wife. Both the mushroom pickers chattered away, interrupting one another in their eagerness to describe their thrilling experience in the forbidden forest, the cobwebs stretching between the trees like veils, the dangerous firing of weapons, the hordes of mushrooms and the magic rings of wood blewits, the pine forest which in the autumn sun smelled of resin, reminding them of Christmas. They both talked at once, but neither Ada nor Rudo looked at each other. The drops of rain scurried down the hairy geranium leaves, which shook themselves, throwing cold showers of heavy drops into the flowerpots. On the veranda roof the rain leaked through the soaked, disintegrating tar paper, which had needed replacing long ago. A stray tickle pushed its way through a crack in the boards and dribbled down the back of Rudo's neck. At any other time he would have cursed waspishly, but now he just hunched his shoulders and shivered as the ticklish drop chilled his hot skin.

His wife gazed at him thoughtfully. His calm reaction had surprised her.

"It's leaking," she said, to convince herself that he really was acting strangely. On any other occasion he would have angrily objected to this comment; he took everything personally, as if she meant to offend or humiliate him. Now, however, he just got up from the wicker chair, flicked a bit of dirt off her skirt and smiled.

"If it leaks, we'll have to patch it up, won't we?" he said jovially.

The rain poured down incessantly, rustling in the lilac bushes, spattering the fallen leaves under the apple tree, breathing damp coolness onto the open veranda.

The wife went into the house to prepare a bed for her friend, and Rudo immediately got up and followed her. He was going to help his wife slip the starched bed linen on the old duvet and pillows. The wife unfolded the sheet and tucked the ends under the mattress, smoothing out the creases with her hand. She had read somewhere that when they have been unfaithful, some men try to silence their guilty consciences by being extra attentive to their wives. But could that be true of her husband? She tried a shot in the dark.

"Look, I know what happened," she said, watching her husband's face out of the corner of her eye. For a moment he froze, then a split second later he screwed up his eyes as if he had received a painful blow between them, but he collected his wits in no time.

"What?"

"I know what happened, but we won't make a fuss over it," his wife said. "I suppose it could happen to anyone...and anyway, you're still in one piece," she added.

He was taken aback and at that moment he didn't know what to think.

"For heaven's sake, what could have happened? You can't think...."

His wife said nothing, allowing him time to recover his composure. A few moments later she quietly slipped out of the room, leaving him standing holding the still uncovered duvet in his outstretched arms as if he was crucified.

Ada was standing beside the geraniums, her upturned palms catching the autumn rain. The little streams splattered on her fingers, sending a shower of raindrops to cool her face and leaving tiny puddles in her palms, which were broken up by further streams of lashing rain.

"So that's the way it is," the wife spoke up, as she stood close to her, her back against the wooden parapet and face towards the dark veranda. She leaned over the geranium blossoms, bending her head back. Little rivulets tickled her face.

Ada was all attention. Waiting in suspense, she opened her palm, so the puddles of water poured off it and the rain pecked at her stretched out palm. Then she quickly clenched her hands and dropped them to her sides.

"A nice day, you say, hmm...," the wife continued. "You had a pleasant day...."

"Very pleasant," Ada interrupted, sounding enthusiastic. "It's a great pity you weren't with us, you really missed something...."

She cut in, "Wouldn't there have been too many of us in that dangerous wood?"

"What do you mean?" murmured Ada, thrown off balance by her best friend's question.

"Hmm.... After all, it is a forbidden zone. And you know me, you know I'm a terrible moralist."

"But.... Who cares...."

"You're right. Really. There's nothing awful about the fact that you were in the forbidden zone, even if it is a firing range. But you know very well that's not what I'm referring to," the woman added meaningfully.

Ada stared at her, horrified.

"Good grief, what a husband you've got! He's been shooting his mouth off, has he? Good grief..., but you can take my word for it, nothing like that happened. I mean it, really. Believe me, it'll never happen again, never again! If I'd had any idea he was like that...," gasped Ada. She was genuinely horrified at the depravity of this fellow, who had hurried off to boast to his own wife that he had been unfaithful to her with her best friend – the beast.

Next morning the two said a cool and almost hostile goodbye. Ada walked away, wobbling dangerously down the path as her high heels sank into the mud.

"I'm sorry, but she's a silly hen," Rudo remarked. "I'm sorry, but I'd rather you didn't invite her again."

Without a word his wife lifted up her smiling lips, to which he pressed a passionate, unhusbandlike kiss. All was forgiven. The game would go on.

PETER ŠEVČOVIČ

- prose writer, playwright, script writer;
born in Bratislava (1935)

Peter Ševčovič worked for the most part as a film and tele-vision script editor.

His literary debut was the novel **Mesto plné chlapov** (*A Town Full of Real Men*, 1963) about a young intellectual in a gigantic iron-works. His novel about builders, **Čakaj nás, Angela** (*Wait For Us, Angela*, 1964), shows the contrast between expectations and reali-ty. In the novella **Mimoriadne okolnosti** (*Exceptional Circum-stances*, 1974) he uses a case of manslaughter to raise the question of the social responsibility of the individual. The novel **Tretinový chlap** (*One-Third Man*, 1976), intended for young readers, is set in Bratislava and describes the period bordering on war and peace. **Kamarátka pre nás dvoch** (*A Friend for Us Both*, 1978) is about bringing up children in an incomplete family. The novel **Maturita ako remeň** (*Tough Finals*, 1990) looks at the question of morality in the period of social transformation.

For the theater he wrote contemporary comedies (**Nie je všedný deň** – *No Ordinary Day* 1960; **Vrabčie lásky** – *Sparrow Loves*, 1978; **Garzónka** – *The Studio Apartment*, 1993), plays about the Slovak National Uprising (**Partia** – *The Group*, **Kvarteto** – *Quartet*). He wrote a series of television plays for adults (**Spor o básnika** – *Dispute About a Poet*, 1967; **Konfigurácia** – *Configuration*, 1971; **Biele vrany** – *White Crows*, 1977; **Prvé lásky** – *First Loves*, 1980; **Exemplárny prípad** – *An Exemplary Case*, 1989), as well as plays for young viewers.

He is the author of many short stories for radio ("**Chlap prezý-vaný Brumteles**" – "*A Boy Nicknamed Brumteles*," 1979; "**Blízka cesta do večnosti**" – "*Near to Eternity*," 1999); as well as of the radio play **Srnka a čierny kôň** (*The Little Red Deer and the Black Horse*, 1992).

In his own words:

In spite of the bad times and the Post-February* norms of spiritual life, my father and grandfather instilled in me the Christian view of the world. Not a showy and proclaiming Christianity, not a pettifogging observation of the rules of one or other of the religions, but the philosophical principle of good as an inner need, helping the individual to face up to the surrounding world, its evils and hatreds. To be humble and meek, but always to remain one's own man. To understand one's enemies. To love them in one's own way as human beings. They did not teach me to hate. After all, understanding those close to us can extract from even the most malicious, the most inhuman world crumbs of good, which benefit all. This has remained within me to this day, even though I often have the feeling that my inability to hate does me harm. This self-inflicted harm, however, gives me inner equilibrium....

Democracy is, apart from other things, the ability to cut somebody to the quick on a political theme in the morning and in the evening to enjoy a drink with your rival while discussing a theme you can agree about. Real democracy is a game for high stakes, but with controlled emotions.

I consider the personal drama of an honest, open, decent person of good character, who cannot be successful in any revolution, to be one of the greatest possible topics for contemporary literature.

(1991)

[* i.e. the post-war Communist take-over – transl. note]

NEAR TO ETERNITY

The housing development on the outskirts of the town was so old that the buildings were of honest bricks and mortar. The double efficiency apartments of a planned hotel that had never become a hotel were originally occupied by university and secondary-school teachers, engineers from important companies, lawyers, as well as doctors from the local hospitals. At that time they were all young, they had their lives before them and so it is no wonder that many of them were now scattered all over the world. Those who had stayed behind were now scraping along on their pensions.

As time went by, they saw the children's playgrounds disappear, the coffee bar in which they had met change into a branch of some bank, and the luxury restaurant with a terrace become a bar with slot machines, where the waitresses glared at the old ladies who had not given up their habit of meeting two or three times a week on the terrace for a lengthy conversation over a single cup of coffee.

In the tops of the spreading trees, once planted by the inhabitants of the development, could be heard the twittering of birds. They had long since gotten used to the roar of the cars on the nearby bypass and they had stopped being afraid of old people. The grey thrush, which Gizela had named Kleo, hopped around the table she was sitting at, in the expectation that she would throw it a bit of stale bread. Mrs. Gizela was stirring her coffee and waiting for Mrs. Ruženka, who was always late, but when she did arrive, surprised her with an unexpected question.

"Have you had your seventieth birthday yet, Gizelka?"

"Last year, Ruženka dear, last year. Good morning!" She watched Ruženka dust her chair and then sit down.

"And your husband?"

"He's six years older."

"You hardly look sixty!"

Ruženka settled down on her seat at last.

"People often tell me that," Gizelka remarked, blushing slightly.

"I'm three years younger than you, but I look older!" said Ruženka, gazing into a little mirror. "My face looks like parchment."

"You can scrape up enough to buy a container of sour cream once a week. I pat some onto my face every day and my skin seems to like it."

"My late husband thought all cosmetics stank. He couldn't even stand the most expensive kind, which he always bought me...."

"I always get up a bit earlier than my Jozef and wash myself with some nice-smelling baby soap," Gizelka began dreamily, "then I tiptoe up to him and wake him with a kiss. He always whispers how delightful I smell. Then I slip back into bed and he wakes me up a second time with a kiss and with some breakfast."

"No one has whispered anything to me for a long time," Ruženka sighed bitterly. "And I don't use any creams."

"You mustn't let yourself go, Ruženka."

"What if I do? I'm alone! My Fedor...."

"...and what if that Fedor of yours should be looking down at you from Paradise?! What if he doesn't like the fact that you don't look after yourself?"

"Him?! To tell you the truth.... In the last year he got more and more grouchy. He would yell at me, he was always quarreling with me, he really hated me. He even hit me a couple of times!"

"And maybe...maybe only because you talked too much. That irritates old men. They want to be left in peace. Otherwise...."

"So what – you don't mean to say you still make love to yours?!" Ruženka burst out.

"Even that happens occasionally."

"At your age – with one foot in the grave!"

"Life can be beautiful even in your old age, even though the days seem almost as alike as two peas. We have loved each other the whole of our lives and we have prepared for death in the same way. Each of us has written a will and had it certified by a lawyer. Then we put our wills in sealed envelopes and now they are waiting in the cupboard for us to die. We did exactly as we agreed."

"No one is going to inherit anything much from me. I have no more now than I had when I was young. In fact, not even that."

"It's the same with us. There's nothing for us to inherit from each other," laughed Gizela. "That's why we both thought up a little surprise to put in our wills. What's that sour look for?"

"We sold a bit of that gold and china when the children ran off to Australia."

"Hasn't Klemka asked you to go and live with them? Your daughter's name is Klementína, isn't it?"

"The last time she wrote was two years ago. I have two grandchildren, but I hardly know anything about them. That's what the world's done to my daughter. Who knows if they're still alive!"

"Our Janík was killed, too. Just before his wedding. Just graduated as an engineer.... We have no one to follow after us. No one'll be left when we're gone.... There'll be no one to put chrysanthemums on our graves. So we don't want to have graves."

"Everyone has to have a final resting place. I've bought a place next to my husband."

"If life continues in the next world, Ruženka, then you simply can't rest forever; and if there is no life there, then it'll be all the same to us."

"But I'm a believer!" Ruženka reminded her quietly.

"All the more reason why you should know there's no need! Is it hypocritical speeches you want? Coffins are a waste, too. They can cremate you in a sheet. Let them scatter the ashes on that beautiful meadow where so many mushrooms grow in the autumn. Those who want to will remember us without all that fuss. And they can light a candle just as well at home."

"But your husband wouldn't be able to visit your grave!"

"Having to change buses three times with his aching joints?! He only goes for the bread and milk because I refuse to buy him beer and cigarettes."

180

"Well, I certainly go and visit my late husband's grave to talk to him."

"We talk at home. I make him a thermos of herbal tea, we light a candle and sometimes we're even up until midnight, just spending a pleasant evening together by candlelight. We talk together like this every day and we always give each other a little surprise."

"What are you going to astonish him with today?"

"I bought some bargain mushrooms. I'll cook them with onion and caraway seeds and bake them in pastry. Then we'll sit down for a chat."

"I go to bed as soon as it gets dark."

"You can watch television."

"But that old piece of junk has given up the ghost and they say it can't be repaired. Well, I can't afford a new one."

"In that case, I would light a candle, put the photograph of my late husband in front of it and I would tell him what I had done that day. Jozef has promised me that every day after I die he'll come and sit quietly with me the whole evening."

"But what if the other world doesn't exist and it's not like that at all? My old man hasn't even come to see me in a dream."

"Well, my dear, me and my Jozef, we've never stopped and we'll never ever stop loving one another. Even though our days are alike as drops of water, every day we live through the good and the bad in our lives together."

* * *

Gizelka's evening was just as she had planned it.

"Mmm! Marvelous mushroom pancakes, Gizka, mar-vel-ous!" Jozef declared enthusiastically, when he bit into the crusty pastry.

"They're patties, mushrooms patties," Gizelka corrected him gently.

"Every day you think of something to give me a pleasant surprise. And people say you're a battleaxe," he said, with a contented expression on his face.

"Eat over your plate...! And who says that?"

"I heard it with my own ears. They pick someone to pieces every day in the shop."

The husband got to his feet with difficulty. His knees ached terribly.

"Get me a cup of milk if you're going there."

"I've got something better in the fridge," Jozef grinned. "Put some glasses on the table. Take those cut-glass ones."

"What's this all about? I didn't know we had a special day today?" Gizelka called out after him.

"Look at the beautiful dew on this bottle!" he said in delight, as he removed the clasp from the champagne.

"I asked you something."

"At our age every day is special in some way. So let this one be, too." He wriggled the cork so that it shot out of the bottle and carefully poured the sparkling wine into the crystal glasses. "Well, cheers, Gizka dear!"

"Throwing money around? Well, then...cheers!"

"Mmm! That's a treat! Drink up, we'll have another...!"

"Squandering so much money...!"

"What use is it to us? We can't take it with us to the next world! Look, Gizka, I bought this for you today, too." He handed her an envelope containing some papers.

"Travel agency...Greece.... A round trip to see the ancient monuments.... Where did you get that idea from?" She was quite taken aback.

"You've been teaching children about it all your life. So you'll go and see for yourself while your legs can still carry you."

"I've always dreamed of such a trip," she looked longingly at the paper, but then something suddenly struck her. "And I'm to go alone? What about you?"

"You know very well that I couldn't manage it with these legs of mine." He lifted his champagne and clinked glasses with her. "Cheers, Gizka, and bon voyage!"

She still felt quite taken aback by it all. However, she didn't refuse his toast. "Cheers, Jožko, here's to your health!" She could not leave it at that, though. "But where did you get the money from?"

"From the writing desk. From the savings book."

"The one we have for our funerals, or the one I don't know about? So you've...." She was about to give him a talking to, but she caught sight of his joyful eyes and stopped herself. "Well, let's drink to our health."

"Cheers!"

They drank the toast and fell silent for quite a while. The soft music from the record player was all that was to be heard. Then Jozef took a deep breath and began, "Another thing I wanted to do for you.... While you were having a chat on the terrace, I sorted out all our papers. In the top drawer you'll find all our documents, in the next one the rest of the money we got for those bonds and the empty savings book.... In the third there are photographs, letters, diaries...."

"I was going to do that...," she drank the last drop from her glass.

"It's a good thing you didn't get around to it.... I wouldn't have been able to find anything."

"You shouldn't have bought that holiday. I'm too old to travel," she said diffidently.

He filled their glasses once more.

"Didn't the doctor tell you last week that you're as well as can be expected at your age?"

"How can you believe her when she prescribes whatever medicines we tell her to? And we never even have to get undressed!"

"Nearly all doctors are like that, Gizka dear. Look at my notebook. Every day I telephone one of my friends. And I don't always get the reply I expect."

"You've crossed some of them out. Why – aren't you friends with them any more?" she leafed through the thick notebook lying beside the telephone directory.

"They – they're no longer alive. And no one let me know."

"You miss them, don't you?" she put the address book down.

"I've gotten used to the idea. When I die, call all those who are still alive..., let them know they should cross me off their lists.... Or, no, it'd be better not to call anyone. Well, let's finish our drinks and let's go to bed."

They drained the bottle to the last drop, but they still didn't feel like sleep.

"Should I make your bed beside me, Jožko, or here in the living-room?" she asked tactfully.

"I would like a bit of a cuddle today."

"I'll be glad to cuddle with you," she nodded, "but you can come here to snore!"

"As usual!" he smiled. "But tomorrow I'll bring you your breakfast in bed and I'll wake you up with a kiss, all right?"

"All right, all right, my gallant gentleman!"

* * *

Jozef began to hunt through the libraries for books on ancient Greek art and Gizelka studied them with interest. Their evening conversations were full of new topics.

"Just imagine, not one of the great Greeks has his own tomb," she exclaimed one evening.

"Not even Aeschylus? Euripides?"

"No."

"Aristotle? Socrates?"

"They all live on in spirit, but there are no graves anywhere."

"Hm...remarkable, but...wouldn't it be a good idea to go to bed?"

There was no need to say any more, she understood. But she couldn't stop herself from making a bit of womanly fuss.

"All right, but you'll sleep in the living-room afterwards."

He was a little put out, but he agreed. After all, he had no choice.

* * *

That morning, four days before her trip to Greece, Gizelka was awakened by the sun shining in through the blinds. After their lovemaking the night before, when Jozef had proved he was still a man, she felt refreshed and younger. She glanced at the bedside table, but the usual breakfast was not waiting for her there. She smiled a little and tiptoed into the living-room.

"Get up, Jožko, it's morning, it's already a new day!"

There was no answer.

She placed her hand gently on his forehead and drew it back in fright. His forehead was cold and unfamiliar. Anxiety gripped her heart and ran through her body, making her fingers tremble. She slowly pulled back the quilt. His hands and feet were an unusual shade of yellow, his body stiff.

When she tried to straighten his crumpled pajamas, in the middle of his back her palm felt the remains of his warmth slipping away forever.

She didn't burst into tears, but just spoke to the dead man.

"So you've died.... The most beautiful way possible. In your sleep. No doubt you were dreaming sweetly when your spirit left your body."

There was no need for her to close his eyes, but his mouth was open, as if he had wanted to cry out at the last moment.

She took the prettiest of the scarves he had once given her and tied it around Jozef's lower jaw and the back of his head, so he would look nice when he was completely stiff.

"You've met the death you wanted. The only sad thing is that it came so unexpectedly. Well, it can't be helped.... I must do something. I'm not used to being lonely, it could drive me insane."

Not long before, Ruženka had written down the numbers you had to call when there was a death in the house.

She phoned the police, but it was busy.

All she got from the doctors was a mocking fanfare.

When she called the undertakers an impersonal female voice announced that the number had been changed and that she should call directory assistance.

At the town hall no one answered the phone.

She therefore pulled the sheet out from beneath the dead man and tried to clasp his hands over his chest. She fluffed up his pillow, combed his hair, covered him with the quilt. She placed two antique candlesticks beside his head, stuck Candlemas candles in them, lit them and opened the windows a little. Lastly she wiped the dust off the furniture.

She took a shower, combed her hair and put rouge on her cheeks. She dressed herself in her black Sunday best and made herself a strong cup of coffee. Finally, she took her husband's will out of the drawer in the writing desk and began to read.

"My dearest Gizelka, when you read this will of mine, don't cry! I'd rather you smiled, remembering what a good life we had together, in spite of the fact that we meant nothing to the world of the powerful and that no one cared about us or cares about us now. We were and we will be just you and I. And that is more important than all those hypocritical fine ceremonies that have taken over this world.

After my death I want you to do everything we have often talked about. I don't want to lie in a coffin, let them cremate me in a winding sheet. Don't show people my dead body, let them remember me as I was when I was alive. I refuse to have any funeral whatsoever, because all those flowery speeches, sentimental melodies, poems and songs, borrowed wreaths, a couple of bouquets and the wake are just meaningless pomp. A ridiculous and exorbitantly expensive gathering of pretense. Let them burn me without any of this, without any parting ceremony. And I want them to scatter my ashes on the meadow without any ceremony. Without you, too, Gizka. Why should you have to see my ashes? What would you or I get out of it?"

She stifled a sob.

"The world never wished us well, it was hard on us. We'll be the same now. Let them dispose of my remains for that pitiful sum the state grants for funerals. Don't give them a crown more! I will be watching to see if you manage it. I'll be with you all the time. Don't you dare put a single heller in the insatiable jaws of this cruel world that made me forget so quickly the dreams of my youth. Be strong and don't give in! Do what I wish, so that I can come to you satisfied and not angry, disappointed and betrayed. You do understand me, don't you, dear?"

She finished reading the will, wept her fill and then, as if by a miracle, she easily got through to all those she needed.

* * *

Three minutes was all the young doctor needed to inspect the body.

"He died because his heart stopped. That's normal at his age," he said, immediately sitting down at the table to write out the death certificate.

"Can I ask what stopped his heart, Doctor?" she said in a quiet voice.

"Old age. A post-mortem would tell us more, but the cause of death is clear to me."

"I'm not going to let them cut him up."

"Quite right. Very wise! After all, he didn't die in the hospital."

"And if I did have a post-mortem done, so I'd know...?"

"It would just be unnecessary expense. The pathologists are up to their eyes in work, and you know, if...."

"A post-mortem isn't the standard procedure nowadays?"

"Well...not really. I don't insist on it. Most of the deceased's relatives refuse to have it."

"I don't want it, either."

She watched quietly as the doctor signed the papers and rubber stamped them.

"Here's the death certificate. Look after it. It's an important official document, you know. Wherever you go, you'll be asked to show it."

He handed it to her and remained standing there, as if he was expecting something.

"Thank you, Doctor. I know there are certain customs, but I haven't the means. I'm sorry."

He found it hard to hide his disappointment.

"Well...it's my duty. But I don't envy you. Funerals are expensive nowadays. Here, I'll leave three undertakers' business cards...call one of them.... They'll arrange the rest for you."

She went with him to the door. "Don't worry, I'm not senile yet."

* * *

She phoned the undertakers on the first business card and they arrived with a black coffin. The one who gave the orders was a skinny little man with glasses, the ones who carried it out were two burly fellows.

"You know, my husband...didn't wish to be buried in a coffin, just in a shroud, she explained with embarrassment when she handed the boss a new white sheet.

He was taken aback, but he said nothing. He asked in an icy voice, "Will you undress him yourself?"

"You'd better do it; after all, there are three of you. He would be too heavy for me. And – you're going to take him away naked?"

"We don't put people in the refrigerator in their clothes. The dead are dressed just before the funeral. Get some clothes ready for him!"

"I'm not going to show him to anyone," she said firmly. "I don't need a coffin either."

186

The head undertaker became irritable.

"We only transport the dead in this coffin. But...go to our office today to settle the details."

"I'll go, don't worry.... I won't have time tomorrow, anyway." She took a bottle of old brandy from the sideboard. "Can I pour you a glass?"

"Of course!" said one of the undertakers with a grin.

She poured out the drinks and put the bottle back in the sideboard.

"I know what is expected, although.... Well, drink to the memory of my Jozef. You'll be taking him to the crematorium, won't you?"

"Goodness me, no.... To the mortuary. But, lady, I advise you to have the funeral as soon as possible, because every day in the refrigerator costs something. Electricity has gone up terribly."

"I told you, I won't be having a funeral. And it's all the same to me when they cremate him."

"Well, that's your business, but stinginess won't get you very far, lady...." He was silent for a moment, hoping to get something out of her after all, then he muttered through his teeth, "Well, then...we'll be going."

She clenched her teeth, to hold back the tears.

"Then go...go."

* * *

A quarter of an hour later the telephone rang.

"Hello," she answered it as usual. "Yes, that's me. Oh, the police. The trouble is, they've just taken my husband away.... To the crematorium. Sorry? Ah, it's enough if I tell you the details on the death certificate over the phone. But what if I didn't tell you the truth?! What if I'm a forgetful old woman who mixes everything up? Don't laugh, I'm not joking. I'm glad you trust me. And I'm glad you're not coming in person. Thank you for the condolences. And now you can write this down: Jozef...."

She put on her glasses and picked up the death certificate.

No sooner had she answered the policeman's last question and replaced the receiver, when someone began ringing insistently at the door. She decided she wouldn't open it, but the ringing was followed by a loud knocking and a woman's shrill voice.

"Gizelka-a! Mrs. Gizelka! Open the door, you must be at home."

"Ruženka?" She opened the door the width of her foot. "I don't have time now."

"I was in the shop and I heard that your husband died in the night. Is it true?"

"I'm making the necessary arrangements. Good-bye, Ruženka."

"Will you tell me at least when the funeral will be?"

"I don't know anything yet," she brushed her off impatiently.

"Well, you don't look very sorrowful," Ruženka said with a smirk, obviously offended.

Gizelka slammed the door.

* * *

The woman on duty at the undertaker's welcomed her with a suitably reverent expression on her face. "Every death grieves us...," she began her general, obligatory introduction. Gizelka's reaction almost took her breath away.

"To the point, Miss...."

"...I'm the funeral director, if you don't mind...."

"As you wish."

The funeral director breathed in and continued as she always did, "So, we will arrange everything to your satisfaction, Madam, in a duly reverent and dignified manner. You can choose the funeral announcements from our catalogue. How you want the deceased arranged from this brochure. For the type of coffin there's this folder. By the way, do you want a burial or cremation? With us you can even select which gravedigger you would prefer..., here are their photographs.... Naturally, we will deal with all the necessary formalities as a matter of course; you don't have to worry about those. Ah, before I forget.... This is a catalogue of standard tombstones. The statues are designed by foremost artists and there are no more than a hundred of each type. You can have a photograph on the tombstone like this.... Or this.... Of course, we will provide both wreaths and flowers. Or we can rent them. In short, please sit down and have a quiet look through everything and choose what you want. The catalogues always have the latest prices. The services we offer really do cover everything."

Gizelka stared in disbelief at the pile of brochures, catalogues and offers in front of her. Then she came to her senses and said in a determined voice, "I'm sorry, Miss...what was it you wished to be called?... funeral director, but you must have misunderstood me.

"Your husband has died, hasn't he, and...."

"He has, and I wish to respect his last will and testament."

"Then that's all right. By the way, we also offer extra...special services, which aren't in the catalogue. You'll find them written there. At agreed prices. Well, Madam, I'm listening."

"My husband's wish was that his burial would cost no more than the state contribution to funerals."

The funeral director looked at her uncomprehendingly: "I beg your pardon?"

"According to my husband's last will, all the expenses connected with his death must not exceed the amount of the state contribution. That is what he wanted."

It was only now that the funeral director burst out, "You must be crazy!"

"Don't lose your temper, please. Last wills are sacred...!" Gizelka calmly pulled the will out of her handbag and handed it to the woman for her to read. She cautiously took the paper and read it with growing astonishment.

"So, you see for yourself. He writes there that if I don't keep to it, he'll come and haunt me."

It was only then that the woman realized what she was being asked to do and anger crept into her voice.

"But that just isn't possible!"

"Why not? Has anyone ever been left unburied in this country?"

"Naked.... Without a coffin.... Only in a winding sheet. And with no rites?!" the scandalized funeral director slowly shook her head. "Is this meant to be a joke?"

"For dust thou art, and unto dust shalt thou return," quoted Gizelka.

"Yes, but, after all...those left behind must treat their deceased in the most dignified manner possible!" the funeral director put on a grave, moralizing tone.

"And are you the one to decide the degree of that dignity?!"

"Dignity is a generally accepted custom!"

Gizelka stubbornly defended her position.

"He always lived as dignified a life as he was able to. His will is dignified, too. It is an expression of our times. And he will be buried in as dignified a manner as the state is able to take care of its old people in their hard lives, as well as after death."

The funeral director gave up.

"As you wish. I'm not going to argue with you. Here you have a duplicated order form for the cheapest funeral, Madam. Fill in the prescribed details and sign it. No one will bury him cheaper," she held out another form for Gizelka to take.

But Gizelka rejected this one, too.

"Look here, Miss...Miss Funeral Director, my husband's body is in the refrigerator, I have already said goodbye to him. You can look after his body, his spirit will stay with me. I'm not going to sign anything else for you."

The funeral director shouted, "But it will be a scandal! A terrible scandal! People will say nasty things about you!"

"I am fulfilling the last wish of a person I loved. The gossip won't last forever, and nor shall we. Good-bye," Gizelka said calmly from the doorway.

"Madam, come back, don't leave! Madam!" the unhappy funeral director called after her, but in vain.

* * *

Gizelka walked out of the building, quickened her pace and mingled with the other pedestrians. On the way, she bought the last few things she needed for her trip to Greece.

When she took her place in the plane three days later and fastened her seat belt, she pulled Jozef's framed photograph out of her bag and stood it on the table in front of her. She gazed at it fixedly with a look full of sad love. Then she smiled a hardly discernible smile, and it seemed to her that Jozef smiled, too.

VINCENT ŠIKULA

- prose writer, poet;
born in Dubová (1936)

Vincent Šikula worked as an editor in a publishing house and for some time as a film script editor. He has been president of the Slovak Writers Society.

In his first book of short stories he wrote about his experiences during military service (***Na koncertoch sa netlieska*** – *No Applause at Concerts*) and in his second book about the village where he was born (***Možno si postavím bungalov*** – *I May Build a Bungalow*), both dated 1964. In the short ballad-like novel **S Rozárkou** (*With Rozarka*, 1996) he unfolds the story of a mentally handicapped girl. The short story collection **Nebýva na každom vŕšku hostinec** (*There Isn't a Pub on Every Little Hill*, 1966) and **Pokušenie** (*Temptation*, 1968) are also about the values of people from his native region. In the trilogy of novels **Majstri** (*Masters*, 1976), **Muškát** (*Geranium*, 1977) and **Vilma** (1979) he portrays the lives of people from this region during the war and immediately following it (this is also the subject of the novella **Vlha** – *Golden Oriole*, 1978). He took authentic experiences from the time when he was making his livelihood as an organist as his theme for the prose work **Liesky** (*Hazelnuts*, 1980). Another book of short stories **Nokturná** (*Nocturne*, 1983) has a similar tone. The novella **Vojak** (*Soldier*, 1981) is a ballad-like story about a man disabled during the war. Next, he published a biographical historical novel **Matej** (1983) about Hrebenda, a distributor and promoter of books. With the short stories in **Pastierska kapsička** (*Shepherd's Purse*, 1990 – including "Babička" ("Grannie")), **Pôstný menuet** (*A Lenten Minuet*, 1994) and the novel **Ornament** (*Ornament*, 1991) he returned home and depicted the complex changes that had taken place in people. The same theme is to be found in the novel **Veterná ružica** (*Weathercock*, 1995). He has published three books of poems and written a number of books for children and young people (***Prázdniny so strýcom Rafaelom*** – *Holidays with Uncle Rafael*, 1966).

191

In his own words:

Everyone should have dreams. I believe in my dreams. After all, dreams are our yearnings, and everyone has those. Take any of our fairy tales, how many yearnings you can find in them! Americans offer our children their mushy supermen, who they have to invent and dress up as water sprites or spacemen. They have a long way to go before they can catch up with what our ancestors expressed in their yearnings long before them. Take one fairy tale after another, they are all dreams. And all of them realizable. Tall, Fat and Sharp-Eyed, The Three Lemons.... Sometimes I pity our children when they sit for hours in front of the television instead of opening Dobšinský's fairytales, dipping into the treasures that can awaken and develop the imagination, give feet seven-league boots, give the mind more beautiful flights of fancy, teach them to dream. People who don't know how to dream, who have no yearnings, can hardly be regarded as rich.

(1997)

Culture must not be, and has never been, forced into a rigid mold. Literature is not a narrow-gauge railway, even though it has almost always been prescribed a strict and relevant yardstick. But the yardstick has always been adhered to and if anyone ignores it, they usually don't last. Because the standard depends on the yardstick and whoever refuses to observe the limits of human understanding or patience, whoever lacks sufficiently clear ideas cannot determine the measure. If someone cannot tell the time, there is no point in talking to him about time. If someone doesn't know the limits of human understanding and patience, there's no point in talking to him about freedom and democracy. If someone doesn't know how to be open to the opinions of others, its a waste of time talking to him about an open society.

(1999)

GRANNIE

Before I started going to school, I spent most of my days with my grandmother.

Neither my parents nor my older brothers and sisters had any time for me, because they were busy working every day. We were the only two to stay at home; Grannie looked after me and I looked after Grannie. Whenever I wanted to go with my mother, they would even explain to me, "Someone must look after Grannie." But they always used to say the opposite to her and on several occasions I heard them say, "Who's going to keep an eye on the boy?!"

I spent whole days with her. She took me with her wherever she went. It's true, she didn't go far from home; she usually led me to the stream, threw a stone into the water and was satisfied she had found something to amuse me. She would sit a little way off and I happily threw little stones into the stream, then bigger and bigger ones, and when some young ducks came to swim there, I managed to hit one of them. Grannie noticed immediately. The duck squawked, Grannie looked around in alarm and shrieked at me, "You little rascal!" She slapped me two or three times on the bottom and dragged me away.

When it rained, we didn't go out of the house. I usually sat at the window with my nose pressed up against the pane. I gazed out into the yard and even tried to open the window to look out into the road, because the rain was making rings in the puddles, large ones and small ones, some of them wobbled, others bubbled and bounced off in little showers. I was curious to see what the ditches looked like, how the water was flowing, carrying more and more rings downstream. I was curious to know what it looked like where there was a lot of water, to see it bubbling along. It seemed to me that some of the rings were tinkling and ringing. When I pointed that out to Grannie, she told me that it wasn't the bubbles and rings that were making that sound, but real bells, because, she said, a little girl and a little boy had died.

"What happened to them?"

"They drowned," Grannie replied in a sleepy voice.

"How did they drown?" I wanted to know.

"The little boy didn't do as he was told. He kept throwing stones into the stream and he didn't keep an eye on the little girl. All of a sudden there was a splash – the girl had slipped into the water. The boy rushed to help her, stepped into the water after her and they were both drowned."

I sat at the window and thought about the little girl and the boy who had been throwing stones into the stream, as I had. I had thrown a stone at the duck and I don't even know how, I hadn't meant to, I had hit it, and his sister had fallen into the water while he was throwing stones.

I expected the funeral to go along the street, but a drenched man dashing along the little bit of road within view was all I saw. A cyclist, soaked to the skin. His head was bent over the handlebars, so the rain wouldn't beat in his face. He appeared and disappeared. Almost immediately he was followed by a cheerful accordion player, cheerfully playing his accordion, not bothering about the rain, on the contrary, even stretching his neck as if he were playing two accordions: one with his arms and the other with his neck, or as if his neck was an accordion, too. A woman was running along shouting something to him, but the accordion player didn't hear her.

When would the funeral pass by? What did a funeral look like anyway?

Grannie suddenly pulled at my leg. "You've opened that window again? What did I tell you?"

I wasn't allowed to do anything. Sit at the window, or even see how it rained into the water, or how a funeral went down the road. Even though it might have already passed by. But all I had seen of the whole funeral was a drenched cyclist and a cheerful accordion player.

The next day the weather cleared up and once again I was with Grannie. First she promised to show me Uncle Novák's threshing machine, which was a little way up the road from our cottage. She promised me that when she woke me up, but later she didn't want to go to Uncle Novák's with me. She said we had to go to church first. We argued all the way there. She wanted to go to church first and I wanted to go see Uncle Novák's threshing machine first. On the way she slapped me again and I dug my heels in: "I'm not going to the church and I don't want to see the threshing machine either."

She already had her prayer book with her, though. Her rosary, too, and when she began to search in her skirts, she even found a lump of sugar. But she didn't give it to me, because she noticed I had a dirty nose. She spat and said, "Ugh, you little pig, you're not getting anything!"

First she spat on the edge of her apron and then she began to pinch and rub my nose between her fingers, pulling the plugs of dried snot out of it. It was smaller in no time, it shrank, I hardly had any nose left, but she kept on chafing it with her apron and twisting it between her fingers, and my nose alone could serve as a really convincing witness to my suffering. She even sang at the same time:

Early in the morning, tomorrow, tomorrow,
we 'll march once more to Komárno, Komárno....

In church she was pious. Before we even went inside, she tried to persuade me to be well-behaved. So when after a while I began pulling at her sleeve and skirt, she kept scolding me, "If you don't behave yourself, we won't go to see the threshing machine!"

"Grannie, what's that stink in here?"

"There's no stink in the church. It always smells nice here."

"What smells nice, Grannie? Is there a toilet here?"

"There's no toilet here. The Lord God is here, be quiet! Be quiet, or I'll spank your bottom!"

"And where's the toilet? Grannie, I need to go to the toilet."

"You can't. You must hold it."

"Grannie, I can't hold it."

I kept looking around me. Suddenly, I ran over to the confessional. Grannie at my heels. She took me out of the church and spanked me the moment we reached the church steps, until I was howling for all the street to hear. Because I was in her charge, she couldn't go back into the church with me. She just threatened, "Since we haven't spent time in church, we won't go to see the thresher either."

Another flick at my nose.

Anyway, she had to take me to see the threshing machine, because I howled at the top of my voice.

As it was, I only saw the threshing machine from some distance. Just through the wooden fence. It stood there, painted a beautiful red, with well-oiled wheels of all sizes and beside it an even more beautiful steam engine to drive it.

Uncle Novák was sitting on a wooden stool just on the other side of the fence and he was rubbing rosin into the leather belts of the threshing machine.

Grannie whispered to me, "That's the machinist. Don't disturb him!"

* * *

On several occasions we went to the cemetery. We said a prayer beside the grave of the little girl and boy who had been drowned and from there we made our way to the statue of the Cross. I knew the way very well. I would have run on ahead, but my grandmother didn't let me. She always held my hand and I had to trot along beside her.

One day a new tombstone appeared in the cemetery and Grannie was in a good mood, because she was wearing a white scarf my father had bought her for her birthday the day before. She had a smile on her face as she led me between the mounds and crosses to the place she had been telling me about from the early morning. When we reached it, we both knelt down. Grannie crossed herself twice – once for herself and once for me. When we got to our feet, she looked at me, then at the inscription, the golden lettering, which glittered in the sunlight. She took out her glasses and put them on, to make the letters even larger.

"Can you see that?" she turned to me.

"Yes."

"And what can you see?"

"A tombstone."

"And what's on it? Tell me what's on it?!" she kept on asking, but my reply had no hope of satisfying her, because I could only see what she could see on the tombstone, and rather less, I suppose, because I couldn't read. She slipped her hands under my armpits and lifted me up. "Look, there's a picture!" she showed me a brown photograph on white porcelain. "Have a good look at it!"

In the photograph was a woman, an old woman. She was gazing out from under the porch roof of her scarf, with its decorative fringe. Her expression was rather stern, but her mouth, which may once have been slightly wavy, though now it just hung down at the corners, into which the wrinkles ran (the photographer had smoothed them out), alleviated this sternness. "That's you!" I exclaimed in surprise. "Who stuck you there?"

She smiled. Then she lifted up the edge of her apron, pulled a thin prayer book out of her skirt pocket and began reading a prayer from it.

For a while I tried to sort out in my head how it was possible for Grannie suddenly to be alive and dead at the same time, and how she had a tombstone in the cemetery even though she was still alive. I didn't rack my brains for long, though. Grannies were like that. They had their secrets, but sooner or later you found them out, because old people also had moments when they were very communicative.

I wandered off a little way and I peed on a grave. She caught sight of me, ran over, gripped my shoulder and shook me and whacked me on the head with her book. She said that demons fond of little boys with a tendency to mischief would crawl into me. Then she ordered me to pray a while, since she had to go off somewhere and she'd soon be back.

I gazed after her. She went over to the Cross, from where she hurried along a path sprinkled with yellow sand, leading to the funeral chapel. What could she want to do? Suddenly she turned off towards the fence. She halted under a chestnut tree and looked over the fence at the meadows, from which wafted the smell of mown hay. I was suddenly afraid she was trying to escape from me. I cried out and ran after her. But she hadn't wanted to escape. By the time I reached her, she had defecated on the grass and spread it out with her stick.

She tweaked my hair and said she would complain to my father that I had been a bad boy and hadn't done as I was told. We went home and again I wanted to run on ahead, but she wouldn't let go of my hand and she even refused to hurry. I was convinced that Grannie's one aim in life was to spoil my enjoyment.

When the mulberries began to ripen, she led me to the end of

196

the yard, sat down on a wooden stool and then she just poked with her stick at the fallen fruit: "Here's one, and here's another."

I had soon eaten my fill and I wanted to run off, but Grannie didn't feel like walking and I wasn't allowed out in the street without her. When I began to bother her too much, she pulled a piece of rope out from under her skirt and she tied one end around my foot and held the other in her hand.

It wasn't long before she began to drop off. At that moment I jerked my foot and it must have hurt her hand. She jumped up and went and tied me to a tree stump. She doubled the rope and made a tight knot, knowing that I would undo a bow, but that I couldn't manage a knot. Once more she sat down, convinced that she could happily doze, but she had hardly closed her eyes when I dug a little stone out of the ground and threw it at her. She got up and spanked my bottom.

When she had fallen asleep once more, I made a hole under the tree, scooping out the soil with my fingers and blowing the dust away, and then I peed in it. Of course, this amusement didn't last long. The hole was soon empty and I no longer wanted to pee. Feeling thoroughly fed up, I looked first at Grannie and then around me. There was nothing within reach to interest me. The ground was purple and stank of mulberries, which made me feel sick. Next to the fence, too far away for the rope to reach, several beer-bottle tops glittered in the sun, for there was a bar next door. The air was hot. When it gets that hot, scorpions come crawling out of the ground, large rust-colored beetles that can fly and have a sting that can kill you. Sometimes a grass snake goes slithering by; its mouth has yellow corners. The largest number of scorpions are to be found near the stream and behind the forge, where the soil is powdery and yellow. The blacksmith has a worn leather apron and red hair, and although he himself looks a bit like a scorpion, he often kills them. He usually does it by going outside with a thin, red-hot rod, peering into their little holes, and when a head appears, he thrusts it in and there is a sizzling sound. Several times I wanted to go and have a look, but I was scared, scared of the insects and of the blacksmith, too.

"Matko, what's Grannie doing?" a voice spoke up from the other side of the fence. I turned to look, wanting to know who had spoken to me, but I couldn't see anything, because the cracks between the planks were very narrow.

Very soon, however, a shaven head appeared over the fence with sticking-out ears and a pointed nose, a very comical, but affable face, affable mainly because it belonged to a boy I knew. His name was Vojtech.

Grannie once had something she had to do and she couldn't be at home, so she had asked this boy to keep an eye on me. We had had a wonderful time and Vojtech promised he would pop in to see me sometime. Maybe he had just remembered and that was why he had come.

"Matko, what's Grannie doing?" he asked again.

"She's asleep."

Another head appeared over the fence, a freckled face I didn't recognize.

"Can't she hear us?" he inquired.

"No, she can't. She's deaf."

"She's deaf," Vojtech confirmed. He jumped over the fence into the yard, followed by the freckled boy. They noticed that I was tied up, so they bent down to free me. I would have let out a whoop of joy, but they gestured that I must be quiet. I wanted to be sure that I would stay free, so I wound the rope around Grannie's boot and the boys tied it with a firm knot.

They climbed up into the mulberry tree. I would have liked to follow them, but the trunk was thick and tall, and I was also a bit afraid that I would feel dizzy up there. I wandered over to the fence and collected the beer-bottle tops.

When the boys had scrambled down the tree, I joined them again. The freckled boy stuffed me with mulberries and then he wanted to shake me off.

"Matko, you can't go with us. We're going to mind the cattle," he said, but I pretended I hadn't heard him.

We went down the yard and when we got to the gate secured with a heavy stone, so I couldn't escape from Grannie, the boys pushed the stone away and let me out in front of them.

However, after a while Freckles began again: "Matko, be sensible! You can't go with us."

"Where are you going to mind the cattle?" I asked, but he didn't give me an answer.

Vojtech thrust his hand in his pocket and pulled out I guess about four marrow seeds and pressed them into my palm.

Freckles looked at me and said, "Now beat it!"

They moved away, but after a few steps they had to stop again, because I was plodding after them.

Freckles shook his finger at me. Vojtech came up to me, turned both his pants pockets inside out, found one more seed and gave it to me.

"I don't have any more," he said. He stroked my head and left me. He didn't bother about me any more.

I wandered through the streets until evening came. When I got home, my father was already there. He was standing under the mulberry tree beside Grannie, who was still sitting there motionless. He bent down over her, in fact he knelt down on one knee, since he couldn't undo the thick string, because the knot had been tied so tight. When he caught sight of me, he wrung his hands, but he didn't say anything. Then he carefully picked Grannie up in his arms and carried her into her room.

I was scared. My father told me that I should have kept an eye on her.

The funeral was two days later. We buried her in the cemetery, where she already had a tombstone.

We buried her. But I didn't. Although it was I who had been with her most often to the cemetery. She hit me with a stick there on several occasions.

I was angry with my parents and my older brothers and sisters, because they didn't take me to the funeral. They said I was too little.

I had looked after her and they didn't take me to the funeral. I cried from early morning because of that.

Once more I was sitting at the window, with my nose pressed up against the window pane.

It was raining. It really was raining. As if the rain was a portent of things to come, a reason for deeper thought than a little boy was yet capable of.

I waited at the window in vain, gazing into the street, but there was nothing to see, it just rained and rained, more and more rings collected in the puddles, splashing, bubbling and spitting irresponsibly in the water. Rain dripped off the wooden gables of the house. When would the procession pass by at last? When would the funeral pass by?

Then suddenly – aha, there it is! I told myself. The oxen trundled on in front, pulling the red threshing machine, which looked like a wide coffin with lots of little coffins with belts, pulleys and wheels stuck on it. Once more I heard those bells and the brass band music playing a mournful march.

Two days later the weather cleared up. It was harvest time. They were bringing the sheaves of hay from the fields and Uncle Novák took the threshing machine from one yard to the next, oiling all the wheels again and again and wiping rosin on the pulleys and belts.

For a long time I thought that when someone dies, they are carried to the cemetery on a threshing machine.

VIERA ŠVENKOVÁ
- *prose writer, translator;*
born in Poprad (1937)

Viera Švenková worked as an editor for literary magazines (*Slovenské pohľady* – *Slovak Perspectives, Revue svetovej literatúry* – *Review of World Literature*) and publishing houses (Mladé letá, Smena).

The dominant feature of her work concerns the emotional, social and ethical problems of contemporary women. Her debut in 1973 was a collection of short stories, **Biela pani Zuzana** (*White Lady Susan*). In her novel **Limbový háj** (*The Grove of Swiss Pines*, 1974) she pictures the quiet heroism of women during the war and the Slovak National Uprising. In the novella **Zátišie s gitarou** (*Still Life with Guitar*, 1977) she uses the love relationship between two students to show a loss of illusions and an attempt to overcome this through emotional relations supported by restraint in thought and behavior. The collections of stories **Malý herbár** (*A Small Book of Herbs*, 1979) and **Jablčné jadierka** (*Appleseeds*, 1987) are sentimental feminine views of the emotional and moral crisis women face, arising from unfulfilled expectations and desires. Her latest book of short stories, **Faraónov úsmev** (*Pharaoh's Smile*, 1999), shows resistance to the emptiness of life and the difficult endeavor to find its inner equilibrium in an over-technical, dehumanized world.

She translates from a number of languages, especially works for children and young people.

In her own words:
The fact that humans are beings capable of culture is a reason for some optimism (although it is jokingly said that an optimist is really a misinformed pessimist). Culture is a way of looking at the world. Sometimes clear-sightedly, at other times blindly. Culture has chosen good as the ideal goal of human history – Saint Augustine spoke

about God's empire, Dominik Tatarka about God's community. In modern times the emphasis has been on the notion of the growing liberation of human beings, the empire of freedom. The result has been rather unexpected – many intelligent people are now talking about the supremacy of evil, the work of the devil. It is clear that, in spite of all our science, and high level of civilization and culture, there are still many things people have not mastered. Many philosophers, however, see clear-sightedly and are warning us in good time.

Many people nowadays find life difficult, for example the unemployed…. But even in their difficult situation they keep to the moral norms, to Slovak traditions, in which preference is given to fortitude and honest work, combined with prayer.

The broad paths of evil and crime attract many, but where do they lead? Good has a better chance of survival, because it can be destroyed only by outside intervention, whereas evil carries within it the seeds of self-destruction. In life we should be guided by the biblical: Do not hate evil, love good! First of all, however, we must learn to recognize evil. A modern philosopher claimed that knowledge is power. If there is enough knowledge and goodness in society, maybe many people will understand that their strength does not lie in money, but that there is something far more powerful in the world and in the universe.

(1997)

PHARAOH'S SMILE

"He who has no traditions and would like to have them,
is like an unrequited lover"

LUDWIG WITTGENSTEIN

He emerged from the pyramid full of energy, his step was light and his head felt airy. A devilish invention, he thought to himself, you lie down in a pyramid, listen to esoteric music and when you get up you feel as if you have been reborn. It's just what you need; if only he had more time and money, he would go there more often.

He turned into a side street, where a bored, pretty salesgirl was wasting her youth in an out-of-the-way stationer's, and boredom, as everyone knows, makes one prone to sin. At that time of day there were usually no customers, but on this occasion a nun was bending over the counter, scrutinizing some paints, as if they were precious jewels and she was asking questions of the bored beauty, who only shrugged her shoulders, unable to help. Matej joined in the conversation, added some good advice, the nun thanked him feelingly, and when her grey eyes rested on him, he recognized her at once, as she evidently did him.

"We met at the college, didn't we?" she smiled.

At the college, he nodded, feeling embarrassed. That was already thirty years ago. As a young assistant lecturer he had taught her, and, knowing him, he had no doubt tried to seduce her. Only he had quickly lost sight of her.

"You weren't there for long," he now recollected.

"I very soon discovered that I wasn't up to it."

"On the contrary, you were very good."

"I'll never make an artist, but I'd like to try it again, painting just for the fun of it, for myself," she dropped her gaze, as if she had admitted to a sin.

She hastily pushed her purchases into her bag and it was clear that any second now she would walk out of the shop and disappear. He tried to detain her by inviting her for coffee – she excused herself, saying she had to catch her bus and she strode off at a brisk pace that said she would not stay. Her skirt swirled around ankles firmly laced in by high-cut shoes, her black habit masking any hint of physical attractiveness.

He entered the nearest bar, where a few solitary, dozing men were sitting along the walls, making it clear they were not interested in company; talking was pointless, words a waste of time. He had noticed with surprise that recently it was as quiet in the bars as it was in church, as if not even alcohol had the power to bring people together, everyone sat looking wretched, buried in his own thoughts, but it suited him not having to talk about himself or apologize for being alive. He exchanged for beer the few coins he had left after his visit to the pyramid. A devilish invention, he said to himself, lying in a pyramid in the position gentle female hands put you in, is one of the few chances you get to pay for the gentle touch of an agreeable young woman. He had lain with a relaxed mind and listened to esoteric music, and when he had awakened from his doze, a song about a meadow in a deep valley was echoing in his ears. What a devilish invention, he pondered in amazement, it didn't evoke thoughts about ancient Egyptian wisdom, about the mysteries which Plato was said to have understood, but it called up his grandfather's favorite song, "I have a meadow in a deep valley...," a long-forgotten song, which he had not heard since his childhood. A hellish invention, a good way of wheedling money out of fools; I'd have done better to spend it on a better drink; a good cognac can give you a light step, too, while after cheap beer you feel sluggish, your legs are heavy, your tongue's unwieldy and your mind apathetic.

Not even his stay in the pyramid had roused him from his apathy. Everything got on his nerves, especially the movement of time, the eternal undulation, soaring high in the afternoon sky and plunging deep into the black abyss of the night, while Matej lay dead drunk from the cheapest beer, stretched out like a log, like the most direct connecting line between yesterday and tomorrow, like an obstacle which time ignores and easily steps over. The nun, who always brings bad luck, as a chimney sweep does good fortune, had taken him back into the past, to the times when he was an assistant lecturer at the college, with women fluttering around him and exposed to seduction. These future teachers of art had a gift for sophisticated visual perceptions, for color, for folds, belts around slim waists, flowing scarves in their hair. It was enough to drive you crazy, absolute hell. Then, suddenly a disarmingly simple girl appears out of the blue, with unforgettable eyes, bright irises set in the clear whites of her eyes, a fine curtain of eyelashes, a high forehead with blue veins at the temples, a few light-colored curls. The face of a madonna, which he never managed to paint to his satisfaction. Now it was a different face, time had left its mark as a tiny fan of wrinkles, but it was still interesting, perhaps a little less kitschy than in her youth. A nun – ridiculous. Can you suppress your physical attractions, and if so, to what extent?

An offer from the Forestry Commission dragged him out of his lethargy. It invited him to join them in an effort to eliminate the consequences of the summer gale; they needed every helping hand since the widespread destruction caused by the wind had to be cleared before winter set in. He was glad of the opportunity to do some physical work. At one time, when it was no problem for him to sell his pictures, in one of those fits of strange behavior Viera had never been able to understand, he had bought a little tractor and, thanks to that, he was now able to make a little extra on the side when his painting wasn't going well, and, more importantly, he could bring back to his yard a couple of healthy logs, interesting pieces of gnarled wood or unusually shaped tree stumps. The timber company let him have them free of charge – as their contribution to a representative of local culture.

When he was at the university there were as many women around him as these wind-felled trees reminiscent of scattered matches and yet he had chosen Viera, a level-headed, practical teacher, who had managed to convince him that if he wished to paint, he had to go back to the place where he was born –

nowhere in the world was more beautiful than this provincial valley, the smallest range of high mountains in Europe, the house he had inherited, where there was enough room for a large studio with a comfortable couch, on which you could lie so pleasantly with a bottle of beer at hand and half-finished pictures along the wall, which, at least according to Viera's for the most part exact estimation, he would clearly never finish.

On days when he didn't have the strength to drive his tractor, he set out on a hike. The autumn forest was ablaze as if gripped by fire, the wind whirled yellow and red leaves in all directions, stirring up inner unrest. Matej was glad when he got above the tree line. As he climbed up the rocky path he avoided meeting the gaze of solitary tourists, whom he kept coming across wherever he went. He never ceased to wonder where so many loners came from. They filled the bars, roamed over the hills, sailed across the seas. He remembered once staying beside the sea, where he would sit painting on a high hill and watch in amazement as solitary swimmers crossed the bay far from the shore, as if deliberately looking for danger, for an untimely death. The mountains are treacherous, injury lies in wait at every step, you can be surprised by a sudden change in the weather, an unfortunate mischance, it is enough to slip on a smooth stone or damp moss above a steep precipice. Yet people really get a kick out of the risks they take, they keep tempting fate, maybe even with a feeling of heroism, as if they were consciously seeking the least painful means of suicide.

It wasn't the blazing forest, dry and lit up by the sun that he would sketch; he was attracted by the shadowy ravines, the marshy twilight. He didn't emerge from his studio for several days, he could see before him fallen trunks like the remains of mammoths or ancient lizards, ominously glimmering moldering trees, crumbling branches like wriggling slippery snakes, the roots of torn-up tree stumps sticking up in the chilly sky like gnarled fingers begging to be rescued. Mire and helplessness, that was what man had made of this Earth created by God. He suddenly remembered his grandfather, who even in the dark forest had felt as if he were in a church and had taken off his hat and clasped his hands when the light had penetrated through the high branches, the slanting rays piercing the darkness as if through high church windows. On the way home he had taught his grandchildren the song, "I have a little meadow in a deep valley, in it the grass, the clover, will never die."

Matej escaped from the house, but he no longer enjoyed sitting beside the window of a coffee bar delighting in the charms of the local beauties strolling past. I'm going crazy, he thought to himself. What the hell's happening to me? Has that nun fixed me with the evil eye? Her pious face rose before his eyes, her milky complexion protected from the sun, snake-like eyes with tiny pupils, their shy yet beseeching expression, somewhat provocative and yet distant, impenetrable, unattainable. On the outside a sweet face hiding a secret. How many such madonnas had artists already painted and who knows what imaginings and desires they put into them. Can there ever exist an innocence that has no idea what hell we carry within us or how dangerous it is to believe that hell is to be found only in others?

He roamed the windy streets, as if he wished to discover whether anyone would greet him any more or at least return his greeting. He was glad when an editor from the local newspaper patted him on his shoulder. In a hunter's outfit, with a tuft of chamois fur in his hat, he looked like the devil out of a folk opera. They entered the nearest bistro, had a drink and in the end bought a bottle of gin as tradition demanded and took themselves off to his studio.

"You're going down in the world, you really are," the editor commented when he looked around. "There used to be more bottles than pictures, and now?" he said, gazing scornfully at the beer bottles beside the sofa, "what kind of a show is that? All you can smell is acetone. At least this gin reminds you of the fragrance of the forest!" They emptied the bottle and Viera went around looking offended for several days: Matej was drinking again, even though he wasn't bringing a penny into the household. Her sharp, teacher-trained voice took on an unpleasant, accusing tone, which drove him out of the house.

The forest had already lost its color, the pine needles and grass were covered with a silvery frost, the paths were icy. Matej strode along at a brisk pace, breathing deeply, smelling the air, wanting to fill his lungs with it to invigorate his brain, clear his mind. Involuntarily his thoughts turned to his grandfather, how on a Sunday he would take the children out to the fields to see whether the wheat was ripe. He would pluck a few ears, crush them in his palm, judging whether the grain was still sticky, milky, or whether it was drying and it was time to sharpen the scythes. Finally, he would sit down quietly at the edge of the field and gaze in front of him, as if unaware of the world around him. "I was conversing with the Lord," he would say when he got to his feet. "Sometimes you have to examine your conscience, right here, in God's countryside, in this most beautiful of churches, before the altar of those azure peaks." On the way back from the fields he stopped in the bar, treated himself to a couple of Sunday drinks and returned home singing, "I have a little meadow in

205

a deep valley, there the grass, the clover will never d...die... hic...."

Matej sat on the hillside and gazed at the dark wall of forest beneath him, motionless in the windless air. The stillness of the trees was not a good omen; it was as if the forest were holding its breath in foreboding. The overcast sky lost its depth, its infinite distance, the trees vainly stretched out for nourishment, for light; in the awesome silence before the storm the only sign of life was the cawing of the crows.

He returned to his studio and pulled out a picture he had started much earlier. Sad lines sketching rolling hills in a gloomy night landscape, lit up by a sickly moon. He turned the picture upside down, the dark hills now hung downwards like heavy curtains, the closed space beneath them included some figures, maybe actors, or rather dancers from a night club, vague figures of women he had once known. They wandered aimlessly across the stage as if half-gassed by poisonous vapor from the marshes at night, which glimmered on the picture alongside them, a dim forest full of uprooted trees, perhaps the product of a sick dream. Or not a stage, but just a wartime shelter, half-darkness, mournful figures, deep shadows. Shadows harm most faces, inscribing in them an augury of extinction, but some they accent, lending depth, spirituality, remoteness. Black robes and a white complexion, in the foreground a beautiful face almost without shadows, arching eyebrows, deep eyes, though at that moment cast down, no shadow could spoil her perfect beauty; in her black hair a yellow rose, for a human hell yellow and bluish shades suffice, they capture our evil instincts perfectly, our vain desire for something time and distance has made unattainable. It looked like a wartime picture, all the men in the world had already been shot dead, they lay in the battlefields, struck down like trees in a gale and here the last seven women were wasting away from sorrow and grief.

A room of sad women, he called the picture to himself. Now all you had to do was wait for them to begin murdering each other.

"I don't want that picture in the flat," said Viera. "It emanates evil."

Recently Matej's works had been driving her to despair. Nobody would buy a picture like that, she claimed, it wouldn't mean anything to anyone, they couldn't possibly understand it. The imploring expression in her eyes said, and the family has nothing to live on.

"I just don't understand you, Matej. What is it you want?"

"Nothing really – or nothing very much."

"And what's that?"

"Inspiration. I'd welcome something.... Let's say a contract with the devil," he joked.

Horrified, she crossed herself.

"You should go to church more often."

He turned the paintings to face the wall. There was no reason to show them to anyone, they were here, they got in the way, there were more and more of them all the time. Unfinished sketches, rough outlines, ruined canvases. With each attempt Matej seemed to sink deeper into seclusion. Very soon the studio would be crowded with unusable, unsellable pictures, among which he would live like a hermit, like a madman.

He couldn't sit around at home any longer. Viera was right, he should go to church more often. In spite of the unsettled weather, he set out on long walks, he roamed through the forest, but he couldn't discover in himself his grandfather's religious feeling for nature, he couldn't bring himself to sit down on a rock and converse with God, face to face, as people with clear consciences used to do. He felt exhausted, partly because the weather changed three times a day, frequent showers alternated with the first snowfalls, and at least three times a day his mood changed too, from the feeling that good – that idea Plato called god – still existed, to the doubt which said that God remained concealed and that the autumn countryside, in which everything decays and turns to dung, was rather proof of the futility of human existence, his own included.

Frozen and tired after his walk, he waited at the bus stop and when he boarded the bus, he caught sight of the nun. They greeted each other, he sat down next to her and nervously showered her with questions about where she had been and where she was going.

"I have a friend in the children's sanatorium. I've been to visit her," she explained.

Involuntarily, he pressed up to her and through the material of her clothes he felt her round female shoulder. "Why did you leave college?" he asked, and when the bus tilted as they turned a bend, he sensed a hint of the outline of her hips and thighs, the bodily warmth of a living person. "Why did you leave?"

"I left of my own accord," she said. "You know how it was, teachers were expected to be atheists. Although she drew back, he couldn't shake off the impression that she had noticed he had touched her, even pressed up to her. She turned abruptly towards the window. "I left to go into a children's home, I helped to look after afflicted children, I found my place."

She stared through the window. The cloud that had suffocated the peaks all day unexpectedly broke up and from beneath it emerged the dark grey rocks dotted with patches of snow like a leopard skin.

"Only now, not long ago, my dream came true," she continued. "I have been allowed to enter the order. At last...." She breathed in, as if something constricted her; maybe nuns really did bind their chests to conceal the sinful outline of their breasts beneath their habits. "At last I am living as I always wanted to."

"Congratulations," he said drily. They were nearing the town. The sky was turning pink in the west, the sun hung low on the horizon, coloring the fantastic shapes of the clouds a fiery red.

They said goodbye at the bus station. The devil has put a curse on me, he said to himself, when he gazed after her. I should at least have asked her to pray for me. He wondered whether to go and see the salesgirl in the stationer's; this beauty behind the counter had always nodded understandingly when he complained that a painter in a small town couldn't choose his models, or even his muse. Damn it, I intended to go to church and instead of that, here I am running after girls; it looks as if the devil upsets all my good intentions. He abandoned the idea of the stationer's and went straight home.

The date of the exhibition was approaching, he needed to concentrate. He spread the fruits of his summer harvest around the studio; his pictures were all flowers – crazy, shameless shapes in fleshy colors, petals curling into each other, suggesting mystery, provocative blooms open wide, deliberately hinting at a similarity to human genitals. He had veiled nothing, it was a glorification of lasciviousness, a sensuous profusion of colors and scents, a conjectured movement of light and a hinted touch of the breeze which flowers expose themselves to, instinctively sensing that this will fulfil their wish and carry off the heavy seeds to fertile soil. Lovers of the Wind – at last he had the right name for the cycle.

"Brilliant," the editor slapped his knees, expressing his satisfaction with the paintings, and especially with himself, for having a nose for artists.

"Of course, you're not implying anything, you're just picturing the innocence of nature, hm, hm...."

"The flower is really the sexual organ of the plant," Matej defended himself.

"Brilliant. Of course, you're not implying anything; you're just an ordinary teacher of drawing and an honest woodcutter. Look at this, look at this!"

Viera outdid herself, bringing a tray laden with refreshments. She produced a bottle of the best whiskey she kept hidden for special visitors. She very much wanted the local paper to present her husband and the coming exhibition in the best light. Look at that, the editor enthused. I take my hat off – what a pity people don't wear hats nowadays and there's no one to bow to you. Artists are like spoiled young ladies, they need to be admired, but fortunately I do have a hat, he said, spinning his little hunting hat with its tuft of chamois fur on his finger. "I take my hat off to you, maestro!"

Viera looked happier. These pictures had at least some hope of being sold. The fact that Matej stayed at home adding finishing touches, completing and spoiling his paintings, had a calming effect on her. At night he turned to her more often than usual, as if he wished to defeat the demons inside him; her body, thanks to many years of habit, became malleable plasticine, adapting itself to her partner's needs.

The preparations for the exhibition required discipline, but he, as always when under great pressure, sought escape elsewhere. He dragged a broad tree trunk under the eaves of the roof and began to chop away at it. He worked as if he were obsessed, swinging his axe as if possessed by the devil himself. He chopped away without stopping, and when the figure of a man began to emerge, he asked himself – was it his grandfather sitting at the edge of a field, or a homely thinker, bent from mental effort, bearing on his shoulders the burden of the world, or someone else as yet unnamed? The frosty breeze carried the ringing blow; every kind of wood gives out a different sound when struck, a hollow groan, as if man was disturbing its dignified peace. Gradually the inner knots, bumps, wavy contours are revealed, materialized time confined between two lines, which people like to think is their space for freedom.

Matej's mind was in turmoil. To hell with it, what freedom? Surely only the freedom to mature towards death after a wasted life. Undistorted people may have had a right to freedom back in times when they knew how to converse with the starry sky above their heads, like the idealist Plato, whom rulers feared, or Matej's grandfather, who, though he did not like going to church, spoke with sincerity of God's kingdom on earth and in one's soul. Matej had been free then, too – the only time in his life – he had skipped along the path at his grandfather's side, free of care, imagining that the whole world was there just for him, that all paths, all towns, all parts of the world were just waiting for him.

He ran his fingers over the tree stump as if he were reading Braille, following the year rings, that ever legible record of time; he was aware of the living wood, which resisted taking on another's likeness, the picture of human ignorance, broken and soulless, emptied, in which at moments there is nothing but despair.

A tree does not deserve such humiliation. This stump was far from the physical distortion of the thinker; it called out for a return to the old Greek ideal. Or would some incomprehensible Egyptian hieroglyph emerge from it?

When the stump began to look like a man sitting, the neighbor's boys stopped by.

"What's it going to be?"

"An Egyptian pharaoh," he replied without hesitation.

"A pharaoh? That king who built pyramids?" the oldest boy asked.

"That's the one," Matej agreed.

Perhaps it will be no more than a memory of dignity, he told himself, of those who knew how to live and die in a dignified manner, like Plato, who some called the Greek pharaoh, like Socrates with his goblet of poison, like my grandfather, reconciled to departing forever, like that village woman who was bitten by a snake and sat on the church wall waiting for death. As usual at harvest time, the village had been deserted. Only children came to look at the unfortunate raspberry gatherer; they watched as her foot swelled up around the tiny wound, turned black, first spreading over her veiny calf, then her knee and finally her whole thigh. The woman sat motionless, tears flowing from her eyes, until they laid her on a wagon and carried her away. He had been lucky in his childhood. He had seen people who knew how to live with dignity and humbly meet their deaths. That did not apply to the figure that was emerging from the wood – pharaohs will rule even after their deaths.

Viera needed his help. She directed him in her strict teacher's voice: you must arrange the invitations, get the wine, I can't do it all by myself. Once more it was clear how dependent on her he was. He carried out her orders without objecting: you should include a few of the pictures that are collecting dust in the storeroom. They're quite good landscapes from the time when you used to paint the Tatra wildlife, the tarns and peaks, such things always sell well. She made no effort to hide how desperately she needed the money.

Quite a lot of people gathered for the opening of the exhibition. A small town welcomes every opportunity for a social gathering. The editor's introductory speech was heard, a complimentary review, which appeared a week later in the local newspaper, some schoolchildren sang a couple of folk songs and then the audience relaxed and pounced upon the drinks and sandwiches. Matej received congratulations, the girl from the stationer's hugged him, it looked like a promise, the nun bestowed on him an admiring glance, the Lord created a wonderful world, but we seem to be blind, sometimes we just don't see this beauty; the editor patted him on the back, I must congratulate you, pal, let's congratulate ourselves, after all, we're friends! Although, I'll be frank with you, there's something a bit obscene about them, but what else can we old-timers do but throw ourselves into pornography or politics, huh? The pictures are all right, but the wine could be better; he turned his nose up at his glass; come on, I'll invite you to a bar near here, we'll have something a wee bit stronger. They retreated to a crowded night bar, where the loud music and drunken chatter made it impossible to hear their own voices. "Here you're suspicious if you don't drink," the editor warned everyone. They sipped their drinks and, arms around each other, they sang, "I have a little meadow in a deep valley, I have a straight, sharp scythe which mows, 'cause it must, the little clover." "Listen here, Matej, what's that straight scythe meant to be? Isn't it a sexual reference?" I tell you, you can find everything in our traditions. Everything! Dammit, there's nothing they don't have!"

"Nothing at all," nodded Matej.

"And how much...how much of that is hidden in it!"

"You're right there...of that."

"Some...some wise man once said that a man without traditions is like an unrequited lover. That's not true of us! We have everything! Pretty songs, pretty girls! We've got it all, we really have!"

"An unrequited lover?" Matej repeated in surprise. "There's no such thing. He died out long ago!" The longer he sat there, the better he felt. "I've done enough running around, I've been chasing around like mad the whole autumn; like a dog following a bus, I didn't know what I was looking for, and in fact all you need is to relax at last and sing that song of ours, *Dance, dance, tralala....*"

"Tralala, we've got it all! Long live tradition!" the editor raised his glass, "May it live and flourish...that.... Let it all flourish," he waved an arm.

"May the thick pine wood grow and become strong," Matej declared euphorically.

They felt like singing and others joined in. They bellowed at the top of their voices, until the bar echoed, tralala, our grass, our clover will never die, never, ne...hic...hic....

They returned home just before dawn. On the snow-covered lawn under the windows there sat a familiar figure. The snowman was an exact copy of Matej's pharaoh. He had a battered saucepan on his proudly-held head and teeth of black coals under his carrot nose. In his lap, on his long, elegant thighs were two enormous balls and a huge erect member. Matej gasped in astonishment, dammit, those snotty kids from next door, they did enjoy making fun of you! But brilliantly! Brilliantly! The snowman bared his black teeth at him in a good-natured smile and Matej suddenly burst into relaxed, crazy laughter.

LADISLAV ŤAŽKÝ

- prose writer, journalist, script writer, playwright;
born in Čierny Balog (1924)

Ladislav Ťažký worked for various organizations, but he devoted most of his time to writing.

His first two books were collections of short stories, **Vojenský zbeh** (*The Deserter*, 1962) and **Hosť majstra Čerta** (*A Guest of Master Devil*, 1962), on themes taken from his birthplace. He made use of his experiences during the war in a short novel **Dunajské hroby** (*Danubian Graves*) and in the novel **Amenmária** (both 1964), which has a sequel entitled **Evanjelium čatára Matúša** (*The Gospel According to Sergeant Matthew*, 1977). He also presents the war in the novella **Pochoval som ho nahého** (*I Buried Him Naked*, 1970) and in the play **Hriešnica žaluje tmu** (*A Sinful Woman Curses the Darkness*, 1966). The theme of **Pivnica plná vlkov** (*A Cellar Full of Wolves*, 1969) is the forcible conversion of private farms into co-operatives. Women are the subject of a small book of short stories, **Márie a Magdalény** (*Mary and the Magdelenes*, 1983). Human humility is portrayed in the novel **Aj v nebi je lúka** (*There's a Meadow in Heaven, Too*, 1985). When writing his novel **Pred potopou** (*Before the Flood*) he used his experience in connection with the building of the Gabčíkovo dam. The short novel **Smrť obchádza štadióny** (*Death Hangs Around the Stadiums*, 1990) he talks about violence in sport. The novel **Kto zabil Ábela?** (*Who Killed Abel?*, 1991) is about responsibility and guilt. The lot of Slovak emigrants provides the subject for the works **Fantastická Faidra** (*Fantastic Faidra*, 1991), **Dvanásť zlatých monarchov** (*Twelve Golden Monarchs*, 1992), **Maršalova dcéra** (*The Marshal's Daughter*, 1993) and **Zjavenie Sabíny** (*The Appearance of Sabina*, 1997). The novel **Útek z Neresnice** (*Escape from Neresnica*, 1999) is about a person's struggle with himself. He writes articles for the press and contributions for the radio (including the short story "Dar na rozlúčku" – "A Parting Gift").

In his own words:

As we all know, no one can escape his own conscience. There is no place where he can hide from it. It is simply impossible to live without a conscience.

Those of us of the older generation who are still alive lived through with our friends and relatives now dead – and are still living through – very serious times. Over each of us hangs the sword of hate, war, the destruction of the individual, of nations and, with no exaggeration, even the destruction of humankind. There is not a day, maybe even an hour, when I am not aware of this *memento mori*, when I don't see, hear or feel in what kind of age, in what kind of world, continent or country I live and to which nation I belong.

My conscience tells me I should not only be a human being, a brother to all people, but also a Slovak, as well as a Slav, which is nowadays a very old-fashioned, historical, patriotic and an almost ridiculed as well as feared category. But I am also a member of human society, which I care for as much as for my nation. I think about what contribution our little Slovak nation should and could make to Europe in the way of usefulness, beauty and delight. My conscience tells me to lay down at least certain moral, social, political, cultural, literary, as well as journalistic principles; not to forget one's family, nation and country at the same time is not easy. With the full responsibility of a citizen, but nevertheless also with the playfulness of a writer, I have more than once tried to work out for myself a basic law, a kind of "Constitution of the Conscience," which would help me to be a useful person, a Slovak, a writer and journalist and in the worst or extreme cases even a politician. I discovered that it is impossible to complete the Constitution of My Conscience, that I shall write it with my life and deeds until my last breath.

(1994)

A PARTING GIFT

It happened a few months before the departure of the occupying forces, that is in the year of our Lord 1990, at the end of May in the central Slovakian town of R. My friend and film script editor, or rather hunter of stories for films, had enticed me to accompany him on a trip around Slovakia. The stories, the themes for films, were to have their roots in the most topical, most burning questions that gave rise to conflicts in lives lived to the full, but they were not to omit the poetry to be found in people's lives, in nature and in the post-revolutionary upsurge of energy and the prospects offered by our easily-won freedom. We spent our time traveling and observing people, but above all in endless discussions about the contemporary political ferment, assessing and criticizing politicians. Whenever we spent a night in this town, we went for a beer or two to a little bar, but if the sun was shining, we preferred to sit on the small terrace with its red and yellow garden chairs and watch life pulsating in the street below. We were sitting like this on that occasion. My friend, an incorrigible smoker, was blowing smoke under my nose, so I turned away and let my gaze fall on the wooded hills which surround this little industrial town. My friend smiled, he was watching a dirty, unshaven tramp who was stopping passers-by and asking them for something. Judging by the gesture he was making with his right hand, it was clear that he was asking them for a cigarette. He was not in luck. Those passing either didn't smoke or didn't want to get involved in a conversation with him. My attention was caught by two officers from the occupying army who were walking in our direction. Their wide peaked caps and long coats were clean, and their boots shone. The officers were well-fed and probably in their thirties; they were cheerfully exchanging opinions and smoking. The tramp was watching them, too, his gaze fixed on their aromatic, burning cigarettes. I felt sure the tramp would ask them for a cigarette when they passed by him. I was wrong. Although the tramp followed them with his eyes as they approached, when they reached him, he didn't move, he didn't utter a word. One of the officers – a major, if I'm not mistaken – sneezed loudly just at that very moment, hurriedly pulling a handkerchief out of his pocket, together with a cigarette, which fell on the cobbled paving. The major looked around, but he did not pick it up; that would have been under his dignity as an officer, he didn't even stop to step on it. The cigarette lay white on the dirty grey paving, the officers had already passed under the terrace and the tramp still stood, staring at it like a snake at a frog, hypnotizing it, so it would not escape, and I waited to see when he would pounce on it, grab it and ask the next passer-by for a light. After a moment, the tramp took one or two steps (his uncertain, lurching movements giving me the impression that he was drunk), he stepped out into the middle of the road, stopped beside the cigarette and once more stared hard at it. Why didn't he reach out for it? I couldn't understand his behavior; I couldn't understand it mainly because I had once been a heavy smoker and I know how strong is the longing for a cigarette, I know that nicotine is a narcotic which divests one of shame and dignity, I know that a smoker such as I had been in the labor camp was willing to exchange a miserable portion of bread, of vital importance for life, for a single cigarette, or.... Show me a smoker, especially one like the tramp in the street below our terrace, who at a time of unbearable longing and physical need for nicotine, has not picked up a cigarette end, even though they don't know who has thrown it away. That is why I really couldn't understand why the tramp was considering the matter for so long and why he didn't satisfy his need with the major's cigarette. I cannot explain to this day what happened after the tramp's long hesitation, while he seemed to be passing judgement. His behavior went against a smoker's logic and completely baffled me. You see, he stepped on the cigarette and he crushed it under foot so fiercely and with such gratification that it seemed to me as if he were fulfilling some higher calling; he squashed the cigarette as though it was the head of a poisonous snake. Even that was not enough. Using the tip of his shoe, he scattered the trampled tobacco across the cobbles, so the wind would blow it away. It reminded me of that awful, degrading funeral of our leading politician, whose ashes were ordered by his opponents to be scattered in the middle of nowhere. The tramp staggered off in the direction of the old town, where crowds of people were gathering. I and my friend sat on the terrace not uttering a word. Each of us was pondering in his own way the incomprehensible verdict the tramp had pronounced on the major's cigarette. What had it been guilty of? Or was it the major who was guilty? Perhaps I had been mistaken and not seen right. The tramp might not have been asking for cigarettes, but for money. What if he hated cigarettes like all those who were once heavy smokers?

"Well, we've got one scene," my friend the script writer spoke up.

"That's not enough, and anyway, what if we misunderstood that scene?"

"The filmgoer will understand it," the script writer assured me and I agreed with him, but added, "Each in his own way."

How would the major have explained this scene, this verdict passed on his cigarette? I understood it quite clearly and simply when the drunken tramp returned a little later, came over to us on the terrace and asked my friend for a cigarette.

Just as he had come, without a greeting, so the tramp left without thanking my friend for the cigarette. We felt pleasantly surprised. We just didn't know whether this was the end of the first scene or whether it was a second mini-scene. Once more we were alone and the pleasant warmth of the sun encouraged us to talk. We turned our pale town faces towards it and each of us became lost in his own thoughts; we longed not to think, not to strain our tired nerves, to relax. But our eyes are like cameras. Our brains turn them off for a while, only to focus a second later on the hills or the houses, while not letting out of sight the pulsating life in the street.

* * *

It was already noon and the sun took our jackets off. Just as an hour earlier our attention had been drawn by the tramp and the major's cigarette, so it was now concentrating on the blossoming cherry trees, dressed up like brides in their wedding gowns. Spring had really only now come to central Slovakia. Everything delighted me, I loved the whole world, not even the strange tramp could put me out. May really is the month for love – that's only too true, as I could see for myself a while later. My friend suggested that we should walk to the middle of the old town, climb up the little hill and have a look at the empty mausoleum of the cursed and now once more respected Father of the Nation, Andrej Hlinka, whose name it was forbidden in the past to mention, but whose name is now mentioned very often, and above all, is misused by various people. I'm fond of the town of R., not for its deserted or despoiled mausoleum, but for its Upper Square, which is really a quaint old village-like town with a beautiful panoramic view, especially of the surrounding hills. Just as I was about to get up and leave the sunny terrace to do as my scriptwriter friend suggested, I noticed from the way his mustache twitched that he had caught wind of something worthy of a film-maker's notice. With a wave of the hand he indicated that I should remain sitting and with his head and eyes showed where I should look.

Coming from the direction of the hotel on the other side of the street, across the cobbles on which the tramp had crushed the major's cigarette, I saw approaching an oddly matched and probably only hastily joined and not yet mated pair of lovers. Walking a step or two in front of the young man was a beauty queen, a gypsy or Indian girl, certainly the most beautiful young woman I had had the fortune to see during our wanderings through Slovakia. I guess she couldn't have been more than sixteen or seventeen. She was not yet in her full bloom, but rather a budding flower of love. Her coal-black hair hung loose on her shoulders. The sister or daughter of Bizet's Carmen? No, just a beautiful Slovak gypsy girl. Or a Romany? Somehow I can't get used to this ancient and latest name for gypsies. A raspberry-tinted mouth slightly open, large eyes, in which two coals were burning, chocolate complexion, slim and enticingly supple figure, her step and movements from the waist sensuous and provocative. I observed all this from the front and the young man from behind. The gypsy girl knew this; she knew exactly how to offer and sell all her attractions and beauty. What boy would not be roused at the sight of this Carmen? Even those who would like to send the gypsies back to where they once came from (if they knew where that was) would look with pleasure at this Slovak Romany, and it wouldn't occur to them, they just couldn't imagine, that in a few years' time this beautiful girl would be no more than a black, faded, scorched rose, whose fire was burning out on the dying embers of unrestrained, uninhibited gypsy love. I noticed that there were already several men standing on the opposite pavement, or in the road, trying to take a closer look at the gypsy girl, drink in the beauty of her body and movements, a body that would never belong to them, which they didn't even yearn for that much any more, because it filled them with fear. That body, after all, belonged to the gypsy girl and who knows who her love had belonged to in the past and who it belonged to now and would in the future. Attention was also drawn to the young man, who was walking at a distance of two or three meters behind her, like a dog following its mistress, on a lead of instinct, admiration and impatience.

Where was this lady taking her faithful little dog? Was he following her smell or her promises? He was very young, obedient and drunk with desire. How old was he?

The script writer guessed twenty, I added another two years. Would the gypsy lead the young man over to us on the terrace? I would have been grateful for a better look, the cameraman would say he wants to take a close-up, a close-up of her face, mouth, eyes, a close-up from the right, the left, the front, because only then does the whole stand out in the picture. No, the gypsy girl didn't bring the young man up to us, the terrace was not the most suitable place to sell her love. She stopped beneath it, leaned up against the warm wall, but in such a way that I could see both their faces. Only now that he was nearer did I notice that the young man was wearing an army shirt, khaki-colored army trousers and army boots. He was a soldier. Ours? No! Whose? If he wasn't ours, he must be a Soviet soldier. Whoever's he was, he was a boy, already a young man in fact, but still a youngster, whose eyes were burning, maybe for the first time, with a desire for love, which accounted for the passion in his eyes and at the same time the shyness, inexperience, even fear that what he longed for might be lost through some foolish action. Yes, he was a soldier from the occupying army; they cut their hair short, like they used to do with our soldiers on military service. His bristling yellow hair and flushed face also helped to make him look scared. His gaze was uneasy, he looked like a watchful deer, he knew he had committed an offense, or at least broken army rules; after all, a soldier is not allowed to appear on the street among civilians dressed like this. He had clearly escaped from the barracks, because when she had passed at the foot of the wall, he had been standing on a ladder behind it, watching the world outside, and just at that moment she had looked up at him and smiled. He couldn't hold himself back, he had jumped over the wall and started following her. He had gazed at her from behind and she had known that he was gazing at her, she had felt his breath, heard his footsteps, looked around and smiled again; she had been glad he was following her, that, after all, was the purpose of it all, to entice someone from the barracks. He was not an officer, it was true, but he was a soldier, who....

We would see whether it was worth the gypsy's while walking past the wall of the barracks. The soldier was an obedient little dog, all he saw now was the movement of her body. For him, she was no longer walking, she was performing a belly dance, which electrified and hypnotized him. He would have jumped over a wall twice that high for such a beautiful, ravishing sight. Looking out of his mind, gripped by desire, at the mercy of his instincts, he had followed her to this spot under our terrace and now he had her before him. She was standing before him, she was all his, she was leaning coquettishly up against the wall and offering herself to him. Now he no longer wanted just to look at her, but to touch her hands, kiss those raspberry lips, stroke that beautiful black hair; for the moment nothing more, really nothing more, just to draw her to him and then, only then would he really want to make love to her, beautiful and ravishing as she was, at that moment he would promise to take her to be, forever and legally, his first, only and last wife, who he would love to his dying day, as no one would ever love her.

My friend and I sat still, as if hypnotized, we were afraid our chairs might creak, we almost stopped breathing, in order not to disturb this mute courtship, in order not to blow on the two flames of this love being born before our very eyes. The gypsy girl, like the most innocent coquette, already knew where her strength and wealth lay, she knew how to show off her charms, for the moment only show off, then later to offer and finally sell them. Goodness, how much beauty there was in her insincere gaze, how much sensuousness and provocativeness in her movements and stance. She lifted her arms above her head, ran her fingers through her thick, long black hair, and at that moment she seemed to wink at the soldier, then she closed her eyes, covered them with a fan of the blackest eyelashes, gently moistened her lips with her tongue and smiled at him, like a child at its favorite toy. The soldier's smile was that of one suffering, he was self-conscious, he didn't know what to do with his hands, he put them behind his back, then a moment later put the left one into his pocket, searching for something or calming something, or he was ashamed of his excitement, then he clasped them as if he was praying, his face begged, he was longing, longing so much for her love, but the little girl was playing with her dear toy, she straightened herself up, pushing out her breasts, so the soldier could see what she had apart from a beautiful face and tempting eyes, then she leaned once more against the wall, but as coquettishly, as provocatively as a model who is not selling just her dress or the belt round her slim waist, but her attractions, too. Fortunately, no noisy waiter came up to us on the veranda, rattling chairs and clinking beer glasses; he would have spoiled the game of Adam and Eve unfolding before our eyes, or was it cat and mouse? In Paradise the tempter was the snake, at the wall it was the gypsy girl, but she was also the mouse or frog which the soldier-snake hypnotizes and literally gobbles up, absorbs into himself, and he, too, enters her, takes her, all of her, and the gypsy saw this in his eyes, in his half-open mouth longing for a kiss; he was just about to touch her, press her to him, first embrace her gently, then hold her a long time in his arms, be with her for a long, long time, with her, but not here, before our gaze. It seemed to me that the gypsy first looked up at the terrace, then the soldier's eyes followed hers and registered our presence, but it might have been an involuntary glance, part of the love game meant to draw them even more to each other, to increase their longing and bring them together sooner.

As an old veteran, the soldier in me was revived, memories returned, my grey hair turned black, my feeble body became younger, my heart filled with love, that kind of love ages ago, when I was a soldier, that love lost and never to return, and in this young frame of mind, I began to wish my fellow soldier luck, I forgot that he belonged to the occupying forces, as they had forgotten, forgiven, us Slovak soldiers, I forgot all the injustices of the world, just love and good-will were revived in me and I wanted to do something to help these two beside the wall, to protect the flames flickering in their hearts.

When the soldier moved nearer to the gypsy and was about to touch her hands and then her cheek, the gypsy kindly, but uncompromisingly placed that hand at his side and like a kitten with its paw she warned him that he mustn't and the soldier's face and hands asked why, why dear, because I really do love you. The gypsy knew this and she told him outright why he mustn't touch her. She told him and she also showed him with her hand, so that the soldier would understand, would be in no doubt what game this was, what kind of love she was after.

"Well.... Don't you have any?!" she whispered, demonstrating counting money with her thumb and first finger. Her face said she was sorry, she would like to, too, but....

The soldier glanced with a puzzled and surprised look not only into the gypsy's eyes, but also – or so it seemed to me – up at us on the terrace.

The gypsy repeated: "Náne lóve!"

"What?" asked the soldier in Russian and his naivete was sincere and convincing.

"Don't you have any cash?!" the gypsy girl repeated and the soldier's face fell, because he had at last understood.

"How much?" he asked, mortified and humiliated.

The gypsy, pushing out her lips as if talking to a child or a deaf-mute, so he would not only hear, but also see, told him aloud, but in confidence, "A hundred!" and she smiled guiltily at the same time, indicating with her gaze that she was not alone. I don't know whether the soldier understood, but I was surprised I had not hitherto noticed a drunken gypsy man leaning up against the wall of the hotel. There was a clear link between him and the gypsy girl, but whether it was her father, brother, or lover, or just an ordinary pimp, I couldn't tell.

The soldier's spirit was prepared to humble itself to passionate love, if necessary to beg her a hundred times not to refuse him; he searched through his pockets, including the one behind him, the one at his knee and the tiny one under his belt. His face suddenly lit up, because from that smallest one he pulled out a piece of paper, probably a ten-ruble note, which the gypsy eyed scornfully and she showed her disappointment with her mouth, too. No, she didn't spit, but it was almost as if she had. Then the young soldier fished out a coin, maybe it was our five-crown one, so hardly enough for one beer, and he held it out on his palm to the gypsy, gesturing that it was his longing heart.

The soldier's money and the heart on his palm softened the gypsy girl a little, she showed it with a hardly visible smile, but nothing more. The business transaction, in which love was bought and sold, could not take place. (Just like in our market economy.) The gypsy said in a very clear voice, "Not enough! You need a hundred! You understand? A hundred! It's the same in your language and ours – a hundred!"

The disappointed soldier still could not take his eyes off his unattainable love. The man leaning up against the wall whistled and waved his hand and the gypsy motioned to the soldier that she must go, but the soldier's gaze still held her. I could see from her face that she was not indifferent to the soldier, that he had lit a flame of love in her that she herself could not put out. She would have liked to get rid of the man propped up against the hotel wall, but he was beginning to be impatient and bad-tempered. So this was the end of the soldier's longing, the end, the definite end of a love that had begun, but not been satisfied, that the young soldier would have remembered when he was an old man. This love would have been his first and most valued gift when parting from this lovely country he had been sent to occupy and force into submission.

I came to my senses, for the second time I forgave the soldier and the whole of his division for the occupation and their own poverty, so strongly did I see myself in him. At that instant I made up my mind.

Putting my finger to my lips, I warned my friend to be quiet and I gestured that he should remain seated. I got up from the table, quickly hurried down below the terrace, went up to the soldier, greeted him "*zdravstvuj!*" shook his hand and immediately left. The gypsy girl and the soldier understood my intervention in their love dealings only when the soldier looked at the green note bearing the figure 100 which had appeared in his palm. The gypsy's eyes widened, there really was not just delight, but also love in them. The soldier handed the gypsy the hundred-crown note, my parting gift to the "liberator" and, with the expression of a confident winner, he looked up at the terrace where I was once more sitting with my friend in search of stories for films. He gave me a Schweik-like greeting, as if he had a cap on his head, that is, he put the middle finger of his right hand to his temple. The soldier's eyes framed the portrait of this mysterious, incomprehensibly kind donor with the question: Why, sir? Why did you take pity on me?

No, my friend, I didn't take pity on you, I just remembered my young days as a soldier and that's why I understood you. May my gift do you good. Take it back to your motherland as a memory of mine!

The soldier and the gypsy girl waved to me as to an old friend and, holding hands, they ran down the street in the direction of the hotel. There they stopped for a moment beside the man who had whistled to call the girl away from unprofitable employment. The gypsy girl shook hands with him as I had done with the soldier and my gift, my hundred-crown note, was passed to a fourth hand. The soldier and the girl disappeared from sight in the nearby woods. The man who had taken my present from the girl came onto the terrace, ordered a large beer and a glass of rum. I don't know why he gave me such a strange, challenging look, as if he was laughing at me, while theatrically lighting a good cigarette.

My script writer friend noted down this second scene in our romantic film screenplay. It was only half a year later that I offered him the third.

* * *

This (third) scene came to my attention, or appeared like a miracle, by a rather unhappy chance. In recent months I have been traveling too much, both with friends who are also writers and with my inseparable scriptwriter friend, on what I call "cultural missions" – discussions with readers in schools, libraries or homes for pensioners. I do it because my conscience tells me that just now, in our turbulent times, our Slovak people need the living word, personal contact with the people who speak to them through the newspapers, radio, television; it is these they want to see with their own eyes, listen to them directly, shake hands with them, ask something in private, confirm their own opinions and not so much to be wiser, but more confident about their decisions.

Traveling around on these "cultural missions" demands a lot of energy; it exhausts me physically as well as financially, but it gives me spiritual strength. At least that is what I tell myself. When such a "cultural mission" took me once more to the town of R., an unpleasant thing happened to me, which ruined a pleasant, friendly evening at the home of K., a painter, who had entertained me royally, in spite of the fact that it was the first time we had met. In small Slovak towns like R. artists like to meet with artists of different trades and they receive them as honored guests. If this unpleasant incident had happened to me at the end of or after my visit, in my hotel room, I would have sought the cause in excessive eating or drinking, which otherwise I don't especially indulge in, particularly on such occasions when there isn't a jug of draft wine on the table. I stress – draft wine. After strongly sulfurous bottled wine I get stomach cramps and strange pains under my right rib, where I have a scar from a gall-bladder operation. That pain then spreads to my chest and I break out in a sweat and the arteries in my throat constrict; in other words, the classic pains which signal a heart attack. I am familiar with this and that is why I am very afraid of such pains and I never set out on a "cultural mission" without a tube of Nitrilex spray in my pocket, two hundred and ten doses of first aid that can save me from getting a heart attack. But I have only used this medicine once abroad and I regretted it. It's true that the pains under my right rib and in my chest disappeared, but I got a terrible headache. My constricted blood vessels stretched so wide that they upset something in my organism. That's why I didn't use Nitrilex at K.'s home, but I begged him to call the hospital and ask for the doctor I used to call Benjamin as a child, who was a friend and also a writer. I was lucky. In a few minutes Doctor Benjamin arrived at master K.'s studio. He came in a wailing ambulance as for an emergency. They put me into it as if I were a corpse. Soon they were transferring me from the stretcher onto an examination table. The nurse connected me up to some black leads, she stuck something on my arms and legs and around my heart and in a few minutes Doctor Benjamin was reading my electrocardiogram. He muttered something about not understanding it, measured my blood pressure, listened to my heart, felt my abdomen, tapped his fingers on my back, stuck his fingers under my ribs and when he pressed the unsightly scar under my right rib, I let out a little yelp. That was all Doctor Benjamin needed. The tomography experts soon took me in hand and a diagnosis of the problem causing my "cardiac" pains was made unexpectedly quickly.

"That's no heart attack," Doctor Benjamin laughed at me, "no heart attack, just ordinary gall stones, sand, so fine you could use it to plaster the walls."

"Me and gall stones?" I began to feel faint. "What are you talking about? I don't have a gall bladder! Can't you see that awful scar?!"

The doctor still seemed to be making fun of me and asked whether I thought that when they took out that bag full of stones they call the gall bladder, they had removed the bile as well? Bile, he told me, is produced in the liver and passes through the bile ducts into the digestive system, and the sand had formed in one of the bile ducts, which when it moved caused terrible pains. But I was not to worry, no one had ever died of sand like that.

I should have been glad about the diagnosis made by Doctor Benjamin, but I once more broke out in a sweat and the pains under my ribs returned as fiercely as an hour earlier at my friend K.'s, quickly spreading to my chest. Doctor Benjamin led me along the spotless corridor as if I were a healthy man, but I had to grab hold of him to prevent myself from falling, because it seemed to me I was having hallucinations. Walking towards me – not walking, floating like a black ghost – was that beautiful gypsy girl of mine, the soldier's hundred-crown love. When she passed us, I halted, so that I could perceive her with all my senses. I looked into her face, I waved her a greeting, I tried to make contact with her eyes, I listened to her footsteps, in order to convince myself that it really was her, alive and not a ghost, I even breathed in the smell of her clothes and body, which, no matter how much perfume is used, carry the pleasant odor of smoke. I was certain it was her and I could have sworn that our eyes met, that she had registered me, too. I gazed at her for a while from behind. It was her, only she had such a beautiful figure, her body held straight, a spring in her step, but like all gypsy women (I often notice them in the street), there was a waddle in her walk. Only her hair was not as long and not as beautifully shining and black as before, and the sweet look had been replaced by a strange, pained expression, a harried look; signs of suffering and old-age had settled in her face. Signs of old age? What had happened to that touching and provocative look of adoration, that charm of an innocent child? When our eyes met, I saw in them more surprise than pleasure, in fact reproach as well, which I didn't understand, but she looked down in shame. And gratitude...?

What had happened to the gypsy girl's gratitude for my gift? Why? Why was there so much sorrow and pain in those eyes? And anyway – was it really her? Wasn't it just a chance likeness? Perhaps the one I had met when I was almost fainting from pain was her aging sister. That is what I thought.

When the gypsy girl paused at the end of the corridor, and not only paused, but even looked around and then covered her eyes with her hand, as if she might be crying, I couldn't tell at that distance, but when with a flirtatious gesture she indicated that her inconspicuous greeting was addressed to me, I was left in no doubt. Yes, it was her, my hundred-crown gypsy girl. But what had happened to her? Was she visiting some seriously ill friend or relative? Maybe the man she had handed her hundred-crown note to was dying, or was someone more dear to her awaiting death?

"Do you know her?" Doctor Benjamin asked me.

"I don't know...I think so...but I'm not quite sure if it's her."

"It would be a good thing if you remembered!"

"I have a feeling I've seen her somewhere, and even that I gave her a little present...."

"What did you give her?" Doctor Benjamin couldn't hide his curiosity.

"A hundred crowns. But not directly...."

"You gave her a hundred crowns?! Do you know what you've done?! You, an old man – you're out of your mind! Do you know what's wrong with that gypsy?"

Doctor Benjamin restrained himself, he didn't tell me what was the matter with the girl who I was convinced was my gypsy, but he suddenly let go of me, as if he were ashamed of me and he said as if to himself: idiot, old idiot! Is it possible? Indirectly.... A hundred crowns!"

Doctor Benjamin was in a hurry to get me out of the hospital. At that moment, I didn't understand why he felt such an aversion for me. What was worse, he didn't even want to talk to me and I didn't understand how an old friend could behave like that to me, much worse than to a complete stranger, who didn't care whether I was in pain, where I was to go from the corridor, whether into his room or outside into the street.

Instead of saying goodbye, Doctor Benjamin looked me in the eye like a judge and asked me sharply, "Tell me nothing but the truth! Did you have anything to do with this girl? I mean sexual intercourse!"

Instead of convulsions of pain under my right rib, I was seized by convulsions of laughter. I really laughed like an idiot.

"You think it's funny? If you knew what disease is destroying that girl, you'd soon stop laughing!"

Then over a glass of cognac, which Doctor Benjamin prescribed for my pains against all logic, I told him the whole story of my parting gift to the young soldier.

Doctor Benjamin told me his version, or what my gift had caused. He didn't disclose the gypsy girl's disease, nor even her name, but he just complained that it was the first case of this disease to appear in their district. The gypsy girl had apparently come too late. Before she had sought help at the hospital, the soldiers had left the barracks, so they couldn't line the whole garrison up in the yard for the patient to inspect and to point out the one who had left her this terrible gift to remember him by. Nor could the soldier walk around town with his army doctor, looking for the girl he had caught the disease from. Who could discover who had infected whom, who was the deadly donor? Wasn't it me, after all?

That cursed hundred-crown note!

That cursed parting gift!

Once more I began to feel ill. But this time it was not a gallstone pushing its way through my bile ducts, but flowing through my heart was a feeling of regret, of guilt, my conscience was pricking me. How could I quiet its reproaches?

JÁN TUŽINSKÝ

- prose writer, journalist;
born in Zlaté Moravce (1951)

Ján Tužinský has been an editor in a publishing house, an editor, literary adviser and director for the radio, a member of the National Council of the Slovak Republic and more than once president of the Slovak Writers Society.

His literary debut was a collection of short stories **Bičovanie koní** (*Whipping the Horses*, 1983) – a critical examination of society, human consciousness and the relations among people. The short novel **Straka nekradne** (*A Magpie Doesn't Steal*, 1985) presents the mental world of a handicapped child. In his book of short stories **Čakanie na šarhu** (*Waiting for the Dog-Catcher*, 1987) he raises the fundamental questions of human existence and the meaning of life. The novel **Kto hodí kameňom** (*Whoever Throws a Stone*, 1989) presents a picture of the life of the inhabitants of a small town against the background of the momentous events of this century. In the untraditional novel **Biliard na streche** (*Billiards on the Roof*, 1992) the author ponders the basic questions of human life against the background of the tragic year 1968. For the short stories in **Krypta** (*The Crypt*, 1992) and **Jeremiášov plač** (*Jeremiah's Lament*, 1997) he let himself be inspired by life in present-day Bratislava. In the novella **Bastard v daždi** (*Mongrel in the Rain*, 1994) he offers a critical analysis of the lifestyle of the Slovak intelligentsia.

He frequently writes articles on current affairs and he has published two books of essays, (**Motiviáda**, 1993; **Bledomodrý svet** – *Pale Blue World*, 1998). The story "Šelest" ("A Murmur") was published in the magazine *Slovenské pohľady* in 1999.

For radio he has written a number of original works of drama (a radio novella **Sadze a sneh** (*Soot and Snow*) and a cycle of dramas entitled **Pentameron**).

In his own words:
Thanks to literature, but also thanks to the fact that through my

own writing I have tried to understand the critical moments and tragedies in my own life, I have not become churlish; maybe I have even been able to appreciate why some things happened, and it is quite possible that as a result my readers have also been able to do the same with regard to all kinds of things. After all, there are few human lives that pass in their entirety without serious personal losses. What I want to say is that one usually does what one has to do.... I write, therefore I am. Even now....

Literature is not so susceptible to the kind of decline that is often talked about in connection with the modern media of the computer age. The latest research in this direction in England as well as in the USA is more than encouraging. British booksellers surprisingly claim that a relatively large number of young people spend time reading books – the very group that are usually considered to be computer maniacs. In this case, therefore, it is a false impression. Books are, after all, the most intimate and most elegant strata of our cultural life. Together with music and viewing works of art they enhance our intellectual lives in the most comprehensive way. The responsibility of the writer for what is written, as well as what is spoken, is therefore still a serious matter. The writer is even to a considerable extent also responsible for what he does not say, or for the fact that when he is expected to say something, he remains silent. We are not going through an easy period. Neither as a society, nor as individuals. Our attitude towards reality is not without obligations. At the very least the writer is expected not to be indifferent to the reality we are experiencing. He cannot and he should not shut his eyes to it. I believe that the general public is still sensitive to the attitude of the writer, or at least a section of the public.... That section which is not indifferent to life.

(2000)

A MURMUR
For Vilko Šikula, because he loved life.

When I was a lot younger, I would have obstinately declared that our ideas are usually more vivid than reality. I don't believe that any longer, mainly thanks to experience, and that advises us that it would be better to come to terms with reality than spend our energies trying to realize our ideas. We have abandoned them anyway in the meantime. Laziness dogs us as do alcohol, cigarettes, women and senseless arguments, thanks to which we cannot look each other in the eye the next day. And maybe not even in the mirror.

228

That is why I can't understand why it all happened.

I was walking through the hushed streets of the town from Michael's Gate along Milan Rastislav Štefánik Street in the direction of the station. It was late at night and a fine drizzle was falling. The asphalt on the pavements shone like the fur of a wet black cat. Lone taxis crawled along after me, as if they suddenly wanted to carry me away, by force if necessary, to some concrete address. But I had no particular destination. At least, so I thought. I had just decided to go for a short walk. Although the seemingly deserted town dampened my spirits. Perhaps that was the real reason why I decided to make straight for the station. I supposed that at the station at least I would come across some people and that they, unlike myself, would have some concrete destination to go to and that I would read in their faces a clear decision to get there. I might meet someone I knew, who was just arriving, and it would look as if I had gone to meet them. So my walk was no longer entirely aimless.

The station building lured me with its yellow light flowing over the damp steps. I hurried towards it like a large butterfly flying into the cool light of the lamps growing out of the asphalt pavement. But my disappointment was all the greater when I found myself in the lit-up interior. Not a soul in sight. I was almost scared by the echo of my own footsteps in that large empty space. It was a mystery to me how I could have arrived at such a deadly quiet time. As if everyone had just left. They had depopulated the town. This is what an evacuation must look like during a war or some natural disaster. A railwayman just passed through the deserted hall, throwing me a puzzled and rather alarmed look and disappeared down one of the poorly-lit corridors.

At first I wanted to hurry after him, but the light from the corridor, where there were usually crowds of people standing in front of the station buffet, distracted me. I soon realized that my attention had been caught by the shadow of a person, who seemed to have been escaping from me into the passengers' waiting-room. It occurred to me why I was alone in the hall. At that time everyone must be quietly waiting in there for their night train.... After all, who would want to hang around a deserted station?

With this justifiable hope, I therefore quickly made my way along the lighted corridor to the place where the shadow of the unknown person had just disappeared. I opened the waiting-room door, but when I stepped inside there was no one there. "But I saw that shadow," I said to myself. "I'm quite sure! I can't have been mistaken...." I walked around the whole waiting-room. I even peered under the chairs and benches, where people usually put their luggage. But there was no one anywhere. The only place I had not yet searched was the corner behind the door, which in my hurry I had forgotten to close, and it hid a little space in the room. When I approached, I heard something like an intake of breath. There was a strong element of distress and helplessness in it. Like the whine of a stray dog. I hesitated for a moment, but then I shut the door. I found myself face to face with the slight figure of a young girl, who was gazing at me wide-eyed. I had obviously frightened her. I must admit that I hadn't expected such a meeting in the middle of the night either, at the completely deserted station. "She can't be here alone," it occurred to me, but I immediately hastened to reassure her.

"Don't worry, I won't harm you. I was just surprised to find you here all alone. It's rather unusual like this in the middle of the night. What's your name?"

"Nelly. And I'm not here alone. They'll all come in a minute.... All those who are leaving.... I must wait for Azorko and Granddad. They're sure to come. Quite sure!"

She said it as emphatically as if I had contradicted her. But it could also have been that for some reason she was not quite convinced that anyone would come.

"Where are they then? I'm sorry, Nelly, maybe I seem very inquisitive, but this is rather unusual. You would expect a station to be fairly busy. Sometimes you can hardly move here. I didn't meet a soul. Then I saw you. But I was very glad. I'd like to meet Granddad and Azorko, too. I suppose he must be your brother?"

"You don't know either Granddad or Azorko?"

Nelly first looked at me as if she thought I was very odd. She quickly realized, however, that I probably *was* very odd. She gazed at me with sad blue eyes and in the quiet, completely baffled, pitying voice of a child, she said, "Of course Azorko is Granddad's dog!"

"Sorry, Nelly, you're right, I should have known," I apologized.

"But you said he was my brother," she reproached me.

"I didn't say he was, I just supposed," I defended myself.

"You thought Azorko was a person."

"I probably did," I admitted in a conciliatory manner, so as not to annoy her unnecessarily. She was clearly alarmed at finding herself alone at night. She was no longer a little girl and not yet a young woman in the true sense of the word. She was certainly still a child who you wouldn't expect to find alone in a deserted station building in the middle of the night. She was understandably wary, but I didn't get the impression that she was really afraid of me. It was more as if she pitied me. Not only because of Azorko. More because of the incredibly deserted station.

Moreover, as if she seemed to know exactly what I was thinking at that moment, she asked:

"You don't believe they'll come, do you?"

She might be defending herself to make it clear that she had nothing to fear. Children defend themselves like this against adults, when they feel threatened. Yet this was clearly not the case here. When she gazed at me thoughtfully with her blue eyes, I had the feeling that she was comforting me.

"Then where are they all?" I asked rather awkwardly.

"They'll come in time," she replied in a serious voice.

"Let's hope they don't miss the train," I allowed myself to comment.

"They can't miss it!" she looked at me in astonishment. "It's their train."

"You mean it's the train they want to take, don't you think?"

"No. They don't want to take it. But it is their train," she insisted, as if I were arguing with her.

"Well, I only hope one arrives. I must confess, Nelly, that I have never experienced such a strange night at the station. It's not just that I haven't seen any passengers apart from you, but I haven't even heard any trains. Arriving, or leaving. I just don't know what to think."

"You don't have to think anything!" she suggested, once more looking at me sadly.

"But you must admit, it's very strange...?"

"Do you think so?" she asked, giving me a puzzled look. "Maybe you just haven't met the right people at the right time."

"Why do you say that?" I felt uneasy, because her words reminded me of something.

"I'm repeating those words, because they were often said to me. That's probably why I don't know whether I can believe them."

"They probably wanted you to believe them," I said, not very convincingly.

"No. They didn't want me to believe them. They wanted me to believe their words. After all, they were only words themselves."

"I'm sorry, I don't quite understand you, Nelly."

"Maybe you do understand...but you don't want to." She smiled sadly.

"No, no, believe me, I do want to, but it seems unlikely.... Strange. Like this night at the station. Do you know what I mean?"

I didn't dare ask the question that would draw Nelly's attention to the large electric clock hanging in the middle of the opposite wall of the waiting-room. I had already been watching it suspiciously for some time. There was something funny about it. There was definitely something wrong with it. But it was only at the moment when I was about to draw Nelly's attention to it that I realized what it was. Of course, it could be a perfectly ordinary problem. After all, why shouldn't the station clock go wrong?

The first thing that caught my attention was the fact that it had been showing twelve o'clock for too long. But that can happen. It was only when I began to observe the clock closer while I was talking to Nelly, that I realized how wrong I was. The clock had not stopped at twelve. When the minute hand was just about to merge with the hour hand and the second hand was going to hide beneath them both, it suddenly seemed to change its mind and began to turn back in the opposite direction. The minute hand appeared to the left of the hour hand for a moment, for almost a minute to be exact, while the second hand moved around the clock face from almost twelve until it got to one and then the whole process was repeated again. "As if time had stopped on this clock," I thought to myself, and that is probably why I sought no other explanation to give to Nelly. I probably wouldn't have found one anyway.

"What am I supposed to see?" She pulled my sleeve impatiently.

"The clock, of course! Can't you see?"

"Yes, I can," she admitted.

"As if time had stopped," I repeated aloud exactly what I had thought to myself.

"Well, it has," she said gravely.

"Just the clock," I objected.

"When the clock stops, time stops too!"

"You can't believe that, Nelly. It's nonsense!"

"But how could they all catch their train, then?" she looked at me, puzzled, but not helpless. In her deep blue eyes there was once more something infinitely sad, and when I looked into them, I felt almost physical pain. But I was also overcome by that sadness you sometimes feel at the station when a train leaves with someone near and dear to you. I can find no satisfactory explanation for why I was overcome by that feeling of sadness when I gazed into Nelly's eyes, but that is how it was.

"It's a strange clock," I said, just to brush off my embarrassment.

"Yes, it is!" she readily agreed.

"This station is odd, too. The only railwayman I got a glimpse of ran away from me, as if he was afraid of me."

"Maybe he was." Nelly smiled for the first time.

"But I only wanted to ask him something!" I objected.

"What?"

"I don't really know," I admitted.

"I can tell you all kinds of things," she smiled again. It looked as if she was making fun of me. But it was the kind of fun adults make of a child in order to help them understand some phenomenon or event. I was sitting opposite her and I was trying not to look at the wall where the station clock was hanging. I didn't want to risk Nelly's rather patronizing tone. But I could see the clock all the time in my mind. "That really isn't an ordinary clock...." How did she put it? Aha! How then could they all catch their trains? Goodness! From the moment I had set out up Michael Street and then up M.R.Štefánik, I had had a very strange feeling. Apart from a couple of taxis, there hadn't been a soul in the street. Just rustling leaves. Rain. Shiny pavements. As if drops of tar were falling on the town. And the silence. Where had so much silence come from in this town all of a sudden? It just wasn't normal for the town at night to be absolutely silent. The noise in a town can die down, but it can't die away completely. Even at night a town can't be like a cemetery. Today, it hadn't been like walking between houses, but along the paths in the cemetery. I realized this and shuddered. After all that, I had been lucky to meet Nelly.

However, when I gazed once more into her face, something disturbed me. Her expression seemed to have changed somehow. Not any particular feature, but she wasn't concentrating her attention on me at every question, as she had before. Her blue eyes also seemed to wander feverishly away from me. They had lost their previous calm, depth and curiosity. She was quite openly staring somewhere over my shoulder. "Could it be the clock?" I asked myself, but I rejected the idea immediately. For one reason, because I had the impression that she was in no doubt about the clock. "No, it can't be the clock," I concluded. Even so, there was something in her face that troubled me. Especially those empty-looking eyes. That was a fact. That's why I waved my hand several times in front of her face. She didn't notice. She didn't react. But why, all of a sudden? I realized there was no point in talking to her just then. Her thoughts were quite clearly somewhere far away. It was as if she weren't sitting with me in the waiting-room of a deserted station in the middle of the night. As if this were a completely different Nelly.

"Can you see me, Nelly?" I spoke up, sounding like a whining dog, in spite of the fact that I knew she wouldn't hear me. It was a quite unsuitable reaction on my part to what I saw and felt. Perhaps that is why I did it.

Not only did she not reply, but she didn't even move an eyebrow. I was seized by a feeling of despair and helplessness. That may be why I suddenly looked behind me. In the direction Nelly's sky-blue and, at that moment, completely motionless eyes were gazing. As if I were seeking help from someone, even though I knew there was and there could be no one else in the waiting-room apart from Nelly and me. After all, anyone who entered, would have to pass by us both.

However, it was clearly otherwise. Not only was the waiting-room behind my back not empty, it was quite full. Sitting on the seats and standing between them I saw people of all ages and variously dressed. Men in Russian shirts, in Tsarist uniforms, women in Russian folk costumes. Generals' uniforms and nuns' habits were no rarity either. A few intellectuals in European suits were debating passionately in groups beside the waiting-room window. They kept pulling their watches out of their waistcoat pockets and looking at them importantly. As if they were the only ones to be aware of the importance of time. The incredible clock on the wall kept showing almost twelve by continuously approaching and retreating from the last minute before midnight.

In spite of the bizarre nature of the scene in the waiting-room, somehow it seemed terribly familiar. Nelly must have noticed that what I saw in the waiting-room did not surprise me as much as it attracted me. The fixed look in her face relaxed. Her eyes took on a feverish, but lively glow. The sadness disappeared, to be replaced by a bright sparkle, which broke into real happiness when an elderly German with a dog that looked almost as old came up to her.

"Granddad! Granddad! I knew he'd come, and Azorko, too! I'm so glad, Granddad! I just can't tell you how glad...!"

The dog wagged its hairy tail excitedly and licked Nelly's hand. The old man couldn't utter a word. He was clearly very moved. He just stroked Nelly's head and tears ran down his wrinkled cheeks. There was something terribly sad and tragic about their happy meeting, and this sadness seemed to descend on me, too. I might for no good reason have succumbed to it, if it hadn't been for the scene which suddenly took place before my eyes. Two men were standing in the aisle between the seats and they reminded me of cocks on a rubbish heap. The older one in particular was waving his arms around and shouting, "Oh, no, sir, as my name is Peter Pavlovich Gaganov! I'm not going to let anyone pull the wool over my eyes!"

It was clearly rather a disastrous sentence. No sooner had Peter Pavlovich uttered it, than the other man stepped up close to him and unexpectedly but firmly grasped his cap, pulled it down over his eyes and dragged him for a few steps around the waiting-room. The chattering stopped completely for a moment and most of those present gaped in astonishment at the two men.

"Good God, what was that meant to be?" Peter Pavlovich Gaganov asked his opponent angrily. "I would never have expected that of you, Nikolaj Vsevolodovich! It's unheard of! Such rudeness! Such churlishness!" stuttered Peter Pavlovich, while his companion apologized awkwardly, "You must forgive me.... I really don't know what's gotten into me all of a sudden.... Such a stupid thing to do...."

He turned on his heel and disappeared among the little group of debating intellectuals. Some of the older generals still shook their heads disapprovingly, but otherwise no one bothered about the incident. As if nothing had happened.

They were a really strange assortment of people. Fortunately, no one took any notice of me. Not even Nelly just then. She was talking to her grandfather and cuddling Azorko. I could therefore move undisturbed among them and listen to fragments of their conversations. The suspicion that had gripped me when talking to Nelly was gradually confirmed. There was something strikingly bizarre about these passengers; that couldn't be denied. But there are things you can't believe, you don't want to believe. Only the strangeness of this night confirmed for me that everything is possible. It was as if reality were being poured through a special funnel and changing its shape in the neck. Time had stopped and I had found myself in its lines of force. In a different dimension. All those strange men and women were in fact very familiar to me and in reality I knew them very well. I knew quite a bit about them, almost everything. Yet I had never seen or heard them before. However, they reminded me of books by F.M. Dostoevsky. I had spent long, sleepless nights talking to them as if to friends, close acquaintances, and they had spoken to me in confidence, seriously, like suffering people aware of life's problems. They knew best its less happy side, and their author had endowed them with exceptional understanding. They had surprised me above all by their ability to love people just as they were. Not only was nothing human foreign to them, but it was as if they knew that this very understanding of our failings and those of our fellow men made them more aware of the beauty of life. I read all kinds of things in their eyes, yet in spite of everything they were able to love. Although it must be admitted that not always were they rewarded with what could be called love. Pain. Cruel, cold and calculating pain. That was often their fate. But they bore it, because they knew that everything in this world is of consequence. Both human life and its victims. "We are sinful, and therefore we suffer," they told themselves. Their creator held this view in the name of love. But he also had his doubts. He suffered. Sometimes in the name of this love. That is why, when he no longer had the strength to put words in their mouths, which through their deeds and actions would convince, he wrote despairingly on the coffin of his first wife, Maria Dmitriyevna, and his words had cut so deep into my heart that they came back to me in the middle of this frozen time in this suddenly crowded waiting-room. "Masha is lying on the table. Will I see her again? To love someone *as yourself*, as Christ tells us to, is not possible. On this Earth we are bound by the law of personality. *I* is the obstacle. Christ alone achieved it, but throughout the ages he has always been the ideal human beings aspire to, and in accordance with the laws of nature should aspire to."

I walked among them and looked with interest at their faces. I listened in on fragments of their conversations, in the hope that I could discover what disturbed me most about the whole of that strange company: why had they met just here and why just at this time?

Close to the window, on two chairs facing each other, I saw two of the brothers Karamazov. They were sitting leaning slightly forward, engrossed in a passionate discussion. Their faces were almost touching.

"No, Ivan, you mustn't think like that about people! Nor about God! God is infinitely kind and his deeds are not measurable in human terms. We see everything very personally!"

"Personally, then?" Ivan looked at Alyosha with an ironic sparkle in his eyes. "You are naive and perhaps too good for this world, Alyosha. They could chop wood on your back and you wouldn't even sigh, you'd be so glad to help them. They confused you in the monastery. Got you all mixed up. They took away your common sense and the only thing they gave you back in return was pompous peace."

"What can be more than peace, Ivan?"

"Knowledge, brother. Man is not and should not be a blind executor of someone's will. God didn't give man free will so that he should become a blind puppet in his hands. If that were true, then all that talk about man's free will is just a stupid lie."

"Control yourself, Ivan. At least for my sake."

"It's just for your sake that I must say things you haven't heard in the monastery. That old Zosima, that holy man, stank. And you in the monastery smelled his stink, but you pretended you were breathing in divine ambergris!"

"Old Zosima was a clean man, Ivan."

"But he stank like a skunk!"

"You know very well, Ivan, that these things are not a question of the body!"

"I know, Alyosha, but it wasn't me, it was you in the monastery who was expecting a miracle. And that didn't happen. The old man's stink took you by surprise. The body is, after all, only the body. There lies the contradiction that concerns you. Holy fanatics. You speak about the soul, but you expected this old man's body to be eternal!"

"Stop it, Ivan!"

"You can't avoid the truth by keeping quiet, brother. The reason why monastery cells are so quiet is that there you have buried alive the bodies of young monks, along with the truth. Do you realize that, Alyosha?"

"There is too much bitterness in you, Ivan. You are very complicated and you have read a lot of books. They have unsettled your soul. Important truths are simple. You might say – banal. It doesn't matter if they are banal, they really do bring the soul peace. Not restlessness, not continual doubts about everything, even about God. What are we in comparison with God, Ivan? How can our limited powers of reason understand the motives, the causes and the results, his great purpose for man in this world?"

"God gave us reason and free will, Alyosha. If that is just a formal declaration, thank you very much!"

"No, Ivan, it isn't a formal declaration, but it is only human reason!"

"But we have been created in God's likeness. Or do the Scriptures lie?"

"No, but how can you be so sure that you can understand everything you have read?"

"I really am not sure."

"You see, Ivan, but you express yourself as if you were."

"I must rely on my reason, Alyosha. I have nothing more suitable at my disposal."

"You're wrong there, brother. Apart from reason, we have been given hearts, that is, faith."

"Now you're going to start talking about conscience...."

"Why not, Ivan?! Enough can never be said about conscience!"

"But people usually talk about it when it has just failed. Where is your God's conscience if he can look on at the clenched little fist of a helpless child, at the unredeemed tears of innumerable children who shake their fists at the heavens, vainly and repeatedly? Innocent, abused children during countless wars.... Where is your God, Alyosha? Where is his half-closed eye, gazing at all this injustice? How, with what arguments do you want to excuse him? No, brother, no one can convince me that God's indifferent

237

gaze can be compensated for with anything else. Not even his eternal redemption can compensate for the tear of a child innocently shed. I'll return the ticket to Him, and you do as you think fit...!"

"Ivan, you shouldn't...."

"He shouldn't either!"

"You are hard."

"Maybe, but not as indifferent as He is!"

A painful sneer appeared on Alyosha's face. His brother's words had touched his most sensitive spot. Tears tricked down his fresh, almost childlike face. His chest lifted and fell rapidly as if he were running. In spite of the fact that neither of the brothers was aware of my presence, I felt embarrassed to witness their passionate debate. I knew I couldn't join in, but as a witness I suddenly felt uncomfortable and so I left them to it. I realized I felt better with Nelly, so I set out in her direction. I saw her talking lovingly to her grandfather and making a fuss over Azorka. But no sooner had I moved in her direction than a tall, lanky man (or to be precise his legs) barred my way.

"A person can take another's life, if he has a noble purpose. I have committed murder for noble reasons! That perverse old woman just didn't deserve her riches. A well-aimed blow with an axe could make several people happy. Wouldn't it be a greater evil if all that wealth lay around somewhere unused? You, as the investigator, think I'm just an ordinary murderer. But there's much more to it than that!" he declared, turning towards a plump man in his forties, who stared piercingly into his cold, steel-grey eyes. There was no hope of somehow getting past his long legs. Both of them were so engrossed in their conversation, that the world around had ceased to exist.

"In any case, Raskolnikov, you took a human life," the man said almost in a whisper, as if he were afraid that someone other than Raskolnikov would hear him.

"A human life!" Raskolnikov exclaimed shrilly. "The things people call a human life! It's shameful to think of it! Shameful, indeed! A rat is sometimes better than a human being. You are an investigator, you're an intelligent man, you should know that sometimes life is worth less than a cheap knife! You know it, but that is hard to say out loud. A herd of moralizing cows always appears from somewhere and begins to moo. Flocks of sheep chase through the villages, bleating as they go. But if they took better notice of the world, they would see those ever-present slaughterhouses, where people drop dead like flies. They would hear the roaring streams of blood. They would see wading through them people who are convinced they are not killing, but only conducting a war in the name of dubious ideals. Always just in the name of ideals. What is the difference, sir? To murder on a large scale in the name of an ideal, or to help someone in particular for the price of one little murder. Don't frown! If we accept that to murder someone is always a sin, then it is always a sin and the blood inevitably dries on someone's hands."

"You're simplifying, Raskolnikov," the other man objected, turning away from him in disgust.

"Do you think so?" Raskolnikov put this vague question, looking with interest at his companion, as if he were amused by his sudden protest. He licked his upper lip several times and with a kind of perverted enjoyment he continued the debate: "Human life either has or has not the value we generally assign to it. If it has, it must also have it when humankind is murdered en masse. If it is a sin to murder, then, I repeat, it is always a sin. If murder is not a sin, then it never is! All that nonsense about ideals, which anyway always turn out to be dubious, is only nonsense and cannot breathe life back into anyone. And if that can't, then anything else is just a waste of words. Nothing more, just empty words. That's how it is, sir!"

"Not quite, Raskolnikov, not quite...."

"What do you mean by your not quite...?"

"In the case of murder, you decide of your own will about the being or not being of another person. You, by yourself and of your own will. In the case of the cataclysms you were talking about, someone else decides for you. You are only their instrument."

"But the result is the same! In fact, even worse!"

"But not with regard to individual conscience."

"Don't be ridiculous! Is their blood any less bloody, just because we don't always know who we have killed? Or is their life less valuable? Or doesn't that blood stain your hands?"

"It's more a question of conscience, Raskolnikov, conscience!"

"Don't be ridiculous, sir. Both the one person and the other very much want to live. Conscience is very broad and everything can hide behind it. Especially human hate and self-interest. A murderer is at least obvious. Nameable. When it comes to it, a murdering soldier is also only clean if he stands on the side of the winners. No conscience, no ideal can free him from the grip of guilt. Only victory. Defeated soldiers are never innocent!"

"You're simplifying!"

"Do you think so?"

"No one has the right to free himself of individual guilt just by pointing to collective guilt."

"So you think that mass graves hurt less...?"

"You are trying to slip out of the noose, Raskolnikov. You are a murderer. Your hands are bloody. Not even a thousand mass graves can cover up your guilt. Blood that has been shed is always blood that has been shed."

"We are not talking about the same thing, sir."

"Probably not," said the investigator.

Raskolnikov fell silent. He curled up in a ball like a hedgehog. His feelings had been hurt. He drew his legs under the seat and I could at last pass along the aisle. I must say, I felt relieved. Somehow I no longer had the strength to listen to this depressing conversation between the two men. I also have to confess that I felt a certain sympathy towards Raskolnikov's arguments, although shivers ran down my back when I passed him and in the blaze of the light bulbs the bare blade of an axe flashed before my eyes.

I wanted to reach Nelly as quickly as possible. She was smiling at me and saying something to her grandfather. He waved at me, too. But when I had passed Raskolnikov, I found myself caught up in a group of people of all ages talking together. An ancient general with colorful epaulettes was nodding his little head in agreement. He clearly went along with what the young man with feverish black eyes was saying. When he looked at me, I had the impression that they were burning into my brain. But he didn't see me. He seemed to be looking through me. It was clear that I was invisible to all those present. They were engrossed in their own problems. They were absorbed in their passionate discussions and clearly did not feel in the slightest inhibited. Nelly was the only one to be aware of me and maybe her granddad and his dog Azorka. But at that moment there were a lot of people between me and Nelly, and I won't hide the fact that the conversation I had the opportunity to hear just then caught my attention. So I didn't try to hurry over to her and her grandfather.

"So you, Prince Myshkin, you are convinced that people are essentially good?" the old general asked, looking as if the question had exhausted him. His nodding head was almost touching Myshkin's shoulder and it seemed as if he might any moment let it rest there while he had a little doze.

"How can people not be essentially good, if they are created in God's own image?"

"Myshkin, Myshkin, you can't take literally anything that is written."

"You may have seen life from its bad side too often, General."

"Probably. But even so, I don't have the best opinion of man. I'm used to seeing him more as an animal. Homo homini lupus! That's what he is, sir. Man is never even by chance more concerned about another man than about himself. He is too fond of life, and therefore of himself.... Then of himself, and finally of himself. That's how it is. Idealists like you can only be useful in the company of old virgins, but even they are usually of the worst human kind. They don't know how to give themselves to others! Tell me, Myshkin, what's the use of a woman who isn't willing to take her panties off?!"

"We are talking about two different things, General."

"No, Myshkin, we are talking about the same thing – about life."

"That's the very reason why I claim that people are good. We must just trust them. Without trust a person becomes an animal. But if you invest in the same person feeling, tenderness and understanding, you'll see what dimensions his inner being can reach. Man is capable of extraordinary things!"

"Extraordinary, you say, Prince?"

"Yes, extraordinary."

"I agree.... But you should see those extraordinary things. You should look at them with your innocent eyes. Lord! What things they are. Shivers would run down your back and you would wake up from your dream. You wouldn't know whether you had dreamed the worst possible dream, or whether you were really in hell. Death is sometimes more beautiful than life among people, believe me, Myshkin. Man has given birth to the worst kind of monster and that monster is constantly devouring him. War is that monster. And man feeds it. Incorrigibly. Again and again and again. As if he had no memory. I could tell you about that human good of yours until it would drive you mad. But what's the point? It would be no use. It's never any use. Even though after every war people say it was the last. The only war that is really the last one is the one that hasn't yet been!"

"You don't trust people at all then, General?"

"You've guessed right, Myshkin!"

"But how can you live with such distrust?"

"Maybe better than you with your belief in them, Prince."

"But what keeps you alive, then?"

"Belief, Prince Myshkin, belief, as it does you...."

"But you said...."

"I said I have a deep distrust of people. Yes, I really did say that. And thanks to the belief that tells me that people cannot be trusted, I can survive everything."

"But people are good, General. People really are good!"

Someone gripped me by the shoulder from behind and pushed me aside as if I had been a piece of furniture or some other object. When I looked around, I saw Raskolnikov's tall figure before me. He was bending over Myshkin in a threatening manner, as if he were going to grab him by the neck and strangle him. But the hand he held out was unexpectedly gentle. Slow. He just made a kind of graceful gesture. As if he wanted to stroke Myshkin's face. Tears ran down his cheeks.

"You, Prince, you are an idiot! A wonderful idiot. You couldn't trust people like that otherwise. No," – he put his hands around Myshkin's neck and kissed his forehead. Myshkin stared at him in astonishment, stuttered a few words and his body began to shudder. His head started to jerk like the elderly general's and foam appeared around his mouth. His body slipped off the seat he had been sitting on and he stretched out on the stone floor not far from my feet. There he began to writhe, his limbs flailing about violently.

"Epileptic!" growled the general.

"Idiot!" Raskolnikov declared openly.

A young girl quickly knelt down beside the prince and tried to put a wooden wedge between his teeth. Raskolnikov caught hold of Myshkin's legs, so he wouldn't hit them painfully on the edges of the seats during the seizure. The old general just looked on with a baffled expression, nodded his little head and kept repeating, "No, no, little dove, you cannot trust people."

It was embarrassing to stand in the middle of this unexpected and unfortunate scene, so I quickly made my way towards Nelly. She was just explaining something to her granddad. He was bending over her and stroking her head. I felt somewhat at a loss. I didn't want to break into their intimate conversation, but it was already too late, they had caught sight of me and Nelly smiled at me. She made it clear they didn't mind my presence. Granddad smiled at me encouragingly, but again I saw in his eyes an emptiness similar to that of blind people, which was mirrored in the eyes of all those I had met in the waiting-room. Nelly was somehow an exception. She looked at me with clear blue eyes, in which I could see my reflection.

"Look at the clock now!" she challenged me.

"Why?" I asked superfluously.

"Just look!" she insisted.

"It's still as odd as before," I asserted irritably, although to an impartial observer at that moment everything would have seemed in order. The little hand was almost on the figure twelve, the big hand too, and the second hand had just started moving from twelve in the direction of twelve. It looked as if time that night was at last to reach its goal. But as I had already seen this situation several times, I was not the least surprised. Feeling a little exasperated, I looked reproachfully at Nelly, convinced that she would understand how disappointed I was. I didn't even feel

242

like making a comment. After all, we both knew how that clock behaved.

"Today is the last time," she said.

"If you mean that clock, I don't believe it," I retorted.

"Their time is up," she indicated the people in the waiting-room.

"What do you mean?" I asked.

"I told you they would all come!" she said.

"Yes, they did," I admitted.

"And they will leave. Their train is already waiting for them...."

"What train?" I asked.

"The train into the void!" Nelly said.

"But why?!" I exclaimed.

"No one needs them! No one wants them here. Don't say anything. We're of no use to anyone. We could be here only as long as we lived in people's hearts."

"What about you?" I asked, even though I had guessed the answer.

"I'm traveling, too."

"But why?"

"There's no place for us in this town. We are humiliated and offended. Who cares about us...? Our time is up.... Look at the clock.

The second hand was moving inexorably towards the figure twelve. It was clear that a moment later all three hands would merge into one. The night would reach its climax and would disappear beyond recall. It would merge with other nights and everything would be repeated. I looked towards Nelly, but she was no longer in the corner where she had been sitting. Neither her granddad nor Azorka were to be seen either. I looked behind me and the waiting-room was empty. As if all those strange figures had been swept away. I glanced in bewilderment at the clock hanging on the wall opposite. It was exactly a minute after midnight. A new day had begun. A railwayman looked around the door. He scowled at me and said, "Don't loiter in the station. You know it's under reconstruction. Something could happen to you and we don't take any responsibility."

I was sure I had seen him somewhere before, but I couldn't remember where. After all, who remembers railwaymen?!

So I once more walked through the deserted town down M.R. Štefánik Street, and a rather cold spring wind caressed my cheeks. I thought of Nelly, her grandfather, Azorka, the brothers Karamazov and Raskolnikov. From time to time the wind refreshed me with a spray of tiny droplets which it threw in my face. In spite of this fresh feeling, I wandered on until I came to the tunnel under the castle walls. A couple of homeless people were warming themselves there over a little fire. I don't know how it happened, but I found myself among them, and I almost fainted when one of them pulled out a bottle of gin, held it out to me and said the words that had been running through my mind ever since I had left that strange station, where I had lost Nelly: "Have a drink, sir, it's turned rather chilly...in this world. You could sleep here, but with the best will in the world – there's no room for people."

So I went on my way.

MILAN ZELINKA

- prose writer;
born in Igram (1942)

Milan Zelinka has worked for the most part as a telephone switchboard mechanic in Humenné.

His debut was a collection of short stories, **Dych** (*Breath*, 1972), partly inspired by experiences he had while doing his military service and containing elements of lyricized comicality, slapstick comedy and absurdity. The stories in **Smädné srdce** (*Thirsty Hearts*, 1974), of which "Modrý boleň" ("The Blue Carp") is one, are set in villages and small towns and are mostly about young people. In the novella **Belasé ráno** (*Azure Morning*, 1978) he is concerned with problems caused by the generation gap. Ordinary people from his native region are also the focus of the short stories in **Slamienky z Makova** (*Dried Flowers from Makov*, 1980). In the novella **Kvety ako drobný sneh** (*Snowflake Flowers*, 1982) he created an eccentric philanthropist who cast himself in the role of comforter in a cancer ward. In his book **Mechanici** (*Mechanics,* 1983) he used the knowledge he had gained from working in telephone offices. The work **Povesť o strýkovi Kenderešovi** (*The Myth of Uncle Kendereš*, 1985) contains tales about a former village teacher. He remained in the Vihorlat foothills in the novel **Z Havranieho dvora** (*From Havraní dvor*, 1988), a panorama of the present with excursions into the past. The novella **Krajina** (*Landscape*, 1992) is a jocular allegory about a rebellion against the misuse of power.

In his own words:
Literature can ennoble man, it can bring people closer together. On the other hand, I realize that the artist cannot change nations through literature. Yet he can influence and change the relationship of man to man. When nations get to know each other better, they cannot make superficial judgements about each other, which can have even tragic results.

(1984)

In my heart of hearts I am really a daydreamer. I think that everyone has the right to beautiful dreams. I like people, especially those loyal devotees of life, who backpack dozens, even hundreds or thousands of miles in search of their dreams, and in spite of the fact that wherever they go they are wounded by the rough side of life, they still believe that somewhere around the seventh bend they will meet happiness in the form of, for example, an attractive girl and that girl will not be a cunning cheat.

Mystery is the essence of beauty. I think that is the main reason why most women try not to reveal themselves too much and too early, bodily and spiritually. It is natural for a healthy, attractive woman to draw a man into her aura of mystery gradually, slowly, but irresistibly, so that the man realizes only later that retreat is no longer possible. While most men first fall in love and only then marry, I married first and then gradually came to love not only my wife, but also the community in general of the place where I was born. It could be said that my feeling for the region in which I live came with my marriage and I later reaffirmed it through hard work.

(1990)

THE BLUE CARP

When Matej Bak caught the four-kilogram blue carp he had long dreamed about, he picked it up in his arms and, accompanied by a little crowd of ten-year-old boys, he paraded it triumphantly three times around the town. Then he was overcome by an unfamiliar feeling of sadness. The boys had gone home some time ago, so he sat down in the little station with his precious fish in his arms and somewhat enviously watched the workers engrossed in their conversations, waiting for the train to Medzilaborce. No one took any notice of the fish, so Matej Bak got up, approached a young railwayman who was smoking near him, touched his elbow with the fish's hard, open mouth and said, "Look, what a carp! Three years I've been lying in wait for him – and now he's mine!"

The railwayman looked at the fish, but said nothing.

"Look," said Matej Bak, shoving the fish under his nose, "look how blue he is!"

The railwayman silently blew out smoke and gazed somewhere over the lines, maybe at the girls who were standing on the other platform, maybe at the hills that rose above the newly-built white blocks of apartments.

"Well, have you ever seen such a carp? It's an asp to be precise,"

Matej Bak went on, displaying the fish from all sides. "Do you know how a carp like this can jerk? Time was if an angler caught a carp like this, he would hold a dinner to celebrate, and the whole street would congratulate him!"

None of the other people said anything either. Girls with handbags slung over their shoulders calmly stood in the gaps between the benches, reading colorful weeklies.

"May I, Miss?" said Matej Bak to a little blonde and he held the dead fish up to the front page of her magazine. "You see how beautiful it would look there! I'll tell you a poem about it. Do you want to hear it?"

He didn't wait for an answer and immediately began, tapping his foot to mark the rhythm:

"I know of two asps,
our stream is their haven.
One is shaven,
the other – unshaven."

The blonde sneezed. Her neighbor put her hand on her elbow and they both began to chatter away about something.

"We're not wanted," Matej Bak said to the blue carp, patting it gently on its mouth. "They don't want us, we disgust them. They don't know how hard it was to catch you and how rare you are! At least you take a look at him, sir," he addressed a respectable man in a hat, pushing his newspaper away from his eyes with the fish. "Look at him, look what a beautiful tail he's got! Look how wide, how graceful!"

"Beautiful," muttered the man in the hat and tried to go on reading.

Matej Bak pushed his newspaper away.

"And do you know why his tail's like that? He lives in clean water. Asps living in polluted waters don't have such graceful and beautiful tails. They split."

"No doubt," murmured the man, trying to get away.

"It took me twenty minutes to pull him out of the water!" cried Matej, when he realized his intention. He moved to prevent him. "He had only one hook in him – and do you know where? Right at the edge of his jaws! If I had pulled for a minute longer, I'd have lost him, I would have had to!"

People began to turn their backs on him. The man in the hat mumbled something and once more buried himself in his newspaper.

Matej Bak looked sorrowfully at the carp, which was now shimmering all colors of the rainbow.

"I shouldn't have killed you.... You could still be alive and no one would know anything about you...."

HANA ZELINOVÁ

- prose writer, playwright;
born in Vrútky (1914)

Hana Zelinová worked for the most part as an editor.

Her debut was a collection of short stories about human relations, **Zrkadlový most** (*The Mirror Bridge*, 1941). The problem of
disappointment with the realities of life is the subject of the plays
Mária (1943), **Ktosi je za dverami** (*Someone's Behind the Door*,
1944), and **Žijem cudzí život** (*I Live Another's Life*,1948). In the trilogy **Anjelská zem** (*Unexplored Territory*, 1946), **Hora pokušenia**
(*Mount Temptation*, 1948), and **Dievočka, vstaň!** (*Maiden, Arise!*
1948) she describes the life of a girl living in an isolated spot in the
mountains. In the novel **Diablov čardáš** (*The Devil's Csardas*, 1958)
she looked back to the post-war years. Then she wrote several books
for children (**Jakubko** – *Little Jacob*, **Sivá húska** – *The Grey Goose*,
both 1959). A girl on the threshold of maturity is portrayed in the
novella **Večer neprídem** (*I Won't Come This Evening*, 1964), and the
maturing of a boy in the novel **Moja je pomsta** (*Mine Is Revenge*,
1967). She dedicated her book of short stories **Kamenný ruženec**
(*Stone Rosary*, 1970) to women; the story "Vlčí rád" ("The Order of
Wolves") is taken from it. In the historical trilogy **Alžbetin dvor**
(*Elizabeth's Yard*, 1971), **Volanie vetra** (*The Call of the Wind*, 1974)
and **Kvet hrôzy** (*Flower of Horror*, 1977) she sketches the saga of
a yeoman's family from the Turiec region. In the trilogy **Hodvábna
cesta** (*The Silk Road*, 1980), **Smäd** (*Thirst*, 1981) and **Kľukatý let
motýľa** (*The Zigzag Flight of the Butterfly*, 1983) she presents a picture of the life of the Turiec tanners. In her latest works – for example, the novel **Hlas starých huslí** (*The Voice of an Old Violin*, 1988*)*,
Nočný koncert (*Night Concert*, 1989), **Víno kráľov** (*The Wine of
Kings*, 1993), **Vranie oči** (*Crow's Eyes*, 1995), **Múr plaču** (*The
Wailing Wall*, 1999) and others – she also alternates pictures of the
present with probes into history.

She is the author of radio and television plays as well as of stories for radio.

In her own words:

Every person carries within themselves something we call a soul and that encourages them to put wrongs right, to tell the truth, to sympathize with everyone who has suffered loss and to shake hands with their enemies. I don't know whether I have captured the nature of the human soul, but all this is in me and I draw on these feelings when modeling the characters and dispositions of my heroes. For this reason I am happy for them, cry and suffer with them and hope with them that human life, however crumpled, will one day straighten itself out, blossom and be fragrant. After all, what else does a person need to live and live his life to the end?

No author much likes talking about his or her own work. That is why to put it in a nutshell, I am glad and I thank God that he gave me the opportunity and time to write. This feeling cannot be expressed; it has the taste of nectar and the fragrance of raspberries. Every time I meet my readers or read their kind letters, I feel a summer breeze. For one thing is absolutely true: If you don't plant a tree, you can't expect to have fruit.

When I was young, not even a large sheet of paper would have sufficed to list all the things I longed for, there were so many. When you are over eighty, you no longer have anything to weigh up, and above all there is no point in regretting and shedding tears over what you have not achieved, no matter how much you longed to achieve it. That is why I, too, smile indulgently when I remember those unfulfilled longings of my youth and adolescence.

The first time I sent a short story to a magazine, at the age of sixteen, I (an impatient child) thought I would never make a writer, although I very much wanted to be one. On that occasion my father said to me, "My child, your bread will be hard if you don't knead it well." Ever since then I have been kneading and kneading that imaginary bread dough and even now in my mind I thank my father from the bottom of my heart for that sound advice.

(1998)

THE ORDER OF WOLVES

The woman beside the bed lifted her head with difficulty and with even greater difficulty she turned it towards the fireplace. All that could be seen in the dark was the white, starched bonnet that framed her smooth high forehead. The remains of the fire were smoldering in the hearth. She could see the cinders glowing and a twig begin to burn. Aspen. Over the years she had been helping her husband to burn charcoal, she had learned to distinguish trees not by their leaves, but by the way they burned. How long had she been helping him? She could only remember that they had called her "white Roxana" and he had been "black Sebastian." Since that time she had grown black and he white. Charcoal and hardship had accompanied her throughout her life; no wonder their blackness had rubbed into her skin. He couldn't be white? Oh, yes, he could. Just look, within reach of her hand lay his head, white as the snow outside the door.

* * *

What a sad story it was, and how much sadder now, on the New Year. Down in the village they had already welcomed it in, and where the master of the house was in good health, he had taken a Candlemas candle and written in the ashes of his hearth the year 1450.

It occurred to her to do the same, as Sebastian was lying in bed and did not even know that the village was welcoming the New Year. However, she thought she should not do it, because that was the task of the man in the house. If he, Lord forbid, were not able to do it, he would never write the new date in the cold ashes again.

That was why she was watching those three glowing cinders and the twig that had almost burned out. She thought she should stoke up the fire after all, because it would soon be as cold in the room as in a kennel and it would be hard for her to kindle a new fire in the morning, but she also knew that on New Year's day the new fire could only be laid on the ashes in which the new date had been written. What now? Should she wake Sebastian and tell him it was time to write the year fourteen fifty?

No, she wouldn't wake him for anything in the world. Let him sleep after his drink of elderberry, at least he didn't feel any pain. He would write it when he woke up and he might not feel the cold if she covered him with the sheep skin from her bed, too.

She therefore got to her feet and stood for a while beside her husband's bed, for her legs had grown numb and her back stiff. She was surprised how light it was in the room. Could those three glowing cinders give off so much light? They must, because Sebastian had covered the window with moss after the very first frost, and on the inside she had hung the woolly skin of that lame sheep the wolf had attacked, but not quite managed to kill, because Sebastian had broken its neck.

Powerful and brave – that was how her Sebastian had been. Always. That knowledge warmed her heart, as it had done all those years living up here, far from other people. A wolf killed like that, or caught in a trap, had eased their hardship. The lords in the castle had gladly paid for a wolf skin, and so they had both wished to have wolves instead of sheep.

Theirs had been a hard life. Hard indeed! How strange she felt today. Why was she filled with regret, why was her heart so heavy just now. Wasn't yesterday the same as today and hadn't she known what she was doing when she decided to come up here with Sebastian? She hadn't muttered any complaints then, nor had she once regretted it; it was only now that she suddenly felt sorry for herself....

The woman slowly moved away from the bed and crossed the room. Under her feet she felt the sprays of green pinewood she had brought in the previous evening to cheer up the room and give it a fragrant smell to welcome in the New Year. When she reached her bed, which black Sebastian had made, she ran her hand over the smooth planks. Here he had waited at the foot of her bed until she had called him to her, when she was still "white Roxana." Here he took from her two sons and a daughter.

On this bed she had covered herself with the softest and thickest sheepskins. She would give them to him now, cover him up, so he would not feel cold.

The woman bent over the bed and grasped a sheepskin covering in her arms. As she pressed it to her, she thought she could hear the stifled bleating of one of the six sheep in the shed.

Carrying the sheepskins before her, she returned to her husband's bed. There she slowly put them down at his feet and cautiously spread them out over the bed. When she had covered him up, she sat down beside him once more.

The sick man in the bed did not stir, not even when the six sheep in the shed began bleating. The woman now knew for sure that she had heard right a while before, but she did not want to get up and go to the shed to throw them some fodder. She just told herself that she would give them more in the morning, when Sebastian got up, too.

She gazed intently at the glowing cinders. One of them had already shrunk and turned grey; it would go out any moment – and when the others burned out it would be dark in the room. If only Sebastian would sleep till the morning, she would crouch at his feet and maybe tomorrow he would feel better.

It would be all right, yes, they had never asked for much. Only what every person could give if he wanted to. Such a person came into her mind. It was now twenty years since he had lived with them: may he rest in peace! He had been a good man, it was hard to believe such people had been driven out of their homeland by their own folk. He had been a Hussite. People called him Joachim, and they did too. As if he had been one of the family –

he had come like that and like that they had taken him in. Only it had been summer then and they had been younger. He used to sit here in this room, beside the window there which overlooks the yard.

The woman looked in that direction. Was it the dim light or her drowsiness that helped her to conjure up the picture of old Joachim over there near the window?

She suddenly felt an urge to touch the bench on which he used to sit. The woman got up and slowly went over to the window. Here she stood for a while and then sighed. That is how people sigh for a good person, yes indeed – a good person.

The woman pressed up to the window, standing on tiptoe to see out into the yard. Then in a voice stifled with fear she said, "Lord save us, there are wolves outside...."

She froze to the spot, pressing her face up to the spruce plank Sebastian had used to board up the window. She smelled the fragrance of the dry moss and the spruce wood, as well as the sour smell of the uncured skin which hung over the window, and she felt the biting frost beside her right eye, as it pushed its way into the warm room through a knot in the wood. She could see footprints in the untouched snow and a black shadow crouching just next to the pile of logs. As she lifted her gaze, she saw another sniffing in the direction of the shed. Then she heard a panting through hungry jaws, as one crept stealthily along the wall in the direction of the shed. How many were there? Three? More? Maybe a whole pack, and just because she had let the fire go out, and in the bitter cold outside they had not seen and had not smelled the smoke from the chimney that would tell them that the head of the house was on the watch and he would certainly defend what was his.

A cold chimney and sad silence gave the wolves courage; they had never come so close to the cottage before. Or had the sheep been restless because they sensed there was something wrong with their master, and that had lured the wolves? Things were not as they should be; Roxana knew that, but she also knew that she would not lift a finger to prevent anything happening.

All she had to do was go over to the hearth, blow on the cinders until the tow and pitch link began crackling, light the torch that was stuck in the iron hook beside the door and go into the outer room. From there a little door led to the shed. She would have to bend down, and if she called out to the black ram, he would come running in answer to her voice, bringing the five sheep behind him. That would save them, because the outside door to the hut was made of slim tree trunks nailed together; it would keep the hungry beasts out.

She knew how to swing an axe, too, and she would frighten them if she suddenly went out with the torch before the smell of warm blood drove them wild – but she did nothing, nothing, because if she did anything at all instead of her husband that New Year's night, Sebastian would never get up from his bed again.

Even if the wolves killed all the sheep and she would have to go down to the manor every day to beg for the baked leftovers of the bread dough and groats, let Sebastian get up from his bed tomorrow!

The woman at the window suddenly could see nothing she had seen so clearly before. She was crying and pressing her face into Limpy's white fleece. What a difference there was: then and now! How happy they had both been that the sheep had survived and the wolf's neck was broken. While Sebastian had skinned it, she had bandaged the sheep's leg with the underlayer of her own skirt. As she gave the sheep water to drink, she had said to it, "Don't worry, Limpy, you'll have lambs in the spring...."

And she did. She reared three of them and then they had cut her throat, because they didn't have enough fodder for the winter. Oh, how poor they had been.... They had always been poor for as long as she could remember. Strange that she had not felt it so much before.

Roxana let the sheepskin fall back over the window and suddenly lost interest in the wolves in the yard. She was thinking of something else. She simply wanted to know why poverty meant something different to her today.

Where she was standing was nearer the table than her husband's bed, so she sat down on the wide bench along the wall where old Joachim had slept in the winter. He had stayed with them for two years and upon my faith they had been good years. So full. Who knows whether anyone can understand how you can have such a feeling of fullness when your stomach is never satisfied and when, apart from the open fireplace and two wooden-plank frames, which poor people use for beds, there was nothing at all in the room. Nevertheless, that was the feeling they had at that time. She and Sebastian – both of them. When Joachim died, suddenly that fullness disappeared. He left behind him an earthenware pot full of honey, two new three-legged stools and a few wooden utensils, but that something that had filled them, satisfied them, had gone and these things only reminded them of their great loss.

If old Joachim were sitting here today, things would be different. It wouldn't be dark in the room and it wouldn't be sad either. Yes, what would this good man have done, a peasant farmer from somewhere in Bohemia, whose grandfather's property had been burned down, whose sons had been killed and whose chapel had been closed? He would have sung, yes, he would have sung that Hussite song from Tábor, which people like him had sung during those fourteen years of fratricidal strife.

Roxana was probably not even aware that she was quietly humming its first and second verse. It didn't matter that the room was dark. There was light within her, maybe that was why those scars from the landlord's whip she received the day her first-born child was dying no longer hurt her. But they had certainly hurt then.

To this very day she could not understand how the hired soldier in the garden could have noticed her, when he was sleeping and she had crept past him barefoot. It must have been that spoiled dog, such a tiny little thing there was nothing to it, with a large bow around its neck. How beautiful that ribbon had been! She had never had such a ribbon to twine in her plaits, but she had promised herself, when she was chasing the little dog away with her bare foot, that one day her daughter would wear a ribbon like that. The new, young "white Roxana." While she was storing this up in her head and chasing the little dog away, a cane whistled over her and stung her back. She didn't have time to cry out in pain, nor to say why she had come; she just ran straight across the flowerbeds to the paved courtyard where they were saddling the horses. She pressed up to them, because it suddenly occurred to her that the cane could not reach her there. What hired man would dare hit the landlord's horse? A serf, yes, but a horse? In this way she escaped a further beating.

When she arrived home, up here, Joachim welcomed her back and without a word helped her take off her bloodstained blouse. They were the only two to know about it. They hadn't said a word to each other, and they excluded Sebastian from their secret. Who knows what he would have done in anger? Only somehow she suddenly couldn't understand why he had always turned away from her when she had taken off her blouse. She would ask him one day: she could now. Her back had healed and who could tell where the soldier was now. After all, would Sebastian fly into a flaming rage over this violent deed? Not now. Not any longer. But then he was young; what had injustice meant to him then? The white Sebastian of today regarded injustice in a different light – that was why it was a good thing he had not been the one to take off her blood-stained blouse.

As these thoughts passed through her mind, she suddenly wanted to hear his voice. The most beautiful thing about Sebastian was his voice. Powerful and clear as a bell, it could be heard above a blizzard. Perhaps the wolves would run away and the sheep calm down if he said just a word or two.

Roxana quickly got up from the bench and walked over to where she knew the hearth must be. She stood there for a while, holding her hand out over the ashes, but they were already cold. She should close the flue then, so the heat would not escape up the chimney, but where was the string? It should be there, on the right side – so she had to stretch up above the hearth to reach the string – and in this position she froze. She thought she must be dreaming, that the forty years had disappeared during which she had, day after day, tied the starched bonnet married women wore around her forehead, cheeks and underneath her chin, for from behind her back her husband called her white Roxana.

"Roxana, my white Roxana."

Between her index and middle fingers she caught hold of the hempen rope tied to the flue, but she didn't pull it, because she suddenly felt weak and her legs gave way beneath her. She leaned with both hands on the stone edge of the hearth and breathed out through her mouth.

"Where are you?" came once more from behind her and only then did she reply, "Here, beside you, Sebastian."

She moved closer to him and stood beside his bed.

"Has the pain gone?" she asked him quietly and tried to guess whether his eyes were open or shut. For if they were open, he was fully conscious and then he would hear the bleating of the sheep and would guess why they were making such a disturbance. But if they were shut, he was not yet awake and he must just be dreaming about white Roxana.

"It occurred to me that your back must have stung terribly then."

Roxana opened her mouth, as if she wanted to say something, but nothing came out. Much later she managed to force out, "How do you know, Sebastian?"

She felt him move on the bed and she also realized that of his whole body, what must hurt most was his back.

"I know," he said simply.

She had to sit down beside him on the bed, and as she did so she thanked the cinders for dying out sooner than they should have. Like this they couldn't see each other and like this they didn't need to feel ashamed.

"We thought, Joachim and I, that we shouldn't tell you. You were like a wild stream then and powerful. And then, it didn't hurt that much," she said slowly, and again it was a good thing that it was dark in the room, otherwise this little lie would be a big lie.

The old man did not reply, his fingers just moved over the

sheepskin cover and found her right hand. They gripped it firmly and they told her that he did not believe her words.

So she went on sitting in silence and with her left hand she stroked his fist.

After a very long pause, he said, "Ever since I've taken to my bed I've been thinking about Joachim, and a little while ago I imagined I saw him over by the window."

The woman realized that she had had a similar impression, but she said calmly, "That was me sitting at the table. It was me you saw."

"Maybe, but even so, I've been thinking about him," he said again, and she replied from the depths of her heart, "He was a good man. We could do with him now."

They could. She had told herself that only a while ago. He would have seen to the sheep, scared off the wolves, laid the fire, talked, sung and rubbed rabbit fat into Sebastian's painful back. Sebastian must have been thinking the same, because he said after her, "We could do with him" – but perhaps for another reason, because he went on, "He would have known how to forgive me, if I had confessed to him today that I killed that hired soldier."

Roxana's hand lay heavy on his, but it was strange, she didn't say anything in response to this confession. She only subconsciously noted that a cold wind was blowing down the chimney straight onto her feet, because they suddenly felt cold, in spite of her sheepskin shoes. Similar shivers ran down her spine, but sweat broke out on her forehead under her bonnet and dampened her hair. She was also aware of the silence all around, which made her husband's breathing and the whistling sound in his chest seem all the louder. As soon as morning came, she would rub it with that rabbit fat.

When had he found out? When? And when had he done it? Would he tell her one day?

However hard she thought, she couldn't think how she had let out her secret. She had cried, it was true, but then she had cried over her first born. How could he have known when she was crying for him and when from physical pain? It was true that she had not slept with him then, so he wouldn't see the wounds crisscrossing her back, but he could easily have thought the reason for avoiding his embrace had been her sorrow. How, then?

What was it he had said a while ago? Whether Joachim would have forgiven him if he had confessed that he had killed that hired soldier. That means he killed him after Joachim's death, because otherwise he would have told him immediately after he had done it. But when had it happened, when? She must find that out, she must ask him before he fell asleep again.

"Sebastian," she said quietly. "How did you...?" she couldn't go on and she didn't even know what more to say.

Sebastian had released his grip on her hand some time before. The moment her hand had become heavy.

"I don't remember. I just know that you cried and cried that night. And whenever you turned around, you cried out in pain. I saw it in the morning."

"How could you when I dressed in the outer room?"

"You forgot to shut the door to the yard when Joachim dressed your wounds. Oh, my white Roxana, that was worse than that little grave in the forest. You know," he went on very slowly and it seemed to her that Sebastian could have had such a voice only when he was a little boy, or would have when he would be an old, very old man. "A poor man doesn't have much. He just scrapes a living. There are more weekdays than Sundays. What he does have is his wife, for better and for worse. Can I help it that you are my heart and that no one was allowed to hurt you?"

Once more his fingers slipped into hers. He desperately held her hand tight and she could feel his heart beat in the tips of the fingers pressing on her palm.

"Roxana, my white Roxana, how I cursed my hands, as large as a bear's, but weaker than feathers, because they had been unable to protect you. They knew how to drag you into poverty, to this place of exile, and how gladly they brought you here, but in all that time they never broke white bread for you, ah, Lord, they were useless."

"Shh, dear husband, don't talk like that," she said quite loudly and then very quietly, "Before you woke up I was thinking about all kinds of things and I told myself that the beautiful thing about my life was the fact that with you I always felt safe and sound. With you I had nothing to fear. Even now I'm not afraid, I'm just sorry that you did it because of me."

She caught his fingers between her two hands when he went to pull them away from her palm.

"You think I shouldn't have done it?" he asked, unable to believe it.

"You shouldn't, dear husband," she said quietly. "I wouldn't have let you go and I would have begged you until you had promised me that you wouldn't do it. You don't know how hard it is to give life. I would have told you that just as I had given birth, so his mother had, too. And he hadn't turned out well? Not her fault, nor his. He ate the landlord's bread, he learned the land-

257

lord's manners. And anyway, he only did what they ordered him to. The root of evil lies elsewhere and neither you, nor we, nor those who come after us, will dig it up. You wanted to revenge my painful back; oh, Sebastian, there will be many more bloody backs before the person is born who will snap the lord's cane once and for all."

"Roxana,...."

She heard him groan quietly, but she calmly went on in a quiet voice.

"I'm a simple, ignorant woman, but I know that one day life will be good on this earth."

"When will that be, Roxana?" he quietly interrupted her.

"One day," she said, but it sounded like "tomorrow."

"Will we two live to see it?" he asked, suddenly impatient and impulsive. "We're already old and I'm ill. And what if it won't be in a year, ten years' time?"

"It will be in a hundred, two hundred, maybe five hundred years," she said as easily as if she were weighing them in her hand. He caught his breath in surprise.

"In five hundred years?" he repeated after her in astonishment and with such disappointment that she had to hurry to comfort him.

"What does it matter that we won't live to see it? The main thing is that sooner or later the day will dawn when there will be no more castles," she said with certainty in her voice.

"No more castles? Oh, Roxana, surely that will never be!" the sick man said dully and slowly, just as if his strength was flowing away with every word. So she had to say, "It will, Sebastian. You'll see, one day...," here she broke off, because it occurred to her that she was contradicting herself if at one moment she claimed there would be no castles in five hundred years' time, and immediately after she assured him that he would see it with his own eyes. Then she shrugged her shoulders impatiently and continued.

"Children won't die of hunger, like ours did."

Silence descended once more on the room and the sheepskin cover over the charcoal burner's chest rose and fell rapidly in response to his excitement and inflamed lungs. His breathing was wheezy and his next words sounded likewise: "And what will there be then, Roxana dear? Do you know that, too?"

Although he could not see her, she nodded in agreement.

"I do. Where the lords used to dance and where they used to saddle their horses, poppies will grow. And on that spot where the little dog betrayed me, wheat will blow in the wind, and where the stocks stood those who were beaten will give the orders."

There must have been something prophetic in her voice, because the sick man on the bed seemed awe-stricken and then he said almost inaudibly, "Are you insane, Roxana, or are you just dreaming?"

She bent over him, so that her mouth touched his unshaven chin. She rubbed it up and down, enjoying touching like this the one she had never ceased to love from the very first day. For him her touch brought back the time when he could not control his desire for her and when he had told himself that life would not be life without her.

Time had stopped for both of them. The wind blew a shower of snow through the chimney onto the empty hearth. She thought that Sebastian had calmed down and that he would soon fall asleep. So she slowly pulled herself away from him, but not slowly enough to avoid waking him from his doze.

"Roxana," he said and then added, "I somehow can't believe that such a time will come, but do you know for certain that it won't be longer than those five hundred years?"

He moved his tired head resting on the sheepskin and continued, "Do you know how many charcoal burners will come after us? You couldn't count them. There are fewer stars in the sky. And they will be as poor as we are."

She was worn out, and hungry, and sleepy, but there was still a ring of conviction in her voice.

"Even if there are as many as poppy-seeds in a field, one day one of them will be the last," she said, and now she felt again the little shower of powdery snow on her face and hands. She lifted her head, thinking she would shut the flue after all, when she froze to the spot where she was standing at her husband's feet. In the opening she could clearly see against the moonlit sky the front paw of one of the wolves.

So they had even gotten up onto the roof. They hadn't given up, even though the sheep had stopped bleating some time before and were pressing up to the door leading into the house. They were so certain of their victory, that a few moments made no difference. They knew that today they would eat and drink their fill, while she did not even know the most important thing: whether she would live to see that New Year's day, that greyish dawn, when the evil of the night gave way to the good of the day. Yes, the wolves were powerful. Just like the lords, the woman thought to herself and she couldn't help smiling at the comparison. Wolves and lords. One just like the other. Inexorable, ruthless, with their whips or canine teeth. And her and Sebastian? Such people were like sheep. Crouching, trembling from fear and waiting for the cane to fall on their backs and the teeth to bite into their bodies. Oh, how weak all the serfs were! Sheep, sheep....

What had she been saying about the future with such certainty that her sick Sebastian had believed her, when she was weak, weaker than flies in August? Why didn't she show that she was a forerunner of those future victors? She must, she must, above all, she must prove to herself that one day accounts would be settled, the cane that had lashed her back would be broken.

She wanted to get up, to go somewhere, but she was stopped dead by Sebastian's choking cough, his heart-rending struggle for breath, his arms thrown wide and the rush of hot blood which blinded her for a moment and fell in a warm shower on her face. She had no time to do anything, just stand in this sudden whirl and then gently settle her exhausted husband back on the sheepskin and cross the hands that were turning cold over his chest. She no longer spoke to him using his name: his blood had sealed her mouth once and for all, and when his body first shivered and then fell quiet, she knew that she was, on that New Year's day, a widow.

She would never know to the last minute how long she had stood over him, but when she moved from the bed, she went straight to the outer room without hesitation and opened wide the little door. She had guessed right. The sheep were pressing up to it and they immediately ran into the main room. She let them go in to hide from danger and she herself went back to where Sebastian had left his wide carpenter's axe stuck in the beam.

She summoned her strength and pulled the axe out of the wood with a jerk. She gripped it firmly in her right hand and with her left she lifted the bar across the door. Then she stepped over the threshold of the hut which Sebastian had built for her, so that she would have somewhere to bring heaven nearer to earth for him.

All this flashed through her mind: her striped skirt, the white blouse over which she had glanced back at her husband. The heat of blood and breath, when she wound her hands around his strong neck. Dozens, hundreds of smoldering charcoal fires, which for them had meant their right to live. Day and night. Rainy and sunny mornings – and now.... Now she was going to get her revenge for all that had ceased to exist a while before. She was going to strike out at that right of the more powerful – at that cane and canine tooth.

She knew she had slashed out well. She only had to swing the sharp axe at the wolf that was waiting beside the shed for its prey.

For me and for Sebastian, she thought to herself implacably and took two steps towards the piled up logs. At the third step she realized whose blood she was carrying on her white bonnet and her chest – and the fourth step she never took. She felt something heavy fall on her from the roof, knocking her to the ground, something that the smell of blood had sent into such a frenzy that it demanded more blood.

She gave it through her torn throat – to two canine teeth, as she had once given it to the landlord's cane. And before she closed her tired eyes forever, a voice inside her said something in reconciliation:

"One day things will be different...."

A DIVERSE CONTRIBUTION
TO SHORT-STORY LITERATURE

Of the approximately four hundred living members of the Slovak Writers Society, over one hundred have written and are still writing short stories regularly or sporadically. If we add to this renowned authors who do not belong to any writers' organization and also those who are registered in other smaller ones, we can claim that for a nation of five million there are plenty of story-tellers in Slovakia, especially if we consider that we also have literature written in minority languages – in Hungarian, Ukrainian, Ruthenian, Romany and even some in German. At a time when conditions for the publication of original works in a society in transition have deteriorated considerably, due to the dreadful pressure of second-rate Western literature which has already flooded the Slovak book market, and the destructive influence of various private television companies in particular, whose superficial stories full of violence, sex and horror are pushing the good book out of the consumers' free time, it seems that paradoxically, as if to counterbalance this, the number of those who need to express their own thoughts and observations through works of literature, and to confirm their own personal identity through writing, is on the increase, although many manuscripts – including ones of high quality – are for the moment waiting with very little hope of publication. Young and old write; quite a few decide to sacrifice their personal savings in order to publish their writings at their own expense. This is true, of course, of all prose genres, but novels and short stories are the most basic and most numerous, as can be seen in the bibliographical surveys of individual authors.

Yes, literature in Slovakia was and still is a serious and indispensable expression of national identity. Its role was determined by the troubled history of this small nation. Literary critic Alexander Halvoník expressed it like this: "Our literature is predominantly serious, philosophical, searching and digressive. A characteristic feature is that there is very little joy in it. What is more important for me is whether Slovak prose really reflects our existence. Here I must say – with all the risks of generalization – that it does. It could even be said that it is too conscientious and thorough in this respect. At the same time, I think it really had no other choice."

What an apt description! For many, many centuries the Slovak word was really the only means of resistance and opposition to social and national oppression, although in the 9th century the language of our ancestors was officially recognized by Pope Hadrian II as the fourth language of worship, after Hebrew, Greek and Latin. The mature culture of Great Moravia left its clear mark on our Old

Magyar neighbors – their language included – who, after the historic battle near Bratislava in 907 and the decline of the Great Moravian Empire, subjugated Slovak territory and its inhabitants for a long time, making them part of the Hungarian kingdom. For centuries Latin prevailed as the official language and, after colonization, German as well in many parts, but the Slovak of our ancestors was only to be found here and there in official documents, and then just a word, title or sentence. One such example is in a notational document from the village of Svätý Michal written in Latin in 1294, where the word "slovenský" [Slovakian] appeared for the first time; 200 years later, in 1488, the Hungarian chronicle of Ján of Turiec has the word "Slovák" [a Slovak]. As a result of expansionist power-politics, the Hungarian kingdom was identified with the Magyar nation, and in later centuries this led representatives of our southern neighbors to declare that the Slovak nation did not exist. That is why during the period of national revival Slovak literature abounds in Defenses – of the nation and its rights, especially with reference to the use of the mother tongue. Although in 1840 the Hungarian Diet passed a law making Hungarian the official language for all administrative and judicial offices, even for church administration and registry offices, and imposed it as the language of instruction in schools at all levels, Ľudovít Štúr, his fellow pioneers and followers in the struggle for the rights of the Slovak nation, demanded above all the right to use the mother tongue freely, and in their endeavors to raise national consciousness they made good use of literature. In fact, until the end of the First World War our predecessors had to chant the Lord's Prayer in a language they simply didn't understand – in Hungarian. Actually, the struggle for recognition as a nation was not over even then, because in spite of the Pittsburgh Agreement on equality, Masaryk and Beneš pursued the idea of a Czechoslovak nation, in which Slovak was only a dialect of the Czech language and the literature written in it was an offshoot of Czech literature. Fortunately literary figures had a better understanding of coexistence than politicians.

Of course, Slovakia now has its own state sovereignty, its people have transformed themselves into a modern nation, and its literature bears all the essential marks of modernity, based on its own evolution, yet also drawing inspiration from other sources in the world without imitating them unimaginatively.

Although those excellent Slovak realistic storytellers from the turn of the 19th and 20th centuries – Jozef Gregor Tajovský or Martin Kukučín – put great emphasis on the mission of their prose works to raise national awareness and educate people, their contemporary Timrava, for example, portrayed the Slovak people with the critical analysis of a Dostoevsky-like scrutiny, although she was by education and way of life an adherent of Naturism, limited to the environment of her native Hont, beyond whose borders she never ventured. Natural talent is also to be found in the short stories or novellas of the leading writers of Slovak prose from the first half of the 20th century – Jozef Cíger Hronský and Milo Urban. Here, too, we find the terms "national" and "human" merging as an expression of the essence of the identity of the Slovak nation.

I think this excursion into history is important for an understanding of the basic tones of Slovak literature, and therefore of this selection of short stories. It is quite clear from this that the short stories written by this selection of Slovak authors will naturally be very varied in theme, genre, period, style, length and so on. A chronological view of the selection from the earliest story (Hykisch, 1963) to the most recent (Tužinský, Ševčovič, 1999) indicates a trend towards more intellectually and philosophically demanding works, expressed in a more modern style.

The feeling that there is a need for a fresh look at Slovak history appears in those works looking back to the Second World War (Chudoba, Hudec), as well as to the twenty years of Soviet occupation after the invasion of our country in 1968 (Ťažký). A classical story by a typical representative of women's literature (Čeretková-Gállová) is followed by stories free of excessive sentimentality (Švenková, Bátorová) and lead to prose with emphatic philosophical and psychological overtones (Farkašová). Alongside classical stories (Ševčovič, Hykisch) are those of authors who use a more modern approach, including the suppression of the story line and an emphasis on feelings (Ferko, Farkašová). A confrontation between dreams and reality (Holka, Tužinský) appears surprisingly often; within a realistic story we find exaggeratedly comic, nonsensical or even absurd elements.

We consider the selection presented here to be an adequate testimony to the variety, intellectual depth and aesthetic appeal of Slovak prose writing. A different selection could have been made, but it would probably have been only of supplementary informative and aesthetic value.

PAVOL HUDÍK